"Pippa Biddle doesn't demonize volunt... others interviewed in *Ours to Explore*. Their stories show how this rite of passage for those wanting to help can lead to so much harm. If you're contemplating broadening your horizons by volunteering abroad, broaden your mind first by reading this book."
—Tina Rosenberg, co-founder of Solutions Journalism Network

"A brilliant must-read for anyone who has a passion for exploration and doing good. Biddle has a beautiful way of weaving a rich narrative together for a thoughtful, compelling, and raw critique of an industry that's long overdue for reform."
—Kelley Louise, founder of Impact Travel Alliance

"Pippa Biddle unwraps the history of what we now call voluntourism, showing us that what's billed as 'development' is really exploitation. . . . *Ours to Explore* should make us all reevaluate what we do abroad and why."
—Sarah Enelow-Snyder, travel industry journalist

"Biddle offers a blistering takedown of voluntourism and a sweeping reckoning with the omnipresent force of colonialism. Her case studies of abuse and malpractice within the industry are damning and revelatory. *Ours to Explore* will inspire critical discussions about building a world where Black and Brown people of the Global South can live free of domination, plunder, and the white Western gaze."
—Nikhil Goyal, sociologist at the University of Cambridge

"*Ours to Explore* is an unputdownable exploration into the collateral damage of good intentions. Immersive, vivid, and thorough, it is required reading for those who seek to help in contexts that are not their own."
—Elizabeth Greenwood, author of *Love Lockdown: Dating, Sex, and Marriage in America's Prison System*

"*Ours to Explore* combines Biddle's experiences as a former voluntourist with real-world examples and perspectives to clearly demonstrate that just because international volunteering feels good doesn't necessarily make it so. An important and accessible read."
—Noelle Sullivan, author of *The Business of Good Intentions: Reframing the Global Health Volunteering Debate*

"In a world of those who believe being an ally is enough, this critical read is a challenge for quality civic engagement and true service-learning opportunities."
—Eddie Moore Jr., founder and program director of the White Privilege Conference

"A well-written look at a thoroughly fascinating and little understood subject."
—Trae Crowder, comedian and coauthor of *The Liberal Redneck Manifesto*

"An essential read for anyone who loves to travel and hopes to make a positive impact in the world. . . . A masterful storyteller, Biddle's stories are full of compelling characters and intriguing experiences that bring the impacts of voluntourism to life. *Ours to Explore* inspires readers to think critically about the best ways to turn good intentions into actions that produce meaningful change."
—Ty Tashiro, author of *The Science of Happily Ever After*

OURS TO EXPLORE

OURS TO EXPLORE

PRIVILEGE, POWER, AND THE
PARADOX OF VOLUNTOURISM

Pippa Biddle

Potomac Books | AN IMPRINT OF THE UNIVERSITY OF NEBRASKA PRESS

All rights reserved. Potomac Books is an imprint
of the University of Nebraska Press.
Manufactured in the United States of America.

Library of Congress Cataloging-in-Publication Data
Names: Biddle, Pippa, author.
Title: Ours to explore: privilege, power, and the
paradox of voluntourism / Pippa Biddle.
Description: Lincoln: Potomac Books, an imprint
of the University of Nebraska Press, 2021. |
Includes bibliographical references and index.
Identifiers: LCCN 2020045911
ISBN 9781640124417 (paperback)
ISBN 9781640124776 (epub)
ISBN 9781640124783 (pdf)
Subjects: LCSH: Volunteer tourism. |
Tourism—Moral and ethical aspects.
Classification: LCC G156.5.V64 B54
2021 | DDC 361.3/7—dc23
LC record available at https://lccn.loc.gov/2020045911

Set in Garamond Premier by Laura Buis.
Designed by N. Putens.

For Ben

CONTENTS

Preface   ix

1. 1866: A Woman in India   1

2. A Certain Kind of Tourism   9

3. Cars, Planes, and Resorts   24

4. The Alternative Tourism Boomerang   35

5. The Age of Voluntourism   43

6. Colonial Pathologies   61

7. Faith, Purpose, and Mission   74

8. The Development Conundrum   90

9. Playing Doctor   102

10. Teaching Children   117

11. Orphanages   123

12. An Indictment   147

13. Turning Tide   156

14. The Future of Voluntourism   163

15. On to an End   179

Acknowledgments   183

Notes   187

Bibliography   211

Index   221

PREFACE

Nothing about the old Julius Nyerere International Airport was remarkable. The construction was simple and unassuming, and, after stripping away advertising and promotional tourism signage, little about it would tip travelers off to where they had just landed. The airport appeared especially nice if your only reference points for African infrastructure prior to arrival were images of bombed Somali buildings and dusty Sudanese refugee camps. It was not until I saw the gift shop selling marked-up Kilimanjaro coffee that I realized that my preconceptions of Tanzania might have been built on everything *but* images of Tanzania.

The temperature climbed upward as I approached the sliding glass doors that connect the baggage claim to the outdoor arrivals area. The comfortable air-conditioned cocoon I'd been enveloped in since checking in for my flight was about to be pierced by some serious heat. When the doors slid apart, I closed my eyes and inhaled the thick air. We, a group of teenage girls, teachers, and board members from Miss Porter's School, a high school for girls in Connecticut, carried our duffels full of donations and gifts to a sagging pink minibus and piled in.

As we pulled out of the airport's relative tranquility and onto Julius K. Nyerere Road, the sounds of Dar es Salaam crashed against the tinted glass separating us from the outside. Constant honking punctuated the cries of young street vendors, calling out as they wove between the bumper-to-bumper traffic. "Ndizi!" "Chungwa!" and "Maji!" punched through the waterfall of noise, replenishing itself through its echoes in a direct refusal of silence.

We passed corner banks guarded by men in green army fatigues with rifles slung across their backs. We saw shiny silver Lexuses parked next to rusted trucks. Young boys carrying bags of green oranges whistled for attention, and cell-phone-minutes salesmen did good business through cracked car windows. Elegant women, babies tied to their backs with brightly patterned fabrics, floated by with circular plastic bins overflowing with market purchases balanced precariously on their heads.

Slowly, the city gave way. The pavement thinned, relinquishing territory to rutted dirt roads that, when it rained, would channel water like a riverbed.

Just as the roads changed, the skyline shifted. Apartment complexes and department stores gave way to smaller cement block buildings, which themselves faded into ramshackle structures slapped together out of scrap wood, corrugated metal, woven plastic food sacks, and other salvaged and reused materials. Every third structure was a hair salon, every fifth a lottery ticket vendor.

With my camera pressed up against the windows, I felt like I had jumped into the pages of an issue of *National Geographic*. It was utterly foreign, and I was completely swept up in it.

When we finally arrived at Bethsaida and the blue front gate rolled open, a swarm of young girls in matching blue and red and green dresses surrounded the van.[1]

Young women grabbed our bags with one hand and our hands with the other. They led us to where we would be staying, a bunkhouse in the rear right corner of the compound built by a Japanese aid group. The bunkhouse was near the small mountain of gravel and stacks of gray cement blocks that marked the bounds of the library we were to build.

The orphanage's buildings were all cement block, open to the air, and predominately single story. The place appeared to be clean, the grounds well cared for, and a sizable vegetable garden suggested healthy meals. The food was simple but good, and the people were kind. Overall, it seemed like a nice place, especially compared to what I had been expecting, and our project was straightforward. Our group of well-educated and enthusiastic teen girls would ostensibly have little trouble accomplishing it in the six days before we left to go on a safari.

The next morning, we showed up at the worksite after a hearty breakfast of hard-boiled eggs, toast, and fresh fruit juice. Boots laced and gloves on, we helped a group of Tanzanian workmen mix bags of cement with buckets of water. As we worked, taking turns mixing the sludge with a few rusty shovels, the men introduced themselves. Their hands were scarred, their arms and legs covered in crosshatched scrapes, and, in place of boots, they wore shredded sneakers or thin sandals to shield their feet from the rough gravel and heavy cement blocks. A few had plastic bags, tied at the ankles, to protect their calloused soles.

That first day, we laid the foundation, a smooth square that seemed small but that we were sure would hold big things. I was confident that this place (an orphanage in Tanzania) was where I was supposed to be and that this job (helping the orphans) was what I was supposed to be doing. Less than forty-eight hours earlier, I had walked off a plane in Tanzania intending to fix a place that I had only recently located on a map. That night, as my eyes closed and my breathing slowed, I did not doubt that I would be successful in doing so.

The next day, we went back into the city to go shopping. We bought piles of boldly patterned *kangas* and *kitenges*, large pieces of fabric that the women used in a dizzying number of ways for everything from clothing to child carriers and that we talked about turning into decorative pillows. After shopping for ourselves, we asked around until we found a shoe store where we could buy the workmen new boots. They accepted the gifts but hesitated at wearing them, worried they would get dirty.

Day 3 was for the walls. I had never laid a brick, and neither had anyone else in the group, but I was sure they would not give us a task we weren't capable of doing.

Thin pieces of string tied to sticks ran around the perimeter of the foundation. The sticks and string were there to guide us, helping us place the bricks straight and level. This is important because if the bricks aren't laid just right, there can be disastrous consequences. If the bricks are placed too far in one direction, the walls will slope out, putting the structure at risk of collapsing after only a few rows. If a brick is placed too far in the opposite direction, the walls will slope in, also risking a collapse. If the bricks are not perfectly level, the rows will be uneven, a hump forming as each subsequent row amplifies the previous rows' imperfections.

There were no specialized tools, and, with our tight building schedule, little time to learn a not-so-simple trade. When we started to stack the second row, I began to understand how complicated the situation was. Without real training, we were far from the ideal people for the job. But I am nothing if not obsessive, so after a morning of confusion and frustration, I spent my free time after lunch on the site with the men, trying to learn to build a level wall without the use of a level.

As the days passed and the concrete set, we alternated between working hard and hardly working. We hung out with the girls between their classes, and group members who were not confident laying bricks or who wanted a break tried to teach English classes or worked on projects other volunteer groups had left unfinished. Progress on the building was slow, and there were grumblings that there was no way we could finish on schedule.

Despite all of this, we were still confident we would not have been told to build a library if we weren't capable of doing it. Skills, cement-setting times, and timeline be damned, we would get it done.

One morning, I woke up long before the lure of breakfast roused the rest of the group, and while I left it out of my journal, I still remember it vividly.

I remember slipping off my top bunk, wrangling my hair into a messy bun on top of my head, making the conscious decision not to brush my teeth. I remember walking out the front door of the bunkhouse under the pretense of jogging around the compound in preparation for cross-country running season. I remember instead checking on the pigs and the half-built chicken coop, an in-progress project started by one of the long-term European volunteers.

I remember wondering why the air couldn't feel that wonderfully fresh and cool all day, and I remember, a few minutes later, wandering up toward the front gate because I was not in the mood to run or read so might as well wander. I remember seeing familiar men on my left and being surprised that they were at the worksite so early, especially since they had been showing up late. Puzzled, I watched them for a moment before I started counting bricks.

I started counting from the row closest to the ground. There were few enough rows that I could have estimated accurately with just a quick look, but for some reason, I felt an urge to know the exact number. When I reached the top of the wall, I was at one row fewer than I knew we had been when we'd stopped work the day before.

I don't know why I stopped to count the bricks except that I was curious as to why the men were working so early. I don't know why, after a short pause, I kept walking, and I am still not sure why I did not immediately tell one of the group leaders. All that I know is what I can remember, and what I can remember is suddenly realizing that the men must have taken down what we had built the day before. In the early hours of the morning, while we were all supposed to be asleep, they were re-laying the cement blocks that, despite our best efforts and massive amounts of enthusiasm, we had failed to lay straight and level.

Rereading my journal today, I think I didn't record that morning because I didn't want what I'd realized to be true. I only told one person at the time, hoping she could explain it away. When she was not able to, I tried to block it out.

Memory is a weird thing. What we remember and what we forget often seem to follow no logical system. I might have been able to forget our failed construction attempt, for example, if the memory of it had not been reinforced by other events and experiences that joined it in muddying my concept of what it means to help. Things like how the representative of Global Crossroad, the volunteer trip provider that was facilitating our trip, told a group of us to plaster a wall in a building that a recent volunteer group had left incomplete. Without any instruction or guidance, we did a predictably bad job. Again, the workmen had to undo and redo our work, this time in full view.

Walking through a woodcarver's market in Dar es Salaam, a long-term volunteer on break from Bennington College told me that the construction issues that we had been experiencing were the least of the orphanages' problems. She said that cases of malaria were commonly left untreated, leaving girls to sweat it out for days as their bodies fought off the treatable disease. It was an accepted fact, she added, that many of the girls also suffered from nutritional deficiencies.

The hearty meals and fresh fruit juices we had been enjoying in the headmistresses' living room (because eating with the girls would be "too disruptive" to their schedule) were nothing, it turned out, like the bland beans and rice that the girls prepared for themselves in huge pots over open fires. Members of our group had requested that there be more fresh produce and meat-based proteins in our meals. The only day the girls would have chicken during our week there was at the going-away banquet they threw for us. After the meal, they wrapped us in traditional clothes, led us up to the elevated stage, and sang to us from below, professing their gratitude for all that we had given them.

Some of these experiences and realizations are in my journal, and some are not. I was trying my best to be optimistic in my entries and made a concerted effort to focus on the positives. I sugarcoated things that felt even a little bit off. Many I left out entirely. I wanted to feel good about the experience. I did not want to look back years later and see all the things I had done wrong.

I had no plans to share my journal, and yet I found myself putting on a show on paper. I switched between print and cursive, thinking cursive would look more adult, more like a "real" journal, but having trouble keeping it up.

I remember trying to come up with things to write that sounded mature or profound. I cherry-picked what I wanted to feel and remember and left out the rest because if I didn't think too hard about it and I didn't record it, it must not have mattered. I didn't want to lose my last little thread of hope—that while the project we were working on might not be wholly good, *I* still was. But holding on to hope is hard work.

When I first met the smart, powerful, and kind young women of Bethsaida, I didn't imagine that I could ever think of my time in Tanzania as anything but wonderful. I still think of those young women frequently and see some periodically, their photos and updates popping up in my Facebook newsfeed. We have all grown up, but while I went from an excellent high school with a price tag to match to a top college, they have had to struggle at every step. With limited access to resources and no safety net, it has been tough for many of them to find stability. While my intentions to be helpful and encouraging and to give back came from a good place, my time at the orphanage did not even begin to address their real needs.

The summer I turned seventeen, I was not ready to see this yet. It was simpler to accept that what I had been led to believe was helpful, productive, and ethically sound actually was. Sorting pebbles out of beans and talking about school and boys and life with girls who were right around my age but from such a wildly different place with such drastically different experiences was one of the most personally fulfilling experiences of my teenage years.

I am a privileged white girl from a privileged town who has gone to schools that cater to privileged people. Before going to Tanzania, I had known what poverty *looked like*. I had seen it on vacations with my family to Ecuador, Brazil, Nicaragua, Mexico, Panama, and Costa Rica, and even, on a lesser scale, during the long drives through upstate New York for summer camp and ski races. But I had not fully internalized it. I had not bonded with people whose realities were so different from my own. What poverty *does* was not real for me until I tried, and failed, to build a library in Tanzania.

It is hard to call something bad when you know that it has done you so much good, and it would be easier to criticize the volunteer work I've done if it did not have so much to do with who I am today. Volunteering has made me more self-conscious. It has made me more aware of my privilege, and it has heightened my interest in global issues.

While this book isn't about me, it is about what I did, why I did it, and how the voluntourism industry successfully sells products steeped in cultural presumptions, privilege, power, and prejudice. While I've chosen to start the book with a deep dive into where voluntourism came from, it is not a sweeping history of the development of tourism globally. If it were that, many things would be missing. White people are not the only tourists, nor were they the first travelers. However, I've chosen to take a Eurocentric view of the origins of tourism because the narrative of voluntourism is rooted in a "West is best" worldview. The early Silk Road is not to blame for my trying to save Africa by building a library. Centuries of people of Western European descent acting on the assumption that they have the right to tread new ground and buy a souvenir along the way is. So that is what I have focused on. Sometimes it's uncomfortable, but that's okay.

I was sixteen when I walked out of the old Julius Nyerere International Airport on June 19, 2009. A little more than a decade later, I am still young and perhaps even more flawed. I spent years trying to hold on to the positives of my time at Bethsaida while ignoring what I knew was wrong. Like maintaining cursive in my travel journal, I am not much good at ignoring things. So I did something different—I started digging. This is what I found.

OURS TO EXPLORE

1 | 1866 *A Woman in India*

She wrote that the streets were narrow and cramped, and the air carried the smells of open sewage and rotting garbage, the evidence of which covered every surface in a thick film of grime. Dark-skinned men with long black hair, rags around their waists their only clothing, sold produce to other men wearing nothing at all. Around them, bodies of all shapes, sizes, and shades squeezed between carriages, carts, livestock, and crumbling brick buildings that lined each side of Chitpur Road.[1]

Arab merchants in bulbous silk turbans walked side by side. Armenians shuffled toward the Opium Bazaar, where they would become rich off the intoxicating drug. Chinese waved fans in a futile war against the stale heat, and traders from Bombay and Northern India in red turbans bragged to each other about the quality of their wares. Periodically, rajas on adorned elephants would lumber through the crowd, forcing beggars and naked children to scuttle out of the way of their rides' massive steps. Ships from around the world brought trade and wealth to the city of almost eight hundred thousand.[2] It was November 24, 1866, and this was British Calcutta (now Kolkata).

Mary Carpenter's carriage had been making reliably slow progress for hours until, suddenly, a religious parade blocked her route. There was no means of evasion or escape, so the passenger and her companion leaned their heads out the carriage's windows. If they could not keep moving, they might as well see what was in their way.

A group of men and boys carried a jumble of objects slapped together into garish idols and draped in broken toys and colorful flags, dragging their feet under the weight. The procession appeared apathetic toward its audience. Only a handful of women watching curiously from behind the glassless window frames of their roadside homes seemed to have any interest in the event. Accessorized with British military castoffs—one wearing a military hat, another a uniform jacket—the people in the parade slowly passed. The flow restarted, and the carriage continued.

As they entered the south end of the city, the road widened and smoothed. Shops with glass windows and neat displays that reminded Carpenter of England replaced ramshackle stalls. A post office offered the opportunity to mail letters to relatives and loved ones. The English Quarter couldn't provide a complete respite from the dust, heat, and noise of the city, but it did offer a taste of English normalcy. Over a dozen churches allowed Europeans to pray in a house of God, and the homes were reminiscent enough of England that even Carpenter started to feel a little more comfortable. Soon after arriving at the home of a local Englishman, she sat down to a light tea.[3]

Once she had settled in and had a chance to recuperate from the trip, Carpenter visited a nearby missionary station and school. Its caretaker, Reverend Mr. Long, a local religious leader, enthusiastic Christian educator, and ardent evangelist, acted as her guide and cultural interpreter. At the school, she watched children in their lessons, encouraged them in their studies, and handed out small gifts.

On their way back into the city, they decided to make a stop at the Kalighat Kali Temple, a large and popular shrine to the Hindu goddess Kali. The temple was set apart from the chaos of the urban sprawl, and its domed roof, tall pillars, and repeating arches were reminiscent of the Mediterranean.[4] The forms were almost comforting, a piece of civilization in a confusing foreign maze. Carpenter had never set foot in a Hindu temple, and the idea of entering a place devoted to idolatry filled her with dread and disgust. But, as a stranger trying to reform a strange land, she felt she had to peek inside.[5]

Carpenter kept close to the reverend as they approached the temple entrance. If he was willing to take a look, it could not be as terrible as she imagined.

Miss Carpenter in India

Nearly two months earlier, on September 5, 1866, Mary Carpenter had boarded a ship in Marseille, France, and set off for India. Her escort, a young British-educated Indian lawyer and Christian convert, Monomohun Ghose, had been called back home and was decidedly unenthusiastic about the prospect of leaving the European continent. Carpenter was more excited. She was already well known for her social activism and reform work in Britain and was ready to test her mettle in a place she had dreamed of visiting for decades. India had been on her mind since the Indian reformer Raja Ram Mohan Roy stayed with her family in 1833. She had been a young woman at the time. Now, at fifty-nine, her dream was coming true.[6]

Carpenter was certainly not a typical Victorian woman. Born on April 3, 1807, she grew up in a devoutly religious and passionately charitable community committed to education. Her father, a Unitarian minister and antislavery activist, taught his children to sacrifice selflessly in the furtherance of "Christian values." At a time when women's education was typically limited to rudimentary academics supplemented heavily with lessons on refinement, her father didn't just encourage advanced learning and independent thought; he demanded it.

Carpenter studied mathematics, physical and natural sciences, Latin, Greek, history, and literature. She learned to have strong opinions, especially on social issues, and as a child became known for speaking her mind. She

was also a born leader. At twenty-four, Carpenter became the superinten-
dent of the Sunday school in her Bristol parish. A few years later, inspired
by the work of British and American social reformers, she helped found
the Working and Visiting Society, a society dedicated to helping the poor.[7]

The society divided Bristol into districts, each of which was then assigned
to a small team of volunteers responsible for visiting the homes of impoverished congregants and Sunday school students. The volunteers kept detailed
case reports on children's welfare and families' health and would notify the
society's governing committee if anyone were in particular need. Carpenter
chose the poorest district for herself and served as committee secretary, a
position she would hold for more than twenty years.[8]

After Carpenter's father died, she struggled with periods of deep depres-
sion and threw herself into her charity work as a form of self-prescribed
treatment. She had already accomplished a lot for a nineteenth-century
woman, but she wanted to work on a larger scale. As a Victorian lady of good
social standing, she had held back from engaging with the most destitute of
Bristol's population. To work with them, even for charitable reasons, would
be seen as inappropriate. Now she was determined to help the poorest of
the poor in a hands-on way. Once again, disregarding societal norms, she
set to work.[9]

In 1846, at the age of thirty-nine, Carpenter founded a "ragged school."
Designed as a private means of addressing the public nuisance of urban
poverty, ragged schools collected homeless or so-called problem children off
the streets and provided them with a Christian education. Starting with just
a handful of kids from the Lewin's Mead slums, her ragged school quickly
grew to serve hundreds of young men and women without stockings, shoes,
or shirts and who slept on Bristol's cobblestones and shipping docks.[10]

As the school expanded, Carpenter became more aware of the nuances of
crime and particularly how children got wrapped up in illegal ways of making ends meet. Children arrested for stealing food would show up at school
a few days later with newfound swagger, commanding respect from their
classmates. Frustrated by the blazon disregard for authority but convinced

that the adult prison system was ineffective at deterring future criminal activity and was cruel to children, Carpenter decided to shift her attention to criminal justice reform.

Carpenter's objections to the existing juvenile justice system were not novel, and her calls for reform were not new, but they were strongly worded for a woman. In 1851 she published her first of many social critiques on criminal reform and the treatment of juvenile offenders and began traveling around England advocating for the cause at meetings and parties.[11]

Despite her regular attendance, she did not speak much at these events. Speaking up in a room full of men would have been interpreted as inappropriate, and she had not yet gained the courage, expertise, nor respect to not care.

Carpenter may have sat silently at the Birmingham Conference of 1851, where the concept of a three-tiered school system for the poor consisting of Free Day Schools for nonoffenders, Industrial Feeding Schools for petty offenders, and Correctional and Reformatory Schools for serious repeat criminal offenders was developed, but she threw herself into the system's execution. Throughout the 1850s and 1860s, Carpenter founded more schools, including the Red Lodge, a reformatory school for girls.[12]

As she approached her sixties, Carpenter conceptualized her 1866 trip to India as a mission in sympathy and sisterhood. She intended, she said, to explore whether her expertise in education and advocacy could further female education and improve the status of women in furthest reaches of the British empire.[13]

The trip from England to India took the better part of a month and included travel by ship, carriage, train, and a period of quarantine. Traveling with her Indian chaperone, Ghose, as part of a large contingent of India-bound men and women, the trip also included exposure to racism and xenophobia. Carpenter saw Ghose endure verbal abuse for his dark skin, his Indian origins, and his presumed Hindu faith, even though he had converted to Christianity. Carpenter defended her anglicized companion, adamant that every Christian, regardless of nationality or humbleness of upbringing, deserved to be treated respectfully.[14]

When they finally pulled into Bombay harbor in the early morning of September 24, 1866, cannon signaled their arrival. Carpenter was met on board by a representative of the governor and invited to breakfast on shore. Stepping onto land in Bombay was like waking up from a dream. After weeks in transit, Carpenter paused beneath the regal coconut palms. The area outside the governor's house was chaotic, but inside the gates, serenity fell like a soft blanket. Native servants served English teas, creating an atmosphere with just enough of India seeping through the walls for the foreign to remain close, but not too close.[15]

Carpenter's trip would last for six months and take her all across India. She visited local jails, where she recommended building individual sleeping cells and hiring a teacher to provide lessons, and private schools, where she emphasized the importance of educating girls. Life for women in India was strictly controlled and confined to the home, but Carpenter believed that by educating women, she could catalyze change.

However, the education Carpenter advocated for in India was very different from the one that she had received from her father. Rather than prioritizing academics, Carpenter was adamant that Indian women first needed to be retrained in what it meant to be a proper lady. Lessons in needlework, poetry, singing, and other "feminine" skills would, she claimed, help to tame their wild husbands and encourage good Christian virtues.[16]

This art of civilized domesticity was, she believed, nonexistent in Indian culture. Men mended clothing and did laundry, both utterly unacceptable in English society—to Carpenter, "good society." She found the apparent inversion of gender norms deeply disturbing, and the entire structure of society was, she felt, evidence of complete social disorder. To set things right, women needed to reclaim their rightful domain.

By regaining control of their God-given domestic virtue, the women of India would be lifted out of the cultural and literal gutters and sewage drains. More peaceful and well-ordered households built on a British system of decorum would draw society away from hedonistic idols and elevate them to a better standard of behavior.

Carpenter's methods were routine and repeated, and each city visit replicated the one before it. She would meet with a British official or two before going to an English burial ground or church. Then she would visit a few schools. At the schools, she would be introduced to well-dressed and well-spoken Indians and give them advice on how to do better. She'd hear students sing or recite, or she would watch them do needlework. She gave gifts to promising students, and she was always thanked effusively for her time.[17]

In each city and at each school, prison, and missionary station, Carpenter was treated as a celebrity. She was catered to, congratulated on her Christian virtue, thanked for her charitable nature, and pleaded with to come back, but she was conflicted about her recommendations. She wrote that the helpless women of India had her sympathy. Still, the joylessness of the Hindu people and their seeming inability to imagine a better life for themselves was frustrating.[18]

The same apathy that blanketed the religious procession that blocked her carriage as she arrived in Calcutta was, she said, pervasive throughout the entire population. To save them was not a lost cause, and she was confident she was equal to the task, but it would be an arduous uphill battle.[19]

A New Type of Traveler

On December 9, 1868, the *Manchester Guardian* published a response to Carpenter's travels around India submitted by the secretary to the Philanthropic Association in Broach. Sorabsha Dadabhai wrote, "I fully applaud the motives by which Miss Carpenter was actuated in visiting these shores some months ago, and I consider her six months' mission as one of pure love and benevolence. However, I can never persuade myself to believe that such transient visits could leave any durable trace behind them."[20] Dadabhai sent the letter to the *Manchester Guardian* rather than to an Indian paper because "there are thousands in India who share in my opinion, and therefore do not require to be informed by me of what they know to be a fact."[21] At the time of writing, Dadabhai knew Carpenter would be back in India soon, and she would travel there many times before her death a decade after she first set foot on Indian soil.

Carpenter was not the first person to travel with the intention of doing good. However, thanks to the advances made during the Industrial Revolution, she could travel faster, for shorter periods, and with greater frequency than those before her. This marked Carpenter as one of the first of a new breed—a type of traveler who wanted to make their mark on faraway lands without having to leave home for years or for good. She was a traveler who pushed for reform, unable to fathom that a different culture could function perfectly well without her butting in. She was nourished in her fight for English social norms by the accolades she received for giving back.

While Carpenter was becoming one of the first of this new type of traveler who feeds on feeling good about doing good, an Englishman was developing a new kind of tour that could cater to the less independent of her kind. They did not know it at the time, but over the next century and a half, the models they each helped to develop would create a multibillion-dollar industry that would reshape the places they loved and affect the entire planet.

2 | A Certain Kind of Tourism

On a spring day in England in 1841, a slim figure of medium height in a dark suit walked along the road connecting Market Harborough with the neighboring town of Leicester.[1]

Thomas Cook was a man of rudimentary education but strong will. Known for his longwinded sermons, he had also gained a reputation in the area for his speeches extolling the virtues of life without drink. Yet alcohol's pernicious hold on his community and society seemed to be growing stronger. Liquor, Cook reasoned, was an escape. If he could offer a more enticing, more wholesome, and still affordable distraction, he might replace the respite alcohol was providing. Conveniently, the Midland Counties Railway Company had recently opened a line connecting the area with larger and more exciting cities nearby. An excursion by rail, he decided, was just what his community needed.[2]

Thomas Cook was born in a poor laborer's cottage in Melbourne, England, in November 1808. There was not much time for education. At the age of ten, he started working for a penny a day in the gardens of a local estate, and, when Thomas was fourteen, his uncle took him on as an apprentice cabinet-maker. Cook was never a particularly talented craftsman, but he learned discipline and deepened his faith. On February 26, 1826, at eighteen, he followed other members of his family in being baptized into the Baptist church by Pastor Joseph Foulkes Winks.[3]

Cook was enamored with Father Winks. When the pastor moved eleven miles away to the town of Loughborough, Cook abandoned his apprenticeship to follow him. In Loughborough, Cook learned the printing and publishing business as he worked alongside Winks in his shop. More importantly, Cook learned the power of a sermon to change hearts and guide minds. After returning to Melbourne in 1828, Cook was appointed as a village missionary and honed his speaking skills while traveling around the countryside, often on foot.[4]

In 1829 Cook met Marianne Mason, a Baptist Sunday school teacher. Mason's quiet patience was the perfect match for Cook's outspoken passion. The young couple was married in March 1833, a few months after Cook took his first temperance pledge—a promise to abstain from all hard alcohol. In January 1834 their first child was born and was named John Mason Cook. Soon after, Cook joined Marianne in reaffirming his pledge to abstain from alcohol, this time including beer, as part of the Teetotal Movement. From then on, the fight against the evils of alcohol was the paramount issue in Cook's life. Later, it would become the driving motivation behind what would grow from a simple day trip on the newly opened railroad in the summer of 1841 to a global travel empire that dominated tourism for more than 170 years.[5]

Life for men like Cook in England was generally static before the dawn of the railway age. Travel, especially leisure travel, was inaccessible for the vast majority of society. The landed aristocracy benefited from inexpensive labor that stayed local. People moving from place to place risked greater social awareness, the dispersal of revolutionary ideologies, and an upheaval of the status quo. Tourism was a nonstarter for all but the richest, and a life on the road was a sign of untrustworthiness and lower social rank. If you weren't rich and you didn't stay put, you were potentially dangerous.[6]

When people did travel before the advent of rail, the process was not particularly comfortable. Scenes of elegant carriages gliding along smooth country roads that fill modern period films and historical novels were in actuality rare occurrences. Most carriages were heavy wooden boxes with minimal ventilation and little to no shock absorption. Roads were rutted, rocky, and often washed out. Carriages were packed with people and luggage and lacked bathrooms. A ride in one for more than a short distance was more often a hardship to be suffered than an enjoyable adventure.

The Industrial Revolution did not immediately smooth out carriage roads or birth a fully mobile populace, but it did shift the tectonic plates of society. With industrial innovations came factory production. Factories needed workers and people flocked to the cities in response, leaving behind many of the expectations, norms, and support structures that had undergirded their lives in small towns.

Steel, Steam, and Social Good

The Industrial Revolution spurred an economic boom and a social phenomenon. For the first time, Western Europe and the United States developed a true middle class, a segment of society made up of factory owners, merchants, doctors, lawyers, entrepreneurs, and others who were not elevated by rank, title, or birth but by the financial solvency that came with industrialization and investment. And yet, just as the expansion of cities empowered the growing middle, the concentration of human bodies within cities amplified the plight of the poor.

In small towns, close ties had formed necessary social safety nets. It was rare that a person of deep faith, good behavior, and with a strong work ethic would be allowed to exist in complete destitution. Meals could be found in exchange for work, and clothing was used, mended, then passed along. It was far from luxurious, and some people did slip through the cracks, especially if they differed from societal expectations for belief or behavior, but by and large the system kept communities as a whole afloat. Mass migration into cities severed these community bonds and ripped holes in the safety nets that buoyed them. Destitute poor overwhelmed cities that had no system for dealing with them. This hit women, children, and those physically or mentally unable to work the hardest.

At first, the newly minted urban middle class tried to ignore this surge in abject poverty. Focused on striving upward, the middle class did not have much time to worry about what was going on in the rapidly expanding slums. When they gave money or goods, it was at a distance and most often through religious institutions: a check here and a bundle of clothes to a women's shelter there. With few exceptions, those with resources were not emotionally tuned in to the plight of those who slept on their doorsteps. Conditions quickly deteriorated, however, especially for poor children, beyond the point where the more privileged who lived among them could pretend not to notice.

In the late 1830s, writer and social critic Charles Dickens blasted through the flimsy wall the middle class had built between itself and the urban poor with his serial "The Adventures of Oliver Twist." From February 1837 through April 1839, the story of a young orphaned boy forced into the inhumane system of workhouses, which used starvation and menial labor as misguided incentives for the poor to raise their lot, played out in the pages of *Bentley's Miscellany*. The story was fiction, but Dickens's vivid illustration of urban poverty lit the match for a social awakening on both sides of the Atlantic.[7]

Simultaneously, the Victorian era kicked into gear. Both English and American society were at the beginning of a half-century of restrained behavior, refined manners, and a pivot inward.[8]

Even before Queen Victoria's accession in 1837, a new form of evangelism was already on the rise. For those who followed the trend, the center of religious life shifted from houses of worship to private homes. A haven of calm domesticity, the family home was, the theory went, the best place to foster and exemplify godliness. Empowered by the entrance of religion into their sitting rooms, women suddenly carried more religious clout than they had when churches were the only place where God resided.

Another piece of the new evangelism that particularly resonated with women was the reestablishment of service before doctrine. Just as the home became the center of spiritual salvation, actively engaging in community service became a means of reaching deliverance. Women were encouraged to become vocal advocates for and actors of their faith, and despite the strict social rules of the Victorian era, middle-class white women became the leaders in hands-on philanthropy.[9]

Charity work offered an avenue for independence and autonomy, creating a space in which a middle-class woman could cultivate a public personality independent from that of her husband or family. This new space offered friendship, fellowship, and increased social status, and was centered on the concept of the "white woman's burden"—a duty to help the less fortunate couched in assumed moral superiority.[10]

Today uncharitableness can be interpreted as an unforgivable character flaw.[11] In the mid-nineteenth century, middle-class individuals engaging in hands-on giving was groundbreaking and society-quaking. However, the enthusiasm for giving in the Victorian era did not immediately translate into productive help. In general, the methods employed by the Victorians were ineffective and at times cruel. Workhouses were particularly controversial. Even so, charity as a middle-class social practice quickly became the norm.

Thomas Cook may not have recognized the connection between his social agenda and the wider charitable movement of the Victorian era. Still, the surge in social concern, volunteerism, and increased autonomy for women among the same class for whom travel was just becoming an accessible leisure activity would have a direct impact on his eventual business success.

Soon after Cook decided that an excursion by rail was just what the good people of his town needed, he convinced the Midland Counties Railway Company to carry a cadre of temperance supporters on a round-trip adventure from Leicester to Loughborough for the deeply discounted price of a shilling each. On July 5, 1841, close to five hundred excursionists met at Leicester Station. Watched by a crowd of as many as three thousand and encouraged by a brass band, they boarded the train. A small portion of the party traveled in a closed second-class carriage, but most squeezed into nine open standing-room-only third-class train cars, from which they waved to the spectators that lined their route, periodically dodging sparks thrown off by the engine.[12]

Compared to the mobility of free white men in America, a tradition that was already deeply ingrained in the social fabric of the young nation, travel was a novelty in rural England. Train travel was a new phenomenon, and the line of open cars full of waving travelers was a unique spectacle. When they arrived in Loughborough, the party processed grandly through town, had tea, played lawn games, and listened to lectures from local temperance leaders before their return trip.[13]

Following his success, Cook moved his family from Market Harborough, which did not have a train station, to Leicester, an ideal travel hub. Over the next few years, he continued to arrange short and inexpensive recreational trips to temperance events. By 1844, three years after that first trip for talks and tea, he had earned a reputation as a travel entrepreneur with a passion for social good.[14]

In the summer of 1845, Cook coordinated his inaugural trip from Leicester to Liverpool, with options for extensions, for 350 people by boat. Participants received discounted tickets for the four train lines they would need to take and a trip handbook. For the first time, Cook received a commission, a modest 5 percent, on the sale of each ticket.[15] It was something, but it wasn't enough, yet, to make a living.

Within a year, Cook's lack of attention toward turning a profit would catch up with him. On July 31, 1846, he declared bankruptcy. Somehow, he was able to keep his home, and that saved him. By 1848 the Cooks were bouncing back. Marianne had opened a Temperance Hotel in their home, and Thomas had launched a new bookselling and news agency and had restarted his excursions.[16]

Cook's clients were mostly members of the mobile middle class: doctors, clergy, and successful merchants, professionals with just enough free time and spare money to take a vacation. Educational and religious groups were reliable travelers as well. Members of the working class were less common customers, but Cook tried to price his trips reasonably enough that a hardworking and savings-minded person could, someday, buy a ticket. In 1877 a Cook trip to Palestine included a man who'd saved for thirty years to afford the fee.[17]

Single women were a core customer base for Cook, who marketed his trips as safe and appropriate for unaccompanied women of good standing. Travelers trusted him, and there were regularly more women than men on regional trips. The accessibility and propriety of solo travel (within a group) stretched the benefits of the new evangelical ethos beyond its urban birth-place, temporarily loosening many of the strict conventions of Victorian culture through a respected social-good agenda.[18]

Over time, the opportunity for middle-class people to see the same sights as the royals and the wealthy began to close the global awareness gap between the classes. Yet the upper classes made it known that the greater geographic mobility among middle-class English men and women was not the same as upward social mobility. Or, at least, not yet.[19]

A Great Exhibition

The Great Exhibition of 1851 was a venue for English braggadocio but also for global education and awareness. For the nation, it was an opportunity to showcase the enormous advances in manufacturing technology and workmanship. For Cook, it was the perfect combination of excursion and educational advancement. It did not hurt that the Crystal Palace, the massive glass structure built to house the exhibition, was dry. Alcohol, he boasted, was not welcome at such an auspicious event. Of the six million visitors during the Great Exhibition's nearly six-month run, almost everyone who was not already living in London traveled there on the country's expanding railways. In the most significant test of volume he had tackled yet, Cook arranged the transportation for 165,000 of them.[20]

For non-Londoners with limited pocket change, there were two ways of getting to the Great Exhibition. The first option was to join a subscription club, a sort of savings plan. Each month, subscription club members paid dues to the club organizers. By the time their trip rolled around, there would be enough money in the club account to cover the train tickets, lodging, food, and admission fees for the group. The second option was to travel with a company like Cook's.

Cook was socially minded and ethically rigorous, but he also knew how to play the marketing game. One of his favorite sales strategies was to hire a brass band to play outside of factories on payday evenings. After attracting the attention of the recently moneyed workers, Cook would launch into salesman mode, selling them "affordable" trip packages that included discounted train fares, guidebooks, and simple lodging. The profit margin on these working-class fares was narrow, but, as with many of Cook's endeavors, monetary gain was not the primary motive. To Cook, attending the exhibition was a once-in-a-lifetime opportunity, and he was excited to give so many the chance to do so.[21]

London was flooded with people from the lead-up to the May Day 1851 opening of the Great Exhibition of the Works of Industry of All Nations in Hyde Park, London, until it closed on October 15 that year. The crowds were unprecedented, and the city's tourism infrastructure was terribly underprepared. Hotels had been reluctant to offer lower-cost accommodations for the working-class "mobs," so many visitors arrived in London only to discover there was nowhere to stay.[22]

A father who brought his family on a discounted rail package from Cook might wake up with a crick in his neck after a night on a hard floor. Once he approached the entrance to the Crystal Palace, however, the differences between him and the doctor, priest, or wealthy businessman who crossed the palace grounds alongside him nearly dissolved. Everyone entered the same building, marveled at the same inventions, bought the same Schweppes ginger beer, pickles, and sweet rolls, and wondered how papier-mâché sculpture could be so strong when paper is so flimsy. The visitors would leave for very different accommodations, but, for a few hours, they had been side by side.[23]

The exhibition was a showcase of English exceptionalism, and many of the machines and innovations spotlighted as particularly miraculous were the same machines lower-class exhibition visitors worked over every day. To see one's tools put on a pedestal is close to seeing oneself exalted, and by bringing hundreds of thousands of people to London, Cook and his competitors had made a strong statement about the nation's more egalitarian future. Low-cost excursions were now a piece of English culture, and there was nothing the upper classes could do about it.[24]

As Cook's travel business developed and the number of people interested in taking train excursions grew, so did the competitors who often copied his routes, sometimes executing them even better. Despite the competition, Cook always stood out thanks to his unique integration of travel offerings with temperance and social-good agendas.[25]

On Iona, a small island off the western coast of Scotland, Cook would pause his tours to give a passionate speech about how wonderful the island was. He would extol the virtues of the people, celebrate how welcoming they were to visitors, and ask his travelers to return the kindness by donating whatever they could to help alleviate their poverty. By 1861 the donations collected from Cook's clients had paid for a new fishing fleet.[26]

And yet, while the people of Iona got a new fleet, Cook was still barely scraping by. Bankruptcy had taught him to be cautious, but he continued to prioritize giving back over financial stability. By 1865 he had taken more than fifty thousand people to Scotland and had launched trips to France and the Swiss Alps, but he was still a small operation in an unreliable and seasonal business.[27]

Other companies had more resources and more prosperous clientele, and Cook was known for letting fellow teetotalers and Baptists travel at deep discounts. He operated his business under the guidance of conscience without much regard for the bottom line, and his profits were anemic. His name had clout, but his lack of a business brain meant that he was in no way an economic powerhouse of international tourism.

Despite all signs suggesting otherwise, Cook was determined to dominate the European continent by sticking with what he had built his name on: inexpensive trips for adventurous people of medium means that discouraged drinking and encouraged social good.[28]

The Next Generation

Since he was old enough to hold a stack of train tickets, Thomas Cook's son, John Mason Cook, assisted with his father's business. He was seven when he joined his first excursion with his father. By age ten, he was guiding groups himself, starting with a day trip for five hundred children. He handled the pressure and chaos well and was only fifteen when his father entrusted him with his first major trip in 1849.[29]

John Mason Cook was exacting. Where his father was relaxed, he was precise. Tall and thickset, his will was iron and his management style was dictatorial. John was not attracted to the job by a desire to work alongside his dad. What his father treated like a side gig, John saw as a business with massive potential. He intended to transform it from a small and struggling operation into a global empire.[30]

John quickly mobilized, and he did his best to keep his father on the road and out of the company's books. It was an excellent time to have the elder Cook leading trips. By the mid-1860s, more than forty thousand Americans were traveling to Europe each year, but with the American Civil War ended and British curiosity about their former colony at a high point, the Cooks decided to expand in the other direction.[31]

In 1866 Thomas Cook led the company's first tour to the United States. The travelers were as fascinated by the lingering carnage of war—bleaching bones, temporary bridges, and torn-up battlefields—as they were by Niagara Falls. They were also comfortable. Americans' enthusiasm for pleasure travel had already spawned a network of tourism amenities (transportation, lodging, food, and guides) significantly more developed than what was available in much of Europe, North Africa, or the Middle East. The true success of the trip, however, was in the company's newfound access to a transcontinental customer base. By 1869 the Cooks were offering all-inclusive package trips to Egypt and Palestine that catered to Europeans and Americans alike.[32]

Even before Thomas Cook's first excursion in the English countryside in 1841, other companies had been taking curious westerners to the Middle East. They had traveled in small groups, relying on local guides, and safety had been a constant concern. Thomas and John were not breaking new ground by entering the Middle East, but they were doing things their way.[33]

A Cook party arriving in the Holy Land in March of 1869 made its first stop in the small coastal city of Jaffa. English men and women in full Victorian dress wandered through the city's fruit tree groves picking lemons, pomegranates, and peaches. The air was heavy with the scent of new flowers, and cypress trees waved in the gentle sea breeze. Veiled women floated through the cramped and crooked streets the travelers took to visit Tabeetha, a school for local girls founded in 1863 by Scot Jane Walker-Arnott.[34]

After camping outside of the city in large circular canvas tents that were easier to control than the unpredictable hotels and guesthouses, members of Cook's group watched as their food, furniture, and mountains of personal baggage were loaded up onto dozens of pack mules. Railroads were few and coaches were rare, so travelers in the Middle East had to hope for a calm horse with a good gait and a soft saddle. They were lucky if they got one of the three.[35]

The harsh climate and long days drained every ounce of energy in the group as they made their way toward Jerusalem along a road that was little more than a stony track. Stories of tourists robbed of everything, even their clothes, kept more adventurous or experienced riders from breaking away from the plodding caravan.[36]

When they finally approached the sacred city, the beautiful and vibrant cityscapes seen from afar were often less pleasing up close, the otherworldly magic traded for the familiarity of urban filth. The travelers could just make out the outlines of donkeys with baskets of stones or bushels of brushwood through the thick dust clouds. Lines of camels carried piles of melons to market. The cries for baksheesh from the crowds of beggars that filled every holy place punctuated the tableau.[37] One beggar became infamous at the time for his successes during the tourism high season. Legend had it that he'd bought multiple orchards with the money he earned from generous European visitors.[38]

Within the walls of Jerusalem, half-naked children followed the tourists like second shadows. Young women enslaved by wealthy Arabs could be spotted by their red pants and jackets, necks dripping with silver. Abyssinian men brought from the Horn of Africa carried heavy loads, and eunuchs slipped through the crowds on urgent errands. Visiting a religious site or historical monument sometimes meant scampering over piles of rotting trash and dodging snarling dogs. Should they wish, tourists could buy slaves to use as servants or concubines for the length of their stay. Many did.[39]

Between the harsh climate, the overwhelming poverty, and the urban disorder, the Cooks had to find a way to maintain an aura of sparkle. The first line of defense were the trip guides, whose job it was to maintain a buffer between their clients and reality, constructing the romance that tourists still expect today when visiting places that are far from simplified fantasies. The Cooks called their guides *dragomen*, the traditional term, but made sure that most of their employees had familiar English origins. A group of true dragomen fought back, penning a letter published in the *Times of London* calling out travel agents like Cook for taking over the industry they had built, but the Cooks and their peers persisted.[40]

The goal was to make travelers' experiences as English as possible. Rather than having their customers stay in local bunkhouses or basic hotels, the Cooks provided travelers with large tents with carpeted floors, iron bedsteads, tables, and camp stools. There were comfortable mattresses, clean white sheets, dozens of attendants, and a team of chefs to cook distinctly British meals. The elder Cook also wanted to facilitate charitable responses that were more controlled than tossing coins and that would literally corral the beggars who, at times, overwhelmed his guests. Handing out food was both finite and fulfilling, and Cook travelers became known for passing out bread to up to a thousand people at a time.[41]

River cruises on the Nile were a particularly effective way of maintaining the luxurious aesthetic tourists demanded. The river formed a natural barrier between tourists and the local flora and fauna, and celebrities of the time, such as Cecil Rhodes and Rudyard Kipling, appreciated the Cooks' ability to create a dream world of white silk suits and holiday fantasy on their riverboats. Florence Nightingale, the oft-exalted founder of modern nursing, compared Egyptians to scampering lizards—present, but hardly a distraction from the beauty of the region. Manufacturing distance worked. By 1899 the Cooks' Nile operation would grow to a flotilla of steamers and sailing vessels.[42]

A Juggernaut

When the Suez Canal opened in 1869, the Far East was suddenly far more accessible to leisure tourists than ever before. Cook arranged the first-ever-documented around-the-world tour, a 222-day trip that covered twenty-five thousand miles by boat, horse, and carriage. And on January 1, 1873, the Cook party became the first recorded organized tourist group to set foot in India.[43]

It was seven years after Mary Carpenter had disembarked in India for the first time, but Cook and Carpenter's paths overlapped in Serampore, a Baptist mission established in a Danish trading community. The two travelers shared an enthusiasm for the religiosity of the outpost in the midst of what they saw as an overwhelmingly unenlightened populace. They even commented on the same thing in their journals, albeit seven years apart: a juggernaut car. "We used to suppose that the car of Juggernaut was a thing of the past," Carpenter wrote in her journal in 1866. "Here, however, I actually beheld it in all its native clumsy hideousness—a dreadful reality."[44]

Juggernaut is the English name for the large chariots or wagons decorated with Hindu gods and used in processions, most notably at the Jagannath Temple in Puri. The vehicles can be huge, towering many stories high, and their engineering often appears unlikely. The carriage of the juggernaut is supported by gigantic wheels that, according to the myth, legend, and Western literature of Carpenter and Cook's time, Hindus would throw themselves under as religious sacrifices.[45] This visual illuminates the modern use of the word to describe something destructive and unstoppable, a force of nature.

The juggernaut Cook recorded seeing in Serampore may well have been the same one that Carpenter had commented on in her journal many years earlier. If so, she would have been relieved. By the time Cook was there, termites were turning it to dust.[46]

The round-the-world trip brought fame, the Suez Canal improved accessibility, and the Cooks' transcontinental business grew. By 1878 the father-and-son duo were formally partners. Soon the Thomas Cook & Son Company was a household institution.[47]

Thomas Cook passed away in 1892 at the age of eighty-four. The *New York Times* called him "one of the greatest revolutionists of our time; but," they added, "happily for mankind, his zeal for change took a beneficent and not a mischievous form."[48]

Guided by John's firm hand, Thomas Cook & Son continued to expand, although it lost most of its altruistic personality. The company passed on to a third generation, which sold it in 1928. At one point, the "& Son" was dropped. Throughout it all and for more than 170 years, Thomas Cook remained one of the most potent travel brands in the world.[49]

Europeans were not the world's first tourists, and Thomas Cook did not invent tourism. He was not even the world's first travel agent, but he did contribute to the transformation of a niche activity and a fragmented market into a global industry. By developing the package tour and introducing a generation to the potential of affordable global adventure, and a smaller yet passionate group to the opportunity to do good along the way, Cook was integral to the creation of the particular form of tourism I'm most interested in. Travel was more than a business to him. It was a social mission.[50]

In September 2019, nearly two centuries after Cook came up with the idea for a humble train excursion to promote the temperance movement, the company's run came to a spectacular end when more than 150,000 travelers and employees found themselves stranded in the wake of the collapsing empire.[51]

Despite this calamitous conclusion, the name Thomas Cook remains one of the most recognizable in travel.

As tourism has grown over the past two hundred years, each expansion toward a new frontier has been an opportunity for those with more to declare that tourists have gone too far. John Ruskin, a "high priest of the Alpine cult," denounced tourists as early as 1864, writing that there was not a single foreign city "in which the spread of your presence is not marked among its fair old streets and happy gardens by a consuming white leprosy." The elite could complain, but tourism for the masses was here to stay.[52]

Cook's core belief that tourism could do good had also taken form as a strong and steady undercurrent within the tourism industry. His passion for altruistic travel would bob and weave its way through time, popping up in places of great beauty and great poverty and eventually becoming an industry of its own—one Cook could never have imagined.

3 | Cars, Planes, and Resorts

The first decade of the twentieth century was good to Western tourists and the tourism industry that served them. The expansion of the European and American colonial empires throughout the nineteenth century had provided literal in-roads as tourism companies, trip providers, and amenities pushed deeper south into Africa, east throughout Asia, and across the American West. The rise of the automobile and the introduction of the telephone transformed tourism in much the same way railways had fifty years earlier: they made movement more comfortable and convenient.[1]

World War I shut down tourism in Europe and North Africa. The impacts of total war, such as food and supply shortages, made leisure travel difficult. If financial resources were not an issue, the idea of vacationing when millions of people were fighting for their lives was at the very least distasteful. But as the world fought, tourism in America boomed. In a nation built on the presumption of mobility and with seemingly endless space to explore, Americans had taken to leisure travel quickly—even if they tended to stay within their own nation's borders. In 1915, in the middle of World War I,

American Express launched a travel arm that would grow alongside Thomas Cook & Son, and its many European competitors, from the other side of the shrinking Atlantic.[2]

The adventurousness of American tourists is best characterized by the most iconic form of American travel: the road trip. Road trips are free-form, self-governed, and constrained only by the amount of gas in the tank and the driver's imagination. When limited by where roads led, early American road-trippers took to pulling on a pair of boots, loading up a pack mule, and going on foot.

From July 1920 through November 1921, Mary Adams Abbott and her adult daughter, Mary Ogden Abbott, traveled a wandering route around the United States from Massachusetts to Seattle, south to Arizona, then east to the Grand Canyon and Idaho. They fished and hiked along the way before boarding a boat bound for New Zealand in San Francisco on December 30, 1921. The women exemplified the free spirit of the American tourist and the freedoms available to bold women with money to spare. A few decades earlier, they would likely have booked a Cook-style all-inclusive package tour. As they lounged upon the SS *Tahiti*, they were on their own.[3]

The Abbott women expressed awe at what they saw throughout their journey. Mary Adams journaled about customs and costumes in Indonesia, and Mary Ogden relished the opportunity to sketch local people. Travel did not, however, seem to result in a greater understanding of or empathy for other cultures nor a reduction of the Abbotts' racial prejudice.

Decades after Mary Carpenter scolded Indian women for letting men do laundry, Mary Adams described the Indonesian New Year celebrations as "a circus at its worst," and the Maori people as "very dark, really quite black sometimes, and rather n—— to the uneducated apprehension."[4] In Tahiti, she lamented that, instead of the picturesque "naked brown bodies plunging into the iridescent water" she had seen in the West Indies, there was "a boatload of nasty fat black slugs."[5]

Travel is undeniably transformative, but every tourist comes (and leaves) with baggage. The Abbotts had packed their bigotry and racism along with their extra stockings.

Innovation

The most significant effect war had on tourism was in the advancement and normalization of flight. The first "airlift" took place in the winter of 1871. With Paris under siege, a small group of citizens and millions of letters were lifted up in hydrogen balloons prone to transforming into floating fireballs. The development of powered flight took another thirty years, and it would be another decade after that before commercial air travel would begin to gain steam.[6]

By 1919 enough planes were whizzing through the air to require regulation. On October 13 the Paris Convention relating to the Regulation of Aerial Navigation was signed. Further attempts at regulation would come in 1925, at the International Congress of Official Tourist Traffic Associations, the origin of today's United Nations World Tourism Organization. The skies were now open to commercial travel to cheers of a more integrated and accessible world—for the Allied and Associated Powers, at least.[7]

Even early in the age of air travel, it was clear that airspace would be a crucial and defendable part of a nation's sovereignty, but now it was a profitable peacetime resource as well. Still, a lack of airport infrastructure (most notably, smooth runways), a small supply of suitable aircraft (both in comfort and technology), and the niggling idea that air travel was simply unsafe limited the expansion of commercial aviation.[8] Many chose to watch planes take off in awe but opted to keep two feet, four wheels, a train car, or a sturdy keel firmly on the earth when it came to their preferred modes of conveyance.

Even with limited planes and significant facility constraints, the ability to access a nation's airspace and airports became a bargaining chip in international politics. Countries took to blocking each other's airlines to protect their chunks of the expanding market in a tit-for-tat battle that carved up the world from above.[9]

World War II accelerated aircraft technology as governments invested in airplanes as war machines. Jumps in technology empowered a scale of violence and destruction that was previously unimaginable, yet they also pushed civilian society toward embracing air travel as a way of getting around. Planes became lighter, safer, more powerful, and more comfortable. Advancements like cabin pressurization drastically improved the passenger experience, whether on a military mission or on vacation.

Commercial flight was not, however, affordable, and neither was it efficient. Routes were roundabout—one could often get somewhere quicker by train than by plane—and tickets were shockingly expensive. A one-way flight from London to Karachi, Pakistan, could run you £162 (around £11,000 or $13,800 today) and only included the bare bones: a reclining seat, tray table, and simple refreshments.[10]

Airlines relied on government financing and carrying freight and mail to stay afloat, and the transition toward passenger-centric flight was gradual. In 1929, 639,000 passengers traveled by air globally. Sixteen years later, in 1945, that number had increased by only a third. But, by the middle of the twentieth century, passenger air travel was finally approaching a viable business model.[11]

With fattening wallets, expanding vacation schedules, and more options for how to travel, the stage was set for another tourism boom. The Holidays with Pay Act of 1938 gave more than ten million Brits access to paid vacations. Britain had followed the lead of France, which enacted a similar law mandating two weeks of paid time off for every citizen in 1936. By the 1950s, surging household disposable incomes and skyrocketing consumer spending meant aspiring travelers finally had the time and the money to take advantage of the opportunity.[12]

Fun in the Sun

Throughout the nineteenth century, England had been the epicenter of the Western tourism market. Its proximity to continental Europe, Africa, and the Middle East and accessibility to reliable land and sea routes to Asia had made widespread international travel easiest for the English. They had opened Egypt and India up to large-scale international tourism, had created European oases in "uncivilized" landscapes, and had mastered the trick of selling what would become known as the "developing world."[13] But by the second half of the twentieth century, the convenience of air travel and American economic success caused trends to flip.

Suddenly, casual international tourism was growing much faster in the United States than in Europe. American tourists became ubiquitous, and American airlines dominated long-haul international routes. At the same time, tourism advertising became the largest source of ad revenue for American newspapers. Americans were on the move, and the Western Hemisphere was the place to be.[14]

In the Caribbean, early tourists picked their destinations along colonial lines. For the English, Jamaica and Barbados were the islands of choice. The French chose Martinique, Curaçao was for the Dutch, and the Bahamas quickly became an American favorite thanks to the short distance between Miami airstrips and Bahamian white sand beaches. Americans also jumped at the opportunity to develop Cuba. By 1915 Cuba had dozens of hotels predominately catering to international visitors. By the 1950s the island was playing host to more than three hundred thousand tourists a year. Unwilling to give up all of the territories it had amassed at its colonial peak, Spain retained its self-given title as "Kings of the Caribbean" by gobbling up sizable holdings in Mexico and the Dominican Republic. Between France, Spain, the Netherlands, the UK, and the United States, the Caribbean was nearly fully accounted for by colonial powers.[15] With only a handful of exceptions, the people buying up Caribbean land were white, those designing and financing the infrastructure were white, and the tourists were nearly all white too.[16]

As competition for travelers' dollars increased, airfare prices steadily declined. In the spring of 1952, Pan Am introduced the tourist-class ticket, which offered fewer amenities in exchange for lower fares. In 1958 the introduction of economy-class fares brought along another cut. For the well off, flights were a luxury adventure complete with gourmet food and smoking lounges. For the mobile middle class, they were the modern equivalent of bumpy carriage rides and third-class train excursions—a necessary discomfort. Anywhere planes could fly, people followed.[17]

Cruises followed the same growth trajectory airplanes had charted. As the list of leisure destinations grew, the boats expanded to comically large proportions, and the passenger volume was on an exponential upward trajectory. Whereas airplanes are a means to an end, the journey is the adventure on the hotels of the seas.[18]

Tourism Enclaves

Even well into the 1960s, international tourism relied heavily on the infrastructure colonialism had wrought. And, just as it had been during the highest points of the colonial empires, that infrastructure was predominately off-limits to locals. In Egypt the idea that Egyptians could be tourists was considered laughable. In Cuba native Cubans were banned from the Varadero resort area as Americans brought their unique brand of racism on holiday with them. Jim Crow beliefs did not take a vacation just because Jim Crow laws did not apply.[19]

The American perspective was particularly well suited to the development of *tourism enclaves*—places where tourism infrastructure is concentrated in a small geographic area. Tourism enclaves create a cocoon of comfort and safety where everything tourists need, and nothing they don't, is within easy reach. For corporations, the tourism enclave model is optimized for the maximization of profits. Tourism enclaves are a prime example of vertical integration. When the same company that owns the resort also owns all of the on-site and nearby restaurants, souvenir shops, grocery stores, guide services, and excursion providers, that company can increase the amount of money pocketed per customer. Instead of receiving a portion of what a tourist spends on vacation, the company gets everything.[20]

In essence, tourism enclaves keep tourists in and keep locals—and local businesses—out, either by force or through geographic restraints. If the destination is a tropical island, tourists want to be on the beach. Hence, resort developers try their best to monopolize the most brochure-worthy real estate by buying up every sand-adjacent parcel and pushing locals inland. This process is a continuation of the "close-but-separate" approach Cook took toward manufacturing paradise on his trips to the Middle East in the 1860s. To this day, local fishers are often still banned from working in areas where guests might see them, and local people remain barred from many beaches by gates, guards, or social pressure, even when the sand is legally public property.[21]

Once developers own all the choice pieces of property, they need to develop them to appeal to the expectations of the tourists they want to attract. Even if locals do not have running water or reliable electricity, tourism demands it. Some of the infrastructure resulting from tourism development may benefit broader communities. Roads that link airports to all-inclusives can also help farmers get to market, but the pavement ends where the shuttle buses stop.[22]

Clumping together is more profitable for developers for reasons other than just the ability to share infrastructure and the curation of a singular experience. The surging demand for cheap trips has cut into profit margins. Isolating people to catch every dollar they spend helps make up for this.[23] As a result, up to 90 percent of the dollars spent by tourists, especially if they are visiting foreign-owned properties, completely bypass local economies in a process known as *economic leakage*.[24]

In the 1970s as much as 70 percent of the tourism dollars that flowed into both Thailand and Fiji were never actually absorbed into the economies of either place. Instead, that money ended up in the foreign bank accounts of the airlines, resort operators, and developers.[25] In the Caribbean, economic leakage hovered around 70 percent through the 1990s.[26] This was not unique to the Caribbean then, and it is not unique today.

In developed tourism markets of the world's wealthier countries, a 33 percent economic leakage rate is to be expected. In developing tourism markets, a 50 percent rate of economic leakage is standard at best and, for many, aspirational.[27] Zanzibar, Tanzania, is one of the thousands of destinations where tourism is the biggest business around, yet the benefits have only trickled down to a handful of local people. Most of the income tourism has generated is accumulating in foreign bank accounts, as reported by nongovernmental organization Action Aid.[28]

The high cement walls of all-inclusives and chain-link fences of cruise ports exacerbate economic leakage even further. All-inclusive hotels have a history of raking in the highest percentage of customer spending while having the lowest economic impact locally.[29]

Over time, the growth of tourism enclaves and the infrastructure that supports them has resulted in many resorts, resources, and amenities being packed together like sunbathers trying to share a towel, forming huge zones dedicated to providing tourists with an "exotic" experience with Western-style amenities. Today, we would recognize these zones as places like Zanzibar, the Mexican beach city of Puerto Vallarta, or the Thai island of Koh Samui.[30]

Cook's Law

The tight hold foreign-owned resorts have on tourist dollars is a modern interpretation of Cook's Law, the theory that the largest profits come from heavy use of a destination by the largest number of people possible and at the lowest possible cost.[31] Local impact does not factor into the equation, but Cook's Law helps tourism surge.

By 1950 the number of international tourist arrivals was at 25 million globally, almost as if the entire population of 1840s England had gone on an international vacation. By 1975 the number of international arrivals had skyrocketed to 222 million.[32] In 2017 more than 1 billion people traveled internationally as tourists worldwide.[33] The entry of China into the global tourism market is responsible for much of this expansion. When Chinese citizens were first permitted to travel abroad for leisure in 1999, they could only travel to a short list of approved destinations. Slowly, though, the list grew.[34] Today, China has joined the United States and the UK as one of the top three nations for outbound tourism, and international tourism generated $1.34 trillion globally in 2017.[35]

If much of the twentieth century was defined by immense globe-encompassing wars of previously unimaginable violence and scale, the twenty-first century is being shaped by a different sort of global competition— the collection, expression, and spending of wealth.[36] Mass tourism has been on a cannibalistic rampage for decades. Big companies have been swallowing up smaller hotels and cruise lines for years before becoming chum for massive conglomerates themselves in a cycle of consolidation and control.[37] Today, tourism is one of the world's largest and fastest-growing industries, and even the threat of a deadly pandemic wasn't enough to stop American spring breakers from partying on Florida beaches in the spring of 2020.[38] Tourism is the largest employer in the world, accounting for one in every ten jobs.[39]

Tourist arrivals in emerging tourism economies are predicted to increase by 4.4 percent per year between 2010 and 2030, twice the predicted rate of growth of more advanced economies.[40] As arrivals increase, emerging economies have set themselves on a trajectory toward claiming the majority of the global tourism market, with projected growth from 45 percent in 2015 to 57 percent in 2030.[41]

These numbers mean little, however, unless applied to on-the-ground realities. In less-developed communities, governments, development organizations, and lending agencies aggressively market tourism as a gateway toward fueling job creation and infrastructure development that will, supporters say, lead to Western-style social and economic progress.[42] However, compounding evidence of the actual impacts of mass tourism development on communities contradicts the assumption that there is a direct relationship between visitor numbers and local economic growth—especially in developing regions.[43]

Each new hotel room equals roughly one new job. However, the majority of the jobs created by tourism in developing economies are low-paying, seasonal, and unskilled with little security. Opportunities for upward mobility are minimal, and management and leadership-track positions are frequently given to imported foreign workers because it is cheaper to fly labor in than to train locals. Unfortunately, these problems tend to be even greater at smaller or locally owned hotels than they are at resorts.[44] Outside resort walls, local businesses near resorts struggle to survive on the pocket change of guests who have already paid for their vacation, meal plan, and excursion package, and have left their wallets in their rooms.

By 1925 tourists in Egypt could travel in carriages cooled with blocks of ice hidden in false ceilings. This luxury was only possible because of local development and advances in infrastructure, and many Egyptians came not just to rely on tourism but to benefit from it. That lasted until their success became a problem. Some of the same communities that accumulated wealth as a result of the development of Nile cruises at the end of the nineteenth century were later "de-developed"—stripped back to their pre-ice-cooled-carriage days to create a more "authentic" experience for tourists. Locals wearing jeans and Jordans were ruining the visual for tourists paying for "authenticity." Destinations must have ample clean water and strong Wi-Fi but are required to reject the rest of the West to appear "real."

Today, we know that the development of mass tourism is as likely, if not more, to augment disparity than it is to increase equality.[45]

Transformation

Tourism has become a social fact, and visiting a new place, whether in another city, state, country, or continent, is a nearly universal experience for anyone with disposable income. It is also one of the most intimate ways in which we attempt to make sense of the world.[46] But for all the ways tourism helps us understand ourselves, for all the impressive numbers and growth projections, and for all the big promises made to the communities to which tourism has been sold as a ticket up, the actual effects of tourism on the ground are startling.

Among socially conscious tourists, a common response to the visible negative impacts of tourism is to try to avoid the places where those scars are visible. The term *authentic* is often used to describe places tourists can access but where their presence seems almost accidental. And yet, just as advances in transportation technology blazed trails for tourism's first growth spurt, today's authenticity-seeking tourists are stomping down the ground for the same types of development that they label "inauthentic." They are a critical piece in the development process of what they despise and are as much myth chasers on the hunt for the exotic as their predecessors were a century ago.[47]

Today, formerly foreign locales now appear almost pedestrian, and places Cook could never have imagined going have been made wheelchair accessible. As we turn the dangerous and the wild into the safe and the consumable, the marks tourists leave on the places they go are not as rosy as the cheeks of the kids on the covers of travel brochures. This is the price we pay to see the world, and our swimsuits, snorkeling gear, and souvenirs serve as convenient blinders that shield us from the worst of tourism's impacts. By the 1980s a growing number of people were beginning to consider this price too steep. There must, they thought, be a way to experience authenticity without also destroying it.[48]

4 | The Alternative Tourism Boomerang

In October 2009 a white woman with an entourage arrived at an orphanage in Malawi. She had been there before, in 2006. That time, she had met a young child named David. She had adopted him after climbing a mountain of legal hurdles, and now they were returning for a visit. As David played, the woman learned how her charity was helping to support the orphanage financially and met some of the children benefiting from her generosity. Journalists covering the visit reported that one child said to her, "You are our god. . . . Where could we have been without you?"[1] Not everyone can be like Madonna, but maybe we can travel like her.

Peer Pressure

Humans are born with a desire to help others. As infants, we show empathy. As young children, we try to assist in the kitchen or around the house even when our attempts are clumsy and ill timed. As we get older, we drop fewer things, can reach higher shelves, and start to acquire the vocabulary to explain the discomfort we feel when life is not fair. Bullying, cheating, and fighting are wrong. So is poverty—not the people who suffer from it, but the thing itself. We try to address the unfairness by giving away our money, our time, and our things. This giving feels good. It is a stimulant that feeds us and fuels us, and we look for partners who like that feeling too.[2]

Up until a few hundred years ago, humans' desire to help was paired with, for the vast majority of our species, a narrow field of vision. Most people could spend their entire lives knowing and living with and caring for the same core group of people. Widespread news media changed that.

In what amounts to the blink of an eye on a geologic time scale, humans were consuming vast quantities of news in papers, on the radio, on television, and online—much of it centered on human pain. Not everyone who is bombarded with visuals of inequity beyond their close social networks leaps into action, but enough do to catalyze and sustain a movement toward global engagement.[3]

The International Red Cross has been a critical piece of the global engagement puzzle since it was chartered in 1863, mobilizing hundreds of millions of people to respond to short- and long-term crises around the world to reduce suffering.[4] A century later, in 1961, President John F. Kennedy gave global engagement a new name and a fresh look: the Peace Corps.

The founding vision for the Peace Corps was that it would be distinct from the forms of development that had been rolled out by the crumbling colonial empires of the preceding decades. Volunteers had to be willing to spend multiple years in less-developed or undeveloped areas, and they needed to be culturally respectful and also, hopefully, tangibly helpful. However, the purpose of the Peace Corps was more than secular missionary work. Volunteers would be tools in a global endeavor to steer communities away from communism and toward a more "American" way of life.[5] The Peace Corps deployed seventy thousand volunteers in the first decade of the program, and the volunteers quickly became a new generation of pioneers who were willing to experience extreme discomfort to bring Western ideals to the wider world.[6]

Other countries launched initiatives approximating the Peace Corps around the same time President Kennedy announced his pet project, or even before. The Australian government started supporting their citizens in volunteering abroad in 1963.[7] Also in the 1960s, the Canadian government began financially supporting the Canadian University Service Overseas.[8] The International Voluntary Service had been founded in the United Kingdom thirty years earlier, in 1931.[9]

Peace Corps positions have never been tourism, and it certainly is not a vacation. However, it has shaped the way Americans conceive of the world—and their place in it. Committing many months or years to a volunteer placement on the other side of the planet is an enormous privilege that few people are professionally or financially situated to take. To the many who are not, those that do are inspiring.[10] The idea of the Peace Corps has inspired altruism at home and wild adventures abroad, and has been integral in shaping a loose desire to help into something tangible and actionable. The Peace Corps, and programs like it, have also contributed to a new era in travel. When those who idolize the Peace Corps book a vacation, alternative forms of tourism can offer a taste.

Good Tourism

Many people point to Costa Rica in the 1980s when looking for the contemporary origins of "good tourism." When Costa Rica decided to focus on tourism as an engine for economic growth, it famously chose to prioritize local ownership and environmental conservation over rapid development.[11] The delayed development of international tourism in Central and South America may have helped with this decision. Costa Ricans could see what had and had not worked with tourism both globally and in their region, and the repercussions of traditional mass tourism served as a cautionary tale. As a result, Costa Rica became an incubator for ecotourism.[12]

Like organic farming as an alternative to commercial agriculture, ecotourism has existed for as long as mass tourism has—although it did not always have a name. Ecotourism began with people who wanted to provide a product that was different than what they saw sprouting up around them, or who simply did not have the financial resources to develop at a large, resort-sized scale. They started small guesthouses, zip-line parks, nature preserves, and back-to-the-roots retreats. These small-time operations quickly picked up speed and, by the early nineties, ecotourism was the fastest-growing international tourism sector. Today, Costa Rican wilderness parks attract millions of people annually. Belize followed a similar path at the same time, offering another example of how ecological preservation and tourism development could go hand in hand.[13]

The rapid growth of ecotourism would not have been possible if there was not a demand for tourism experiences that fulfilled travelers' moral desires better than sprawling resorts and cruise buffets. They craved something different than what was on the main tourism menu. Where mass tourism is big, they wanted small. Where mass tourism is foreign, they wanted local. Where mass tourism is high impact, they wanted to leave no trace.[14] They were interested in human rights and global issues, and many wanted to feel like they were experiencing things as they are: the culture, the people, the environment, and, often, the poverty.[15] They desired authenticity. They wanted something that felt *real*.[16]

However, building the infrastructure for ecotourism was not as simple as dropping a bunch of hippies in a forest with a bottle of water, binoculars, and a bag of locally made trail mix. Ecotourists expect some level of discomfort in exchange for an authentic and environmentally responsible experience. However, like their mass tourism counterparts, the majority of ecotourists still want the core comforts they are used to at home. By pulling from the history, mythology, and natural resources of a nation, ecotourism can offer travelers feel-good vacation experiences that position the tourist as the socially aware, ethical, morally responsible heir to the grand tradition of exploration. And while there probably will not be a Pizza Hut within walking distance, ecotourists will still have electricity, running water bathrooms, and perhaps even a fan.[17]

If you try to visualize ecotourism, you probably imagine small lodges made from locally sourced materials tucked into secluded areas. That is not all of ecotourism, but it is its origins. In East Africa, the richest biota on earth has become an ecotourism lodestar.[18] Tourists are drawn to the region because they want to see *The Lion King* in real life, so preserving the environment while building tourism infrastructure has been paramount to development success.

On the water, a number of small-boat cruise companies offer intimate ecotourism experiences to aquatically minded travelers, especially when compared alongside their full-scale skyscraper-sized cruise ship counterparts. Alternative cruises often include lectures and documentary screenings instead of off-Broadway musicals and casinos. They carry passengers through the Panama Canal, up the Amazon, down the Nile, around Baja California, and along the Alaskan coast (not all on one trip, though) with a focus on hiring native people, especially naturalists, with local insight. As with many ecotourism options, these experiences come with a sizable price tag. Traveling green is rarely cheap.

Despite widespread stereotyping of ecotourism as a wallet-friendly way of getting around, ecotourism and budget travel are a bit of a mismatch. Smaller hotels with fewer rooms and more local food options are expensive to run. They are often less conveniently located than resorts, and either offer constant transportation services or pass the burden of finding a ride on to their guests. Add in airfare and à la carte meals, and even "rustic" ecolodges often add up to a whole lot more money for much less rum punch than their all-inclusive counterparts. For many tourists, the cost and inconvenience are worth it if ecotourism providers are following through on their promises. But how can average travelers know that the "eco" options they are paying a premium for are actually doing what they brag about on their websites? Most of the time, they can't.

Government subsidies and grants for environmentally friendly development projects have turned going green into a lucrative business strategy. The commodification of environmental friendliness has resulted in widespread greenwashing, or the use of eco-friendly language and messaging, without following through. In the world of mass-market ecotourism, "green" often means whatever will result in the highest profits. Some industry groups have tried to create ecotourism, ethical tourism, and sustainable tourism certifications to counteract greenwashing and hold ecotourism companies accountable, but a lack of consensus on what constitutes "green" has fragmented these efforts, resulting in many labels that carry little clout. Other certifications are misleading and more for marketing than meaning.[19]

Ecotourism does, as a whole, have a less negative impact on the ground than conventional mass tourism, and the terms *alternative tourism* and *sustainable tourism* are often used interchangeably to broaden the scope of "real" or "good" tourism beyond ecotourism.[20] However, like ecotourism, both designations suggest results that don't necessarily manifest. Not every alternative tourism project is environmentally, culturally, and financially sustainable in ideation or application, just as not every project marketed as ecotourism protects or improves the environment. Refraining from washing towels every day may save water, but it shouldn't garner the label *eco resort*.

What alternative tourism development does do, whether in a large hotel or scrappy tour guide operation, is to push back against economic leakage, sometimes inadvertently, by identifying potential linkages—opportunities to keep tourism dollars within a community.[21] These links may include buying food locally, hiring and training local workers, bringing on local guides, and getting visitors outside of resort walls and into local markets and restaurants. Like ecotourism, alternative tourism developments are generally smaller-scale and more dispersed than conventional tourism developments. There is a higher percentage of local ownership and community participation, and there can be an emphasis on environmental and cultural literacy.[22] Sometimes, there is volunteering, but alternative tourists don't need to be picking up bricks to feel like they are using their vacation to make a difference.

An Old New Option

For alternative tourists, including ecotourists, feeling like a good person is absolutely critical to the experience. We may not be able to measure how good we are on a ruler, but humans are continuously judging ourselves and others on a moral scale.[23] We have an impulse to help, but each person ultimately has a choice whether to give in to that impulse or ignore it. When we do choose to help, we have options. There may not be a point value assigned to each, but tipping your hotel server a little extra certainly ranks lower than staying at a locally owned ecolodge with an on-site turtle sanctuary, which itself is dwarfed by, say, joining the Peace Corps.

For most of us, the Peace Corps is a no-go. However, even the most conventional traveler encounters opportunities to engage in an economy that has existed for as long as humans have been helping each other at the cookpot: the moral economy.

Giving has never solely rewarded the recipient. The giver also benefits, and the moral economy is the manifestation of those benefits into tangible outcomes: job promotions, leadership positions, and, ultimately, cold hard cash. The moral economy is the accumulation (or loss) of social, political, and monetary capital as a result of one's behavior. The more moral or ethical a person appears to be, the greater their power.[24] If altruism means giving up resources to benefit others, the moral economy offers an opportunity to counterbalance the expenditure.[25]

It has long been said that the good guys come in last. Today that is not so true. Being good or at least showing goodness can put you at the top of the pile. The vast majority of people on earth may never be able to give as much or as visibly as Madonna, Angelina Jolie, or George Clooney, but we can try to mirror how they present themselves. We can strive to be informed and to act ethically. We can become more aware of how we are impacting the planet, champion social causes, and try to do good while we travel. A 2008 survey found that 80 percent of the 1,600 people surveyed were interested in using their vacations to do just that.[26] What *good* means, and what it looks like, are less overwhelmingly obvious.

As more people have tried to reap the benefits of the moral economy while on vacation, the limitations of ecotourism have become increasingly apparent—especially the lack of transparency. Travelers who want to see their good choices manifest into positive outcomes need more than local produce and solar panels. They want to see the smiling, thankful, local faces of the people they've affected through their morally superior vacation decisions.

Toward the end of the twentieth century, the ideological schism between what tourism offers and the image morally minded travelers seek to cultivate created an opportunity for a new vanguard to be built upon an old frame—something that could handle the high volume that ecotourism struggles to carry sustainably while making mobile middle- and upper-class tourists feel like they have done good. Volunteer tourism, or voluntourism, seemed to offer it all.[27]

For those looking to use their time off to invest in the moral economy, however, even the word *tourist* is packed with negative connotations. These individuals use other words to describe themselves and their trips: They are *adventurers, travelers, nomads, explorers*. They go on *expeditions, adventures, treks, safaris,* and *odysseys*.[28] By combining volunteering and tourism, voluntourism trip providers appeal to these anti-tourist tourists by distancing themselves from the tourism establishment while building upon the legacy of reformers such as Mary Carpenter and cause-conscious entrepreneurs such as Thomas Cook.

Over the last two decades, voluntourism has surged, bringing more people into the fold of those who want to use their vacations to have a visible, hands-on impact.[29] It is framed as authentic global citizenship and often called the most ethical way to travel. While voluntourism is only a small slice of the massive tourism pie, claims of its growth potential are enormous. In classrooms and board rooms and to investors, voluntourism is pitched as the future of ethical travel.[30] In reality, voluntourism has more in common with the mass tourism establishment it contrasts itself against than nearly anyone could have imagined.

5 | The Age of Voluntourism

Early in 2006 a documentary that told a gripping tale of how power and greed can destroy communities, and even countries, started making the rounds of college auditoriums. On a trip to East and Central Africa, Jason Russell, a young filmmaker, had seen something most in the West had barely heard whispers of. The Lord's Resistance Army, led by Joseph Kony, was ravaging a large swath of Central Africa, forcing children to become soldiers in a ruthless battle for land, money, and power. Jason's film, *Invisible Children*, would go on to inspire millions of students to try to help the children exploited, maimed, and killed by Joseph Kony and the Lord's Resistance Army.[1]

When Emily Scott saw *Invisible Children*, she was a student at Chapman University pursuing a degree in peace studies and conflict resolution. The film compelled her to do something. If she could not go directly to the heart of the conflict, then she would get as close to it as she could—Kenya. As she planned her trip, Emily was not sure what help she would be able to provide, but she wanted to work with children. So she decided to go to an orphanage.

"It was an organization in the slums that had an orphanage and a clinic, and I had no real, applicable skills," she remembers. "I kind of did my best." It wasn't her first time muddling through volunteering at an orphanage. She had traveled to Romania two years earlier, in 2004, and had spent a few weeks at an orphanage there. The conditions were bleak, and the experience was both saddening and scarring. She left certain she would never put herself in that position again. A few years and an *Invisible Children* screening later, she changed her mind.[2]

Emily's decision to go to Kenya despite her previous negative experience, and even the promise she'd made to herself never to repeat it, was less surprising when examined in context. Many of her classmates and peers were working voluntourism into their school breaks. It was the thing to do if you were young, able, and wanted to give back. She managed to convince herself that her first trip had been a fluke. Romania hadn't worked out, but a different place could, so she booked a flight. Five years earlier, the United Nations had declared 2001 the International Year of Volunteering in recognition of the growth the industry was experiencing.[3] It was also a signal of what was to come. Emily was in the middle of a voluntourism surge.

Definitions

In the first decade of the new millennium, voluntourism was growing in response to prominent social crises, increased awareness of environmental issues, and natural and human-made disasters of terrifying proportions. People felt spurred to give back by events like Hurricane Katrina and the 2004 Indian Ocean earthquake and tsunami, partially because it was easier to see the immediate impacts and the lasting damage than ever before, whether on TV, online, or (with a cheap plane ticket) in person.[4] Emily was just one of the millions of people looking to get in on the "good fight."[5]

However, even as voluntourism was becoming popular on college campuses and in high school auditoriums and church fellowship halls, a deeper understanding of the voluntouristic impulse was scarce. Research on voluntourism was anemic, and the published papers, studies, and books that did exist tended to circulate between researchers, jumping from desk to desk without making a splash in the pool of public opinion. Furthermore, the research predominately served to affirm voluntourism rather than questioning the assumptions supporting the practice.[6]

There were even questions of whether voluntourism should have the word *tourism* in it at all, as if, by engaging in the moral economy, it should be entirely set apart from resorts, cruises, or even Costa Rican zipline tours. Could it be, researchers asked, that voluntourism is a social phenomenon, not a product?[7] Was the trip Emily Scott purchased a moral imperative delivered in the shape of tourism, but not really tourism at all? But the moral economy and the traditional capitalist economy are not mutually exclusive membership organizations.

Voluntourism products may carry morally valuable clout, but they still cost cash.[8] And while academics pondered the implications of voluntourism being, or not being, a product of and participant in capitalism, trip providers— the for-profit and nonprofit entities that sell voluntourism products—have embraced their place in the traditional economy, even if they renounce the vocabulary of capitalism.

Different ways of branding voluntourism land better in different age, faith, and geographic market groupings, especially as participation has expanded beyond the West to affluent Asian and African communities. Terms such as *volunteer vacation*, *alternative spring break*, *mini-mission*, *mission lite*, *service-based tourism*, and *service trip* have been substituted in to obscure the tourism side of voluntourism products.[9] The variety of terms has caused widespread confusion, but they are all describing the same thing: voluntourism.[10]

Amid this confusion, it is time for a working, dynamic definition of the practice—one based on the core pillars of voluntourism, not merely what it purports to be or aspires to create.

Voluntourism can be defined in six parts:

1. *Voluntourism is short term.* Most trips are less than four weeks, but they can be as short as a handful of days or as long as a few months.[11]

2. *Most voluntourists are white.* According to the United States Current Population Survey, a monthly survey of tens of thousands of households, from 2004 to 2012, 87 percent of people who volunteered abroad were white.[12] While there has been an increase in participation by people of color, and especially by people from Asian nations, the vast visual majority of voluntourists are white.

3. *Most voluntourists experience financial privilege.* Household income is a strong predictor of voluntourism. Looking again at the Current Population Survey data from 2004 to 2012, most international volunteers come from homes that are at or above a middle-class income bracket. After reviewing that data, Professor Benjamin Lough found that 63 percent of individuals who reported volunteering abroad came from a household that earned more than $50,000 per year. The 9 percent of volunteers who come from households with an income of less than $20,000 were mostly young and in school. The number of lower-income voluntourists was trending down as of 2012, while the number of people of financial and social privilege taking part was rising.[13]

4. *Voluntourists are unskilled at and often unqualified for the work they undertake.* For a few thousand dollars, someone with no medical training can pay their way into playing the role of surgical assistant in an underresourced hospital.[14] The most common activities, though, involve children, including teaching, orphanage volunteering, and assisting with pediatric medical care.[15]

5. *Voluntourism is a combination of tourism and volunteering.* Some trips focus more heavily on traditional tourism, with an afternoon or two of volunteering mixed in. On others, volunteering is the sole focus, with no time for beach excursions or day trips. Most are somewhere in between.[16]

6. *International travel is not required.* Just as a New Yorker can be a tourist in San Francisco, an Oregonian can be a voluntourist in Alabama (and vice versa).

To sum it up:

> Voluntourism (*noun*): Any combination of unskilled volunteer work, or skilled volunteer work (e.g., in medicine or education) done by someone unqualified, and traveling on a short-term basis. Voluntourism is typically done in less developed regions by people from more developed regions. International travel is not necessary for an experience to qualify as voluntourism. Most trips are shorter than four weeks.

I use this definition throughout the rest of this book, but even in it, something is missing. Built into the concept of voluntourism is another presumption: the presumption of *progress*, the assumption that positive intentions will result in positive outcomes.[17]

Without the assumption that voluntourism results in improvement, there is little reason for anyone to take part, or, at least, there should be little reason for the product to sell as well as it does. However, I have yet to find the words necessary to describe in the objective way a functional definition requires the deeply held belief that voluntourism results in beneficial changes. Yet this belief remains an ever-present element of the practice.

The Economics

Without oversight and with ever-increasing demand, voluntourism trips have become one of the fastest-growing tourism products globally.[18] No longer on the fringes of the tourism industry, voluntourism is now mainstream.[19]

A 2008 MSNBC and *Condé Nast Traveler* survey found that out of 1,600 respondents, 80 percent were interested in giving back while traveling, and 62 percent were intrigued by the prospect of voluntourism.[20] In the years since this survey, it is likely these numbers have only increased. Today, young people in the world's top volunteer-sending countries—the United States, the United Kingdom, Canada, Australia, and New Zealand—insist that volunteering is the most effective and reliable way of giving.[21] As these people come of age, their ability to buy voluntourism products only grows.

The actual statistics on how many people are signing up for voluntourism trips leave a lot to be desired, but what data does exist illustrates precisely what Emily Scott noticed before booking her trip to Kenya—voluntourism has long been on the rise. Estimates for the number of people taking part in voluntourism annually run from 1.6 million to 10 million.[22]

There is no shortage of trip options for these buyers. The Volunteer Vacations guide, a series of print voluntourism guides, boasted 75 options in 1987.[23] In 2005 a single online trip database, GoAbroad.com, offered nearly 700 voluntourism options.[24] Only two years later, a prospective voluntourist could browse 3,441 trip options in 150 countries through the Volunteer Abroad database.[25]

While this observation is anecdotal, as someone who has watched dozens of friends and relatives buy voluntourism trips over the past decade, has spoken to hundreds of voluntourists in detail about their experiences buying trips, and who has bought trips herself, I feel comfortable asserting that the majority of buyers assume—unless they are explicitly told otherwise—that the trip providers and destinations that sell voluntourism packages are nonprofits. Small surveys on the ground have backed this up. For example, a survey of one hundred tourists in Siem Reap, Cambodia, who reported interest in volunteering at local orphanages found that 60 percent of those surveyed did not even know that orphanages could be run for profit.[26]

Many nonprofit voluntourism hosts and trip providers do exist. However, over the past decade, voluntourism has taken a sharp for-profit turn.[27] Following the overall trend of consolidation in the mass tourism industry, more and more small trip providers have been gobbled up by larger brands that are turning a profit on altruistic intentions.[28] Voluntourism is often marketed as an inexpensive vacation option, but there is room for a healthy profit margin thanks to the low costs of operation. A traveler can book a bare-bones trip package with housing, a volunteer placement, and basic food for as little as a few hundred dollars a week. Group trips can be even cheaper. There are higher-end options, and prices have risen as the voluntourism market has expanded. Still, while many trip providers charge thousands for the very same simple experience, augmented by a few language classes and excursions, even those opportunities tend to be advertised as steals.[29]

Low operating costs and rising widespread interest add up to big money. By 2008 more than 1.6 million people were volunteering abroad and spending an estimated $1.7 billion to $2.6 billion for the opportunity.[30] These figures likely fall significantly short of reality, as tourism data tends to fail to take two significant areas of voluntourism growth into account—faith-based voluntourism, such as mission trips, and domestic voluntourism, voluntourism outside of participants' community but within their country. These omissions mean that a substantial portion of voluntourism, especially within the United States, is not being included in the global tallies. Likewise, the figures do not include the ever-growing gap-year industry.

Gap years, or the practice of taking a year off between the final year of secondary school and beginning university, are a well-cemented tradition in Europe, Australia, and New Zealand. The gap-year industry in the United Kingdom has been estimated at well over £5 billion per year.[31] The market for gap years in the United States is smaller but growing. Ethan Knight, executive director of the Gap Year Association, estimates that forty thousand students in the United States are choosing to take a gap year each year. Each student, he says, spends around $5,000, putting the domestic market at around $200 million, and growing at an average rate of 20 percent per year since 2006.[32] While not all gap years involve voluntourism, many do, and voluntourism has long been a vital portion of the gap-year marketplace.

As a low-cost, high-margin activity that requires minimal infrastructure investment, it is unsurprising that companies ranging from mom-and-pop operations to tourism goliaths have been getting in on the voluntourism action.[33] There is money to be made in selling doing good.

One family, the Kielburgers, became particularly influential players in the voluntourism industry by working both sides of the for-profit and nonprofit coin. It all started back in 1995, when twelve-year-old Canadian Craig Kielburger learned about child labor in Pakistan. Upset and confused that kids his age were being worked to death to make products for Western consumption, he turned his anger into activism. Joined by his brother, Marc, and heavily supported by their parents, the young brothers built an awareness campaign that grew into a nonprofit they named Free the Children. Today, it's called WE Charity.[34]

WE Charity shares its branding with ME to WE, WE.org, WE Movement, WE Schools, WE Families, WE Villages, WE Day and other events, initiatives, organizations, and enterprises. Together, they offer service-minded people everything they need to inform their community about global poverty, raise money to fight it, book a trip to see it for themselves, and buy a Rafiki bracelet to remind them of their journey. The profit structure is ambiguous in a way that can only be purposeful, and the online branding makes it nearly impossible for even a tech-savvy kid, let alone the adult with the wallet, to tell where the nonprofit side ends and the for-profit side begins.

If you have the patience to dig around, the pieces of the puzzle can be fit together. WE Charity is the nonprofit that works on the ground to provide impoverished communities with education, clean water, job training, and other development initiatives. Then there is ME to WE, which looks exactly like WE Charity but is the for-profit voluntourism trip provider the Kielburgers created in 2009 to capitalize on young people's impulse to take action. ME to WE has brought thousands of young people, families, and corporate volunteers, and more than a handful of A-list celebrities and social media influencers, to WE Charity projects on voluntourism trips. ME to WE also sells products made by nearly two thousand artisans in Kenya and Ecuador. Kids are encouraged to resell the products as a fundraising tool, donating their profits back to WE Charity. Bridging WE Charity and ME to WE are WE Day events, nonprofit celebrations that promote giving back while pitching the for-profit products—trips and physical goods—as convenient ways of doing so.[35]

The various arms and branches of the Kielburger's empire are complicated, but they have a good reason to keep everything under one umbrella: money. ME to WE has publicly committed to donating at least 50 percent of net profits to the WE Charity, although they report donating a much higher percentage than that minimum—over 90 percent—annually. Over the years, ME to WE, a for-profit, has injected millions of dollars in cash and in-kind donations into the WE Charity, a nonprofit.[36]

Much of the money ME to WE gives to WE Charity comes from the substantial trip fees ME to WE charges. ME to WE trips are at the higher end of the voluntourism spectrum, and, in 2019, a fourteen-day ME to WE trip to Ecuador for university students with flights started at $4,295. Visits to historic sites, community-building activities, and unspecified volunteer work are all included in the package. Projects have included working on school building sites, digging wells, and planting crops.[37]

This model is not necessarily bad. Using a for-profit to raise money for a nonprofit is, at its essence, simply harnessing the power of the market to further a mission. However, it is frustrating that the average young person considering a ME to WE trip would likely assume that they are giving their money to a nonprofit in the first place (because who pays to volunteer for a company?) and wouldn't know where to look to learn otherwise. In addition, for-profits are held to a different standard of disclosure than nonprofits, so it's harder to look inside ME to WE to see the path money takes than if it were a nonprofit organization.

In July of 2020 WE Charity became embroiled in an ethics scandal when Prime Minister Justin Trudeau's government tried to award a contract worth as much as $43.5 million to the nonprofit without disclosing that members of his family had been paid hundreds of thousands of dollars to speak at WE events, such as WE Days.[38] As outcry spread, accusations of unethical hiring and management practices, as well as erratic and concerning behavior from leadership, gained fresh attention and brought a new level of scrutiny to bear on a behemoth built on the idea of doing good.[39]

Projects Abroad—a designated for-profit, despite its use of a .org domain extension in the United States—is not cheap, but it does skew slightly more affordable than ME to WE. In 2019 a two-week medical internship in Argentina for fifteen- to eighteen-year-olds complete with homestay and language lessons went for $3,000. There were also options like a four-week trip to

Ghana that included teaching classes and caring for special needs children for $3,155—less than $800 per week. That trip was open to anyone over sixteen and, as is the norm, required no experience.[40]

For trip providers, the market is growing, and the product is attractive. They just need to fine-tune their offerings to the right frequency to convey the perfect message to stand out in a sea of package options vying for the attention of buyers who are, typically, seeking a once-in-a-lifetime experience.[41] The not-so-stealthy secret is to tap into the natural urges and socialized desires that draw people to voluntourism in the first place.

The Buyers

The only reason companies like ME to WE, Projects Abroad, or any of the hundreds, if not thousands, of other trip providers can exist is that they have buyers. There is a market for the product they peddle, and while definitions and economic breakdowns of voluntourism are useful to understanding the global scope of the industry, they fail to illuminate fully why people are buying the opportunity to give back. Why, more than 175 years after Cook's first temperance rail trip, is voluntourism still popular? Slavery is illegal, women can vote, top hats are out of fashion, yet voluntourism remains and has only grown stronger.

The Natural Reasons

The reasons millions of people buy into the idea of voluntourism each year are rooted in the very core of who we are as a global community. For many, the pursuit of service—not just voluntourism—is a moral obligation.[42] But we are also adventure-seeking creatures. Not everyone craves wild explorations, but the desire for increased connection is a piece of the human condition. When we itch for that connection in other places and with other peoples, we call it *wanderlust*. One of the biggest hurdles when it comes to scratching this itch is access to places and communities that do not have websites, airports, or well-established tourism infrastructure. Voluntourism trip providers offer a way in to otherwise inaccessible or difficult to access spaces.[43]

We are also continuously seeking out positive attention and emotional fulfillment. It is hard for us to control our cravings for the feeling that other people's gratitude creates. When we please our parents, a teacher, or a coach, our neurons start firing, our hormones start rushing, and we want to feel that good again. Voluntourism promises to deliver that feeling, nonstop, and without the pressure to commit long term that exists throughout our normal lives.[44]

The Socialized Reasons

Travel is known to be transformative. Add service work and expectations of transformation skyrocket. Voluntourists want to find themselves and lose their insecurities. They want to be happier, more appreciative of what they have, and to gain a broader perspective on life. Personal growth and a greater sense of self are two of the primary motivations for voluntourists.[45] Lives can be made meaningful through giving, and trip providers promise to deliver.[46]

Whether it is even possible for voluntourists to become the self-actualized beings they imagine by installing cookstoves, painting walls, or handing out shoes is not thoroughly questioned. The performance of caring is, ultimately, the most important act.[47]

The potential for personal development has helped voluntourism become a rite of passage for young people who want to prove they can make it in the real world.[48] In the United States, in particular, voluntourism trips are linked to the lingering image of the great American frontier and the pioneers who conquered it.[49] When there is no wild and dangerous land to conquer in our own countries, the natural place to look for pain, discomfort, and self-righteous satisfaction is somewhere else—somewhere wilder, poorer, or simply unknown.[50]

Oftentimes when voluntourists return from a successful trip, they are invited to stand on a higher rung of the social hierarchy in their community, especially in faith communities. Peace Corps volunteers and their international equivalents will likely always have the top spot when it comes to international do-good-ery. However, Peace Corps–lite experiences offer an identity to wear proudly in a more manageable package. With it, voluntourists gain access to a community of those who have been *there*, who have seen *it*, and who want more of their peers to do the same.[51]

The other positive results voluntourism trips provide to travelers are frequently both visible and valuable, more tangible than higher social standing, and more lasting than temporary emotional fulfillment. For years voluntourism experiences have been such a favored topic for college admissions and scholarship essays that some colleges have started to discourage them.[52] Time building a school in Kenya or teaching English in Honduras can also give job applicants a competitive edge. The presumption of ability, when combined with societal clout, can transform social capital into economic capital, the transmutation of value in the moral economy into hard currency.[53]

Voluntourism as a way of doing good while reaping personal rewards relies on the concept of Western benevolence, a belief that improving the world is a responsibility that sits squarely on the shoulders of the wealthy, the powerful, and, more broadly, the West. By some accounting, it is a logic with merit. Western countries have a long history of interfering in places they chose to "civilize." Taking on the responsibility of fixing the mistakes they made could, possibly, be a restitution of sorts. But if that is the prevailing logic, it is pulled from the same fire from which colonialism was born.[54]

Local volunteering can achieve some of the aims of voluntourism. It can serve as a résumé booster, and it purports to result in personal growth. However, historically, local volunteering does not carry the same status as doing a similar or even the same activity further away from home. Slogging through a few shifts at a local soup kitchen is not treated as equally altruistic nor impressive as doing the same thing in another place.

Most travelers dream of, plan for, and raise or save the funds for a voluntourism trip over many months, if not years.[55] When a spark ignites the powder—an *Invisible Children* screening, a best friend returning from a week saving South Africa, a church group putting a group together—they make their move. They buy a trip. They book a flight. They arrive in Kenya or Tanzania or Cambodia or Romania. And they save the world?

Marketing

We live in a world where even our unarticulated desires have become commodities that can be bought and sold, and the industry that has resulted from the contemporary clamor for voluntourism experiences is one of parrots repeating each other ad nauseam. The same keywords and taglines are plastered across websites and social media without regard for where one trip product ends and another begins. Eerily similar photographs of predominately young, predominately white volunteers working with predominately younger, predominately darker people could be swapped from one brochure to another without anyone taking notice.

When one trip provider finds success with a term or phrase, the rest follow in droves. The word *authentic* is a notable casualty. The use of *authentic* as a descriptor for everything from people and places to chocolate bars and stretch denim had numbed us to the term, so new ones—*community-focused, immersive, unfiltered*—have been thrown into play. For-profits and nonprofits have blurred together, and everything looks the same. Through attempts to sound unique, the industry has become monotone.[56] The difficulty differentiating trip providers and their products from one another is confusing and infuriating for travelers trying to do their research. However, it makes analyzing the industry as a whole a lot easier because treating it as predominately monolithic isn't a gross oversimplification.

Despite the blending together, a central pillar of marketing voluntourism is division. Voluntourism cannot exist without the creation of the "us" and the "them" Western benevolence provides set within the vocabulary of "global citizenship."[57] It is the haves versus the have-nots, the westerners versus the rest-erners, the potential voluntourists versus those they might save.

These invalid binaries rely on prejudice and false privilege and yet are essential to voluntourism. According to trip providers, the developing world is in crisis, and only the helping hand of the voluntourist—who knows of better and can dream of bigger—can save it.[58] This is a cliché, but clichés are a tradition in marketing any product. Instead of a sneaker or a romantic escape, voluntourism offers the chance to save the world. To maintain the façade that this is a worthwhile endeavor, trip providers construct barriers between voluntourists and communities for buyers to imagine climbing over.[59]

One of the most efficient ways of building barriers is by creating otherness, and one of the most reliable ways of creating otherness is through imagery. Drive toward a major airport and the power of travel imagery quickly becomes clear. Billboards plastered with sunny beaches remind us that we do not have to be wearing two layers plus a raincoat. We could be on the beach![60] There is no separate playbook for voluntourism marketing—the words and images just change.

Whereas marketers may sell a resort in Jamaica with sand, sex, and the promise of paradise, voluntourism in the same country is sold with images of shacks, shoddy electricity, and children with bare feet and bloated bellies. Images of poverty take center stage, while images of local creativity and ingenuity are omitted. Homegrown success stories disappear behind foreign-funded advancements.[61] In reality, both sides are nearly always present, but by erasing one, local agency is traded out for manufactured helplessness.

The next step in marketing voluntourism is to target the product toward the most receptive and accessible consumer: young people. The United Nations defines *youth* as individuals between fifteen and twenty-four years old.[62] Globally, the youth travel industry was worth an estimated $173 billion annually in 2012.[63] An explanation of voluntourism's growth spurt is buried in that pile of cash.

For trip providers, it pays to have access to young people where they gather: namely, schools. High schools and universities have become battlegrounds for voluntourism marketing. The combatants range from old-guard organizations like Habitat for Humanity to the adolescents like ME to WE and to the many single-region and mom-and-pop operations that run only a few trips a year to a small number of destinations.

In the fight for students' attention, trip providers hand out flyers, hire students to hang posters, encourage the formation of trip-centric clubs, and offer classroom visits by trip representatives. Sometimes, there are even large-scale events on and near campuses targeted at selling voluntourism to the student demographic.

In the nineteenth century, Thomas Cook gave talks about his travels and social beliefs that doubled as sales pitches and attracted thousands of people.[64] Today, WE Charity and ME to WE have ambitiously scaled up this model.

WE Day events are stadium sized and celebrity studded. Students cannot buy a ticket—they must earn their spot through service. ME to WE creates these high-budget experiences with the help of huge sponsors (such as Allstate in the United States and Virgin Atlantic in the United Kingdom) that whip people into a frenzy of goodwill. Then, they offer the audience a way to express that enthusiasm: buy a trip. Millions of young people, educators, and families have attended WE Day events in the United States, Canada, the UK, and the Caribbean.[65]

Trip providers that cannot rent stadiums rely heavily on word-of-mouth marketing led by past customers. Encouragement from friends is a crucial factor for people progressing from being interested in the idea of voluntourism to booking a trip.[66] At the same time, negative word-of-mouth does little to dissuade people. The industry is distributed over such a large area (the entire globe), that it is easy to shrug off stories of bad experiences as outliers while embracing a good experience as indicative of the whole.[67]

In the end, what makes voluntourism function as a consumer product that satiates socialized and natural desires is its accessibility. According to the marketing, voluntourism is affordable, accessible, and safe. Many trip providers give their low trip fees top billing, emphasizing savings above local impacts and even personal gains. For travelers motivated by a bargain, there is no better deal than being able to fundraise to cover the costs of a vacation—even though most voluntourists are well off.[68]

In addition, some high schools and universities require or strongly encourage volunteering before graduation. Voluntourism trips are a convenient way to fulfill these service requirements in one go.[69] Instead of showing up at an assisted living facility every Thursday for a semester, a student can fulfill their service requirement while on vacation—no experience necessary. The lack of oversight, qualification matching, and training pervasive in voluntourism is the icing on the accessibility cake.[70]

Two Fallacies

There are two commonly accepted reasons why people take part in voluntourism that are incorrect or, at least, inaccurate and overly narrow.

The Age Fallacy

The first false assumption is that the majority of voluntourists are young. A little more than a quarter of people in the United States who reported volunteering abroad between 2004 and 2012 were between 15 and 24. That is a lot of young people, but they are nearly balanced out by their older compatriots. Fully 20 percent of voluntourists during that same period were between the ages of 45 and 54.[71]

We can blame voluntourism marketing for the mismatch between perception and reality when it comes to the average age of a voluntourist. Images of voluntourists shared by trip providers skew young. This could be because those using the platforms the images are sourced from, especially social media, skew young too, or simply because youth sells.

Despite the marketing of voluntourism as a youthful activity, several factors beyond a desire for adventure may be attracting older travelers to voluntourism trips. Older voluntourists could be continuing to do something they have done since they were young. Others may be traveling alongside their younger family members.[72] Some may have wanted to take a voluntourism trip for a long time, but the resources and free time have finally matched up with the dream.[73] That, especially, would explain why the number of voluntourists fifty-five and up has grown rapidly.[74]

The Gender Fallacy

The second fallacy is gender. Academics, industry insiders, and observers generally accept that the vast majority of voluntourists are women. Volunteering Solutions, a voluntourism trip provider, has shared that 76 percent of the more than ten thousand volunteers in their database identify as women.[75] Some estimate that up to 80 percent of all voluntourists globally are women.[76] Professor Benjamin Lough is one of the few people who vocally disagrees.

He has analyzed international volunteering by United States residents extensively, combing through hundreds of thousands of responses to the Current Population Survey over eight years: 2004–2012. Through his research, Lough found that the widely held assumption that women make up the vast majority of international volunteers is way off. The gender breakdown of individuals from the United States who reported going abroad to give back between 2004 and 2012 was nearly fifty-fifty. Only slightly more women (52 percent) reported taking part than men (48 percent).[77] The survey did not consider domestic voluntourism, but Lough believes the trend would carry over.

Lough was not surprised by this finding. "It's something I'd actually anticipate," he says, hypothesizing that the percentage of voluntourists who are women is so often miscalculated because of who is doing the counting. The idea of parents being more protective of daughters than they are of sons is a stereotype, but he believes it holds water when it comes to voluntourism. "Parents," he says, "want their daughter to go with an organized program," whereas boys get freer rein. This is not just true for young people, he adds; "it's for adults as well."

Women, Lough believes, are more likely to travel with trip providers regardless of age. Society gives men more freedom to travel on their own (however sexist that may be), so they appear to work directly with organizations on the ground without the support of a middleman more frequently than women. Most of the available data on gender in voluntourism has been collected and published by trip providers. Their customer pool limits their perspective, which leads to the discrepancy between the narrative that the vast majority of voluntourists are women and the reality uncovered by Current Population Survey.[78]

Eternal Optimism

Breaking down the motivations for voluntourism does not mean that each motivation should be examined in isolation. The weight each carries is unique to the individual and the circumstance.[79] And yet, regardless of gender or age, voluntourists around the world, from the United States and Australia to Taiwan and Switzerland, share the same hopes, desires, and dreams of feeling good by doing good.[80]

The orphanage in Kenya fell short of Emily Scott's expectations. She remembers crying in her room because she didn't feel like she was making the difference she had convinced herself would be a natural result of her positivity and enthusiasm. "It totally broke my heart," she remembers. She was going to spend a month sweating and sacrificing, and nothing was going to be different when she left. Yet hope is a resilient thing, and voluntourists have a nearly supernatural ability to find possibilities for positivity in even the least encouraging circumstances.

After a particularly rough day, Emily decided that making a difference in one kid's life would be enough. Even if nothing else changed, that would be okay. She left the definition of "a difference" purposefully vague.

6 | Colonial Pathologies

It is impossible to examine voluntourism without accounting for the imperial projects, especially the British, American, and Dutch colonial empires, that laid the foundation for the global tourism industry.[1] Mary Carpenter traveled to India during the British Raj and spent most of her time there with British and Dutch officials, entrepreneurs, and missionaries, and the Indians they trusted. Thomas Cook's travel empire expanded into new markets in the wake of colonialism, following Western comforts and conveniences across the globe.

Like the overwhelming majority of American and Western European travelers, both Carpenter and Cook's clients ventured forth with the expectation that the cultures they traveled to would reform to fit the desires, thoughts, and values of visitors.[2] Building upon Edward Said's foundational conceptualization of the *Other*, a romanticized exotic continues to be constructed through comparison against the Western metropolis.[3]

The Other is what Western civilization is not, and what the West embodies is what the Other must strive toward, willingly or otherwise. There are

Others in every community, in every town, in every country, but the most common Others on a global scale are the populations of developing communities, regions, and countries. Billions of people have been set apart by this method of differentiation. Colonialism is not the only reason this division has taken place, but colonialism is heavily to blame for the entrenchment of Othering in contemporary culture.

The term *colonialism* is itself slung around a lot, so it may be helpful to offer the definition I believe to be most comprehensive: Colonialism is a form of imperialism. It is a state in which one entity exerts political, financial, or military control over another entity, especially through the physical movement of foreign individuals into a geographic region. Not limited to nations, it has also been practiced by corporations, religious groups, and individuals for centuries.[4]

Colonialism was the reason why Mary Carpenter could stay in the English Quarter of Calcutta, now Kolkata, and drink tea in homes with just enough of India seeping through the walls to feel foreign, yet still enough of home to stave off most discomfort. It is why the marchers in the parade that blocked her route to one of those homes wore the castoffs of the British Raj—a military hat, a uniform jacket. It is also why it was relatively easy for her to funnel local women into British-style schools. It is why the founders and funders of those schools could insist that they teach British principles, reinforcing British ideas of what is "proper" and "civilized": wash, clean, cook, mend, do not let your husband help, and hold yourself like a "lady."

The Cooks also leaned heavily on colonialism. Palestine and Egypt fell under the Ottoman sphere when Cook tours were first exploring the region, and the travelers had colonialist ideals to thank for the hotels, restaurants, and other amenities they relied on during their stay. The people who benefited the least from these advances were the inhabitants of these regions themselves. John Mason Cook was adamant that the Cooks' Nile River trips were ushering in an economic tide that would raise all ships: international tour companies and local entrepreneurs alike. Evidence that this proved true is scant, although John did take a group of Egyptian teachers and students on a Nile tour in 1892 as a charitable, educational experience.[5]

What benefit this single trip had is not documented, and Western tourists pressed into Egypt with colonial fervor parallel to the British projects in the country, reshaping the ancient and holy landscapes to fit their expectations. In the process, locals were pushed to the fringes to make room for visitors eager to see how locals lived.[6] Thomas Cook's and Mary Carpenter's travels should be seen in this context, as should Sorabsha Dadabhai's letter about Mary Carpenter, published in the *Manchester Guardian*.

In the Caribbean, the legacies of slavery, European exploitation, and American political control played a critical role in how the region transitioned into becoming a tourism destination. Slavery is foundational to Caribbean tourism, and it remains a key piece of many of the issues that continue today, from economic leakage—the flow of money out of the country—to job discrimination.[7] Islanders must be poor but happy, entertaining but inconspicuous, and must relinquish the best beaches in the name of tourism. These expectations produce a theatrical choreography in which locals are encouraged to let themselves be tourist attractions, stepping aside when they aren't needed to set the scene.

Women

Women have mostly been exempted from critiques of imperial projects. They often receive a free pass because they followed their families or partners to foreign postings rather than having sought out roles in colonizing enterprises themselves. In the case of female travelers at the height of the colonial empire, their keen interest in social reform, such as imparting Western family structure and its accompanying gender roles, suggests a softer approach to domination than the harsh tactics of foreign governments. However, their work was no less imperialistic in intention.[8] Whether traveling for leisure, following their partners, or pursuing philanthropic missions, female travelers were delivery mechanisms for assumptions of Western cultural superiority, and the presence of Western women in foreign places was a byproduct of violence.

Mary Adams Abbott was a bold adventurer who could, in many ways, be seen as a role model for adventurous and independent young women today. She did not allow 1920s social norms to hold her back as she explored the globe and recorded her journeys in an often gripping and, at times, humorous journal. She was also an unapologetic racist and white supremacist who lamented that the "English New Zealanders have intermarried with [the Maori] rather disgustingly."[9] Her racism does not make her any less adventurous, but it should disqualify her from role-model status. It also reinforces how individual travelers contributed to the mechanisms of colonialism and the narratives of privilege and power—even from the comfort of beach loungers and boat decks.

Power and Image

Privilege is complicated and multilayered and goes far beyond race or economics. There is financial and racial privilege, but also educational privilege, geographic privilege, gender privilege, privilege of sex and sexual orientation, and, yes, religious privilege. A poor white man who dropped out of high school and a wealthy Latina woman with an Ivy League degree both share space on the winning and losing ends of the privilege spectrum depending on which aspects of their lives are included in the equation.

Voluntourists are mostly winners in the privilege lottery, and they try to make up for their position of power by obsessively striving to even the scale. They wish to give things away—time, energy, clothes, technology—to make up for the amount they have.[10] While the urge to help others have what you enjoy is understandable, how voluntourists attempt to pursue their goal is problematic. It is further complicated by one of the most important pieces of a good voluntourism trip: It must be easy. Further, hosts should be welcoming and kind. They should invite voluntourists into their homes seconds after meeting them and smile for pictures anytime a camera is pointed in their direction. They should be the poor, but happy poor.[11] Simultaneously, voluntourists want simple projects with visible results, free time, flexibility, and private space, often in communities where having your own bed, let alone your own room, is a luxury.[12]

Heddwyn Kyambadde grew up a member of the Ugandan Pentecostal Watoto Church. When he was a child, the mega-church had a children's ministry that placed homeless or impoverished children into family-style homes run by "mothers." Heddwyn's mom helped manage the program, and she would bring him along when she visited the facilities.[13]

"I would watch the children be very casual around me and my mom and the mothers," Heddwyn remembers, many years later. But if visitors or volunteers were coming, "they would change themselves." They would rub dirt on their faces and bodies; their English would suddenly become more fragmented and broken. "They would play the part."

When the time came for the volunteers or visitors to leave, Heddwyn remembers kids crying and running after the vans, reaching up toward the windows begging for a little more, anything more, despite the fact they had what they needed. The action, he felt, was another performance. Heddwyn's mother was upset when white people held Black babies for photo opportunities, but hosting voluntourists was the norm, so they did it.

The kids dressing up in dirt may have served as a way of reclaiming power. They could not stop the volunteers from coming. They could not control what the orphanage director and teachers let the visitors do or where they could go. They could not leave nor refuse to engage. The way they could claim agency was by trying to get as much out of every visit as possible. To capitalize on the opportunity, they had to play the part.[14]

As he got older, Heddwyn started working in the church media department, and his bosses gave him a list of pictures to take and footage to capture for promotional and fundraising materials. Certain subjects were always in demand, especially crying children. Heddwyn knew to snap that whenever an opportunity arose.

One of the most emblematic images of contemporary voluntourism, one that represents both what it is and what it strives to be, was taken on October

28, 2015. It is of a young girl, wrapped in layers of blankets after being pulled from the sea, tightly cradled in the arms of a volunteer. Photojournalist Giorgos Moutafis took the photo a few hours after a ship laden with refugees sank off the coast of Lesvos, Greece, leaving the girl among hundreds waiting in the water for rescue. In the photo, the young girl serves as a stand-in for every child struggling for a safer life, and the volunteer holding her represents everything good about wanting to make a difference—sincerity, commitment, and a bias toward action. It is an intensely intimate photograph of a profoundly human moment.[15]

Soon after it was published, the picture was all over social media. It was pure, honest, emotional, and intriguing. Who was the girl? And, even more pressingly, who was the volunteer displaying such pure altruism and selfless giving in the midst of a humanitarian disaster? The girl was named Mina, but few people ever learned that. The volunteer was Erin Schrode. Soon, millions would know her name.

A few days after the photo went viral, a young volunteer approached Erin Schrode with a straightforward request. The picture was beautiful. She wanted one just like it. In this new version, though, she would play Erin, and another refugee child would take the place of Mina. It would only take a moment to stage, and the image would be precisely what she needed to impress people at home.

It was, Erin remembers, "the most reprehensible thing I've heard in my life."[16] She refused but knew that despite her rejection of the request, someone else might have helped the young woman get her perfect picture.

The young woman was practicing a core tenet of voluntourism: pics or it didn't happen. Ultimately, the photographs a person collects are a testimony of who they are. When we have the right pictures, they confirm our most intimate identities.[17] But, as Erin experienced, this process of identity confirmation is also one of construction and, often, staging.[18]

Mainstream travelers might want to show that they live a life of leisure by asking a beach attendant to catch them peeking out mischievously from under a wide-brimmed hat. An ecotourist may ask their guide to share the photos of the moment a monkey reached toward them as they cruised along a zipline. A tourist interested in sustainable development may ask a friend to take a photo of them alongside women dressed in brightly colored local costumes in a mountain market. For voluntourists, images as tools for identity creation and affirmation are even more important because to be a volunteer is not just a temporary name tag, but, often, a piece of a person's very identity.[19]

Erin Schrode is a hardworking, passionate, and informed woman who was an activist for social justice long before she first volunteered on the shores of Lesvos. Still, she probably would not have later appeared on CNN to talk about refugee issues ahead of area experts, regional activists, and the refugees themselves, if not for that one powerful image. For most voluntourists, the results are less dramatic but equally seductive. By choosing to spend their vacation volunteering, a voluntourist constructs a story of who they wish to be, not just away from home, but throughout their life. The presentation of evidence, whether film or photo, is part of the narration of that chosen identity and necessary proof of their profound altruism.[20]

Pathological Altruism

Heddwyn Kyambadde's photography job was short term. His goal was to go to college: an American college and, preferably, a Christian American college. A "cliché go-out-and-save-the-world college," as Heddwyn calls it now. But soon after he arrived at Biola University in California—a good Christian boy at a good Christian school—things started happening that reminded him of the kids he had seen rubbing dirt on their faces, or the pictures he had taken of children crying. Soon, he realized that what he was witnessing at Biola was where everything he had seen at home in Uganda started.

Heddwyn was in an "experience room" for an on-campus conference when all of the pieces finally, jarringly, fit together. Each experience room was themed around a location on the globe and involved a skit meant to immerse and educate the conference participants. One was the Uganda room.

The first thing Heddwyn noticed about the Uganda room was that there was sand on the floor. Uganda is landlocked, and he'd never seen beach-style sand there. Then he noticed the broken desks, scattered chairs, and letters and numbers scrawled across a blackboard. His Black peers were playing the teacher and students, and as the skit started, the "teacher" recited the alphabet incorrectly. When the teacher instructed the students to parrot it back, a white student jumped out and exclaimed toward the onlookers, "We need to help them! They need help!" The message was unambiguous. Ugandans were helpless. Their teachers couldn't even recite the alphabet.

Heddwyn hadn't expected the Uganda room to show a perfect place, but he didn't realize the complex reality of his country would be traded out for a caricature. For a moment, the room even made Heddwyn question his own knowledge of Uganda. "I thought, maybe I don't know what is going on in my country? I grew up pretty wealthy. Maybe, this was what was actually going on."

"There is something about religion," Heddwyn says, "that gives ... I don't know if you can call it entitlement, but 'because I do good, I have leeway. Because my heart is that of a minister, it's ok.'" It is permission enabled by intention. He remembers when his peers asked a Sri Lankan student at Biola to stop cooking traditional food in the communal kitchen because they thought it "smelled like poop." Then they excused their prejudice by saying they would love to go on a mission trip to her country someday. If the purpose is pure, the action is okay.

Power lines tend to fall along color lines, and prejudice and ignorance reinforce the us-versus-them structure voluntourism relies on.[21] Over time, the guilt that drives the urge to invent differences, and to use those differences as excuses to exercise power, becomes pathological.[22]

Pathological altruism is a psychological phenomenon that occurs when someone tries to do good, sees negative consequences as a result of their actions, and insists on continuing nonetheless.[23] The term is attributed to Nancy McWilliams, who used it in her 1984 paper, "The Psychology of the Altruist." Pathological altruists push forward as "messiahs of development" in the face of evidence that contradicts their intent.[24]

Some communities have devised ways of capitalizing on voluntourists' pathological altruism, from pretending to convert to Christianity to get the most from missionaries to using voluntourists as mules for items that are unavailable locally.[25] Or, as Heddwyn saw, orphanage residents rubbing dirt on their faces to get the most from visitors. Yet these responses do little to solve the imbalance of power voluntourism thrives in. They are intriguing anecdotes within a mess of inefficiency.

For thousands of years, feeling concerned for others and scrambling to save them has helped humans stay alive.[26] Today, it may be helping voluntourists do harm.

Whiteness and Faith

When Heddwyn Kyambadde first arrived on Biola University's sunny California campus in 2008, he was greeted by a mural that had already caused more than a decade of debate and will likely continue to be a point of conflict on the Biola campus for as long as it remains. The multistory mural by Kent Twitchell, titled "The WORD," depicts a Jesus modeled after a Russian Jew.[27] The year 2008 was a particularly heated one for Twitchell's Jesus, as the campus erupted with debates over what it meant to live, study, and work on a campus where a Russian Jesus looked down on all of them, every day, as they sought an education and a relationship with God.[28]

It took Heddwyn a little while to understand what the fuss was about. Today, he recognizes his inability to see the issue as itself problematic. At the time, though, he was not comfortable with any of the slots his classmates were trying to fit him—a Black African—into, so he struggled to connect with the conflicts that arose from those identities. His accent does not match the Hollywood stereotype of a man "straight out of Africa," so, he says, "sometimes people would forget that I'm African. People would say things and then expect me to be the 'angry black man,'" even though "I didn't understand racism. I came from a community where I was the majority. I thought that everything I was experiencing was adjusting to a new community."

This uneasy adjustment lasted until Justin Timberlake wore a black suede-looking suit to an awards ceremony. Heddwyn was watching the red carpet coverage with a room full of students when someone piped up. "Did they have to carve up all of your brothers for that suit?" Suddenly, painfully, Heddwyn realized that the friction he had been feeling was not an adjustment period. It was living in America while Black.

The crux of the mural debate was whether Jesus was white. The only times Heddwyn can remember seeing a Black Jesus growing up was during church pageants when a local would put on a blond wig. He was not tied to the idea of Jesus being white; Jesus just *was* white. The black suede incident was illuminating, though, and it reframed his understanding as to why the Jesus mural was such a flashpoint. When white Biola students who insisted that the mural was an accurate representation of fact learned that the popular image of Jesus was not what we now know he would have looked like, Heddwyn saw them fall to pieces.[29] A few, he says, left the school for other universities where they felt their understanding of Christianity would be better represented.

A significant portion of voluntourists are guided toward voluntourism by their faith, predominately Christianity. Many go on mission trips, but some take part in secular experiences, relying on their faith to guide them without the structure of a religious group. One of the arguments put forth for *why* Christians are particularly qualified to engage in voluntourism is that they are following in the footsteps of Jesus Christ.

It is not explicitly stated that the idea of a white Jesus is evidence of white voluntourists' unique qualifications for carrying out his work. However, the subtext beneath much of the marketing of mission trips is that white westerners are the ones to save the world because they look like the man who saved us all. The most obvious of the many issues with this perspective is that Jesus was not white.

When Heddwyn returned to Uganda after university, he noticed that white people listened to him more than they did his colleagues. He was even hired to oversee people who had been doing their jobs for over a decade and who could easily do his too. He believes a core reason for this was his Western education, which was accepted as a stamp of approval from the global white establishment. His practical qualifications mattered less than the name of the school on his diploma.

The debate around Twitchell's Jesus, as well as Heddwyn's other prejudice-centered experiences at Biola and after returning home, illuminate what has come to be called the *white savior complex*. The white savior complex refers to the actions white people take when they feel that they have to save the world—and so, therefore, they should be given free rein to do so however they see fit. The *white savior industrial complex* is the network of businesses and nonprofits that support and encourage people in executing on their privilege-based assumptions.[30] The white savior industrial complex is a system, and the white savior complex is a psychological phenomenon or state of belief. Together, they empower each other in a way that breeds inequity and deepens prejudice.

The broader *privileged savior complex* is a race-ambiguous version of the white savior complex that recognizes financial, geographic, and other forms of privilege. All three—the white savior complex, the white savior industrial complex, and the privileged savior complex—are fed and fueled by the moral economy, the parallel economy that rewards people who behave altruistically with status and financial gain.

Many people, especially white people, bristle at the idea that race has anything to do with their desire to give back or with the more ready access they have to other communities when they slap the word *volunteer* on their name tags. This discomfort is understandable. If we have more than enough money, we can give some away. If we have benefited from access to a high-quality education, we can pass it along by teaching others—formally in classrooms or informally in our workplaces. Even if we live in a privileged region, we can find those in our communities who are struggling and aid them by supporting soup kitchens, community centers, or other local initiatives. But we cannot change the color of our skin. Skin color is a visible characteristic that we cannot do anything about except to acknowledge it. If you are white, to acknowledge your whiteness means to accept the baggage that comes with it, which includes the white savior complex.

But what of those who claim not to see color?

A common rebuttal of the white savior conversation is that if one does not recognize race or "see color," none of these conversations about whiteness and privilege apply. Claiming not to see color is not related to the medical condition of colorblindness. Instead, it is a claim of not assigning meaning to skin color. To assert such a thing is simply absurd. Humans assign meaning to all things. Invisible and visible, learned and innate, novel and pedestrian, there is nothing we don't react to some way, and that reaction is an assignation of meaning. Every human, no matter their race nor privilege nor background, has made and continues to make assumptions in which skin color plays a role. This includes when deciding who to help and where to volunteer. The predominate skin tone of a population is a factor prospective voluntourists consider when deciding where to go because they want the destination to feel "authentically different" from where they are from.[31]

Smile and Play Along

Despite the confrontation of whiteness that needs to happen in voluntourism, race is not the strongest signal of the uneven power dynamics inherent in voluntourism. Rather, it is the belief that, against all evidence, what one is doing is right and good, that most brightly spotlights the colonialist perspective pervasive in voluntourism.

Race matters. White privilege is real. The white savior complex is real. But pathological altruism and the damage it causes relies on a comprehensive imbalance of power—and that imbalance of power does not reside in race alone. If a pro-tourism billboard tells locals to remember to smile because tourists may be watching, the requested performance is not only for the pleasure of white tourists.[32]

Tourists, particularly American tourists, can travel almost anywhere on the planet with a passport, a few recommended vaccines, and minimal prep work. The same is not true for others. In 2017 only 3 percent of outbound international tourists were traveling from a country in Africa.[33] Even within their own borders, many voluntourism hosts cannot afford to access the same activities, such as safaris, that voluntourists do on their days off.[34] By the time I left Tanzania, I was bored with zebras. Many of the young women at Bethsaida shared that they had never seen one. It is not that 97 percent of Africans are travel averse nor terrified of striped horses. For them, the door to tourism, global adventure, and even voluntourism simply is not open. They are supposed to smile, to play along, and to stay put. They may inhabit the world, but it remains ours to explore.

7 | Faith, Purpose, and Mission

Go ye therefore, and teach all nations, baptizing them in the name of the Father, and of the Son, and of the Holy Ghost: Teaching them to observe all things whatsoever I have commanded you: and, lo, I am with you always even unto the end of the world. Amen. —MATTHEW 28:19-20

A passage of the Bible commonly referred to as "the Great Commission" has inspired millions of people over hundreds of years to spread their faith. Some have used violence. Others have planted churches and founded schools aimed at converting people. Some have become outspoken street preachers who yell at passersby, warning them of the dangers of hell if they do not accept Jesus Christ. Others have woven their faith into their daily actions at home. Many have traveled across the world as missionaries. Millions have chosen voluntourism as a mechanism for practicing and spreading their faith.[1]

Globally, there is a direct positive relationship between religiosity, especially Christianity, and volunteering, which is to say that religious people are more likely to volunteer.[2] In the early 1900s, the evangelical revival movement in the United States and Europe led to a surge in missionaries.[3] Today, around 130,000 American Christian missionaries go overseas each year, intending to do good for God.[4]

There is little research specifically exploring the influence of religion on voluntourism numbers. Despite this, a cursory glance at the voluntourism industry reveals the undeniable and deep connection between faith and service, especially in the United States.[5] One of the most influential and controversial Christian groups offering voluntourism experiences—although they do not use the term *voluntourism*—is Youth With A Mission, or YWAM (pronounced "Why-Wam").

The idea for YWAM appeared to founder Loren Cunningham in a dream. He was a twenty-year-old on a trip in the Bahamas with a touring choral group when he felt God wanted him to help others spread their faith. YWAM was established four years later, in 1960, with the mission of attracting young Christians of all denominations, particularly recent high school graduates, to go forth for God. Cunningham set out to train his recruits in discipleship before sending them to impoverished places around the world as advocates for their faith.

Over the following decades, YWAM built short-term mission programs, training schools for evangelism, and a Discipleship Training School (DTS) for teaching biblical foundations. By the organization's fiftieth anniversary in 2010, they reported more than eighteen thousand volunteer staff and more than a thousand ministry locations, making YWAM one of the largest mission organizations in the world. Short-term trips for youth remain at its core.[6]

YWAM trips today have two central components. First is the Lecture Phase. The Lecture Phase is education-centric, combining the original DTS concept with intensive evangelism training. Lecture phases happen at training centers around the world, and there are hundreds of training centers in the United States alone. Class sizes ranging from a handful of participants to more than a hundred. After completing the Lecture Phase, which can last up to a few months, participants enter the Outreach Phase. The Outreach Phase is the voluntourism piece of the YWAM experience. Together, the experience is called Discipleship Training School.

The Outreach Phase of a DTS can take place over a few weeks or stretch to more than three months. No matter the length, the number-one goal is to spread the word of God. However, DTS programs can also include taking part in development projects in addition to direct evangelism.[7]

YWAM does not make an annual report readily available, but it's possible to estimate the ministry's financial might by tallying up the visible line items. Participants pay thousands of dollars for the DTS experience. The training schools are managed independently and set their own prices, but a Lecture Phase at YWAM East London cost $1,265 in 2019, with the Outreach Phase varying from $2,110 to $2,530, depending on the placement location.[8] Also in 2019 YWAM Yosemite in California offered their Sierra Discipleship Training School for $3,000 for the Lecture Phase and then an additional $2,500 plus $1,200 airfare for an Outreach Phase in Nepal, Thailand, or Lebanon.[9] Buyers who have their heart set on a YWAM experience can shop around for the best deal, but it appears that they should expect to fork over around $4,000 before paying for airfare.

YWAM staff members run the DTS experiences, but YWAM's 18,000-plus staff members are volunteers. They have to pay their way or convince their friends and family (and, often, their church community) to finance them. All staff members are also required to have participated in a DTS.[10] If 18,000 staff members have each completed a DTS, with an average cost of $4,000, $72 million has run through YWAM's veins before even accounting for participants who do not become staff members, and other forms of income, such as donations.

YWAM's skill at turning the practice of faith into an accessible global experience has made it a household name in the world of short-term missions.[11] Many other short-term mission groups have tried to follow in their footsteps, often with mixed success.

In 2016 Luket Ministries, a small Oklahoma missionary group working in Eastern Uganda, released a music video cover of Justin Timberlake's hit single "SexyBack" with a new look and a fresh set of lyrics. The group of young white women who starred in the video traded the skimpy outfits from

Timberlake's music video for *gomesi*, the traditional dresses of the Baganda people. Instead of bringing sexy back, they were, they said, bringing missions back ("I'm out to serve God, it's my pact"). Nearly immediately, Luket came under fire for the video. Eventually, the group removed it from social media and offered an apology. They hadn't aimed for cultural insensitivity. They were just trying to attract young missionary-minded voluntourists to their cause.[12]

Large mission groups like YWAM and smaller ones like Luket rely on the same selling points as secular voluntourism to attract customers. Poverty must look fun, enthusiastic engagement is more important than expertise, and anyone who can buy a trip is capable of saving the world. From Mary Carpenter advocating for Christian values in a "heathen" India to Thomas Cook's travelers handing out loaves of bread to Luket Ministries releasing a music video, religion—particularly Christianity—has always been part of voluntourism.[13]

Barbie Saviors

On March 7, 2016, a new Instagram account posted for the first time. The post featured a close-up shot of a brunette Barbie doll running a hand through her hair and was captioned: "Just thinking about my upcoming adventures . . . #excited #africa #adventure #blessed #blessedlife #blessedbygod #blessedbe #mission #stayprayedup #hereiamlord #trustgodbro #disciplethestreets #greatwhitehope #barbiesavior."[14]

On March 29 a blond Barbie wearing a head wrap cuddled up against a Black child. The caption exclaimed, "Orphans take the BEST pictures! So. Cute. #whatsyournameagain #orphans #wheredemorphansat #kingdomcome #blackbarbiesarethecutest #strangers2secondsago #attachementproblemsarentcute #notazoo." The post received more than three thousand likes.[15]

On April 16 Barbie proclaimed herself a qualified teacher because "I'm from the West, so it all works out." The hashtags included #theyteachmemorethaniteachthem, #whichmakessensecuzicantteach, and #PhDindelusionalthoughtprocess. It received more than five thousand likes.[16]

If a stranger walked into a preschool in the United States and started taking pictures of children, he would be kicked out immediately and someone would probably call the cops. Despite this clear social taboo, pictures of and with young children, often taken in much the same manner, have become a voluntourism souvenir so standard that not having one is a sign of a failed trip.[17] Turning complex issues into eye-catching images has consequences. When we distill trauma and inequity down to singular snapshots, it is easy for the allure of the image to outstrip both the context within it and the meaning behind it.[18]

Photos have a profound ability to reveal the invisible, but they are equally good at simplifying what should be complex.[19] The flattening of a community into the photographic format can easily lead to further reduction as people become something to be stared at, their neighborhoods transformed into habitats that outsiders can roam at will, cameras up.[20] This process has been called *zooification*.

Zooification is the transformation of a complex community into a tourism exhibit.[21] These simplified versions of reality are curated, distributed, and then replicated by the next round of well-minded intruders through more images.[22] There is no conversation on consent, and the most popular images become the most popular objects: children.[23]

The @BarbieSavior account went viral in 2016 by taking these stereotypical voluntourism images, replacing the people with Barbies, and giving them a humorous twist. The images they chose to replicate, captions they wrote, and hashtags they included made it clear who the pictures were targeting— voluntourists, and especially short-term missionaries.

For each person laughing in the comments, as many (if not many more) were angry. Everyone wanted to know who was behind the account that was turning well-meaning do-gooders into the butt of the joke.

Confrontation

In the summer of 2018, American Emily Worrall was eating dinner with coworkers at a restaurant in Jinja, Uganda. Just as she was finishing, a woman marched up to her table and shoved a phone in her face. Emily had been watching the woman and her friends, just a few tables away, as they whispered and passed a phone back and forth to show each other something on the screen.[24] Now, they wanted confirmation. Was Emily Worrall Barbie Savior?

Jinja is a small city with, Emily says, a disproportionately high percentage of missionaries. They all know each other, and she had been one of them once. She was living in Kampala now, and she had hoped to get through a night in her old stomping ground without notice.

Emily's first mission trip to Uganda had been more than a decade before. In 2007 she was part of a group of seventy or so short-term missionaries. Many of the group evangelized, but she was assigned to volunteer at an orphanage. She loved it, and she returned to the same orphanage in 2008 and 2009. After three stints there, she decided that she was ready to launch her own NGO.

Emily went on to found Ekisa Ministries, a faith-based Christian organization that specializes in working with special needs and disabled children, providing families with therapy and educational services and young foreigners with voluntourism opportunities. Ekisa serves more than one hundred children in Jinja and accepts voluntourists over the age of eighteen to work with them directly. The minimum suggested stay is six weeks. No qualifications are required.[25]

The picture on the phone screen shoved in Emily's face was not of her, but it did show something she had created. There was a Barbie photoshopped into a stereotypical "third-world" scenario and a sarcastic caption with snarky hashtags. The woman was right. Emily Worrall was half of the creative team behind Barbie Savior. After only a few hours back in the town where her journey had started, she was being called out.

Emily created @BarbieSavior with Jackie Kramlich, a fellow former voluntourist and missionary who had also worked in Jinja. When they launched the account in 2016, Emily was still part of the leadership at Ekisa, Jackie was in the States, and they both needed a way to process their frustrations about missions, voluntourism, and faith. They knew other people would probably see the account. It was public, and the hashtags they were using weren't exactly subtle. Still, they didn't think much about the reaction their posts would garner from people they knew. The internet is big, and their humorous critique of the industry they had devoted their lives to was sure to be swallowed by the void.

To their surprise, the pictures quickly attracted attention from the global voluntourism community, and "Barbie Savior" entered the alternative tourism vocabulary as a term for anyone who believes they are doing good while being blind to the repercussions of their actions—a pathological altruist. Those critical of voluntourism began using "Barbie Savior" to bundle the motivations, actions, intentions, and outcomes of the industry together into one catchy concept. Trip providers and voluntourists began using it to differentiate themselves—Barbie Saviors were real, but they weren't one. Once mainstream media caught on, it was only a matter of time before it landed in Jinja. Emily and Jackie were caught off guard by the attention, but they were also still anonymous.

Their anonymity was creatively liberating, but it was also necessary. Emily was still working in the same industry she was comically excoriating online. If her coworkers found out, her career at Ekisa—the organization she had founded—would be in jeopardy. So she tried to play it cool. When someone would mention a new post to her, which happened almost daily, she would pretend she had not been drafting it with Jackie sometimes mere hours before.

Emily and Jackie did not know how to label the Barbie Savior project when journalists first started reaching out to the account for an interview, a statement, anything to further illuminate the viral phenomenon. Eventually, it came to seem something like an art piece. "It's open to interpretation," Emily says. "We put it out there, but we don't defend ourselves. We don't apologize."

At the peak of the project's virality, Emily and Jackie quietly took credit for their work. Not many people noticed, but word made its way to Jinja. And so, when one of the women who had been whispering throughout dinner walked up to Emily's table and shoved a phone in her face, she nodded. Yes, she was one of the people behind Barbie Savior. As the woman tried to escalate the situation, Emily walked to the bar and bought a pack of cigarettes.

When she rejoined the group at her table, she pulled one out. "I'm sorry. I quit, but I need one of these." The apology wasn't necessary. None of her tablemates had been able to follow the altercation. They didn't know why the woman was waving her phone around. They didn't know Emily was Barbie Savior. Now they knew they were dining with a legend in the voluntourism debate, but they still didn't know the full story.

Back when Barbie Savior was first gaining steam, Emily had been fighting two battles within herself. She was losing her faith in God, and she was losing her faith in voluntourism. In response, she decided that she either needed to reframe Ekisa, the organization she had founded, or leave it. When she explained her vision for a new Ekisa to her team, they were not receptive. When she told them that she didn't identify as Christian anymore, they recoiled. Christianity was central to the identity of the organization. If she wasn't Christian, they weren't willing to work with her.

Emily accepted their verdict. As she managed her transition out of Ekisa, Barbie Savior was an outlet for processing her feelings about her work, her faith, and herself.

After leaving Ekisa, Emily moved to Kampala and found a job at an NGO she truly believed in. Eventually, she was assigned to take a small film crew a few hours outside of Kampala to document a project. Jinja was along their route, and the crew asked to stop there for the night. Emily knew she couldn't avoid Jinja forever, but she was anxious. She suspected that her return would not go unnoticed, even if just for a night. And then a woman challenged her, and she answered, "yes," and now she was sitting at her table, smoking a cigarette, filling in the crew on the epic tale behind the excruciatingly awkward showdown.

Finding a Mission

In certain circles of Christianity, maintaining the idea that a voluntourist can be a savior is a matter of survival. There are those who save and those who need to be saved, and the line must be clear for the product hanging in the balance—mission trips—to remain viable.[26]

In 2018 Emily broke her near-silence on Barbie Savior when she joined the Failed Missionary podcast, a project focused on power, privilege, place, and what it means to try—and fail—to give back, often in ways that are damaging to communities. Emily had met Corey Pigg, the host and co-creator of the podcast, after she visited an online forum for liturgists looking for someone to talk to about missionary work. They clicked immediately.[27]

Corey grew up in Missouri, and at seventeen he attended a worship event that changed the course of his life. He likens the experience to Hillsong, the Australian mega-church known for its Pentecostal and evangelical beliefs and celebrity members, including Justin and Hailey Bieber. The church Corey attended was not a Hillsong church, but it delivered similarly charismatic services centered on enthusiastic celebration.

"That was my first encounter with a God that was interventionist," he remembers. "To an impressionable boy that already doesn't feel like he fits in with his family, it was like electricity running through my body. Even to this day, I think that whatever that was, there was some realness to it. It woke me up."

He quickly became infatuated with his newfound faith, but his family was wary of the sudden change. They tried to intervene, but the church crowd Corey had surrounded himself with insisted that his family's attempts to get him to step back were tests of his belief in God. "Why would I want my family," he asked himself, "when God is a lot cooler?"

When Corey graduated from high school, he chose the path of ministry. The next step was to select a place to practice. He had two criteria for a mission: he didn't want to be somewhere hot, and he didn't want to lose access to "modern" conveniences. These requirements eliminated many of the most popular mission destinations in Africa, Asia, and South and Central America. Eventually, he picked the least boat-rocking faraway option he could come up with: Germany.

There was another reason Corey fixated on Germany—artist missionaries. He had learned about a group of missionaries in Germany who were

YWAMers, members of Youth with a Mission, who used their art to spread their faith, and he wanted to become one of them.

At the same time as Corey was planning his future following Christ, he was struggling to come to terms with his sexuality. YWAMers adhere to an oppressively heteronormative set of guidelines for behavior. In a 2019 letter to the YWAM community from David Joel Hamilton on behalf of the Global Leadership Team of YWAM, he wrote that YWAM believes "all sexual activity (heterosexual or homosexual) outside of this God-ordained arrangement [of one man and one woman] is sin." "Our Foundational Values," he went on to write, "are a whole package. They are not a buffet line from which one can choose some that one likes and leave behind those which one does not like. . . . If you read through these values and do not see yourself joyfully embracing them, then you most likely are not called to be a YWAMer."[28]

YWAM was rejecting a piece of who Corey was, but they promised to fill that void and more. Just as he chose to be a missionary over becoming a college student, he decided to try to suppress his identity in favor of the missionary life he was craving. "You had to assimilate or go home," Corey remembers. So he tried to assimilate.

Looking back at his decision, Corey thinks that therapy would have been a healthier option. "I chose to give service to God, thinking that would heal things. That was the worst thing I could have done," he says.

Over the next seven years, he visited more than thirty countries and lived in four: Germany, China, South Korea, and closer to home in the United States. Some of it was exciting, like the times he entered China illegally with short-term mission groups.[29] But most of what they did was rather boring. He remembers twiddling his thumbs in the forests of Germany while living off of money donated by members of his community at home. He went on mission trips to other countries a few times a year, then used the photos and videos he collected to raise money to cover the other nine months. He eventually became a YWAM staff member, a volunteer who drummed up donations in lieu of pay.[30] Slowly, he became more fragmented than he had been when he joined YWAM. By the end, "I was a dead person," Corey remembers. "I was gone."

"I felt so shameful," he says, "because I didn't have the words to tell friends or family about why, all of a sudden, after seven years, I just gave up." It would take years of therapy and what he calls a process of "deprogramming" for him to articulate why he needed to leave YWAM. Even years later, he continues to struggle with the fact that he supported and promoted a group and a lifestyle rooted in fraudulent ideologies and harmful actions.[31] "You realize a lot of the lies that you let your brain get twisted around, and a lot of the people and figureheads in your life that you just gave yourself to," he says. To move forward, he had to disentangle himself entirely.

The idea for the Failed Missionary podcast came toward the end of that process of disentanglement. Corey had lost most of his friends, and his family wasn't as immediately warm and welcoming as he had hoped. They were confused by who he had transformed into and wary of what he had come to represent. He hoped that the podcast would be a way to reach back out into the world he had left, and he envisioned it as an ecumenical project. He would bring people from where he had been spiritually and ideologically while with YWAM together with those who shared his new, more skeptical beliefs. The two opposing groups would have conversations that grappled with faith, privilege, and purpose through a missionary lens.

However, Corey quickly realized that using conversations on missions as a meeting ground was not going to work out well. Early in the podcast, he had to cut guests out of episodes after they acted shocked and upset in front of their followers that they had appeared in the same digital space as people like Emily Worrall. Corey insists that he was upfront with his guests about what to expect. He never tried to catch someone in a gotcha moment, and the former guests' indignance was, he thinks, a performance for the benefit of their enraged fans. The point of the podcast was to bring people with varying views together, but it was being used by the most dogmatic to entrench their base. "There's white privilege," Corey says, "and I've also come to like the term 'Christian privilege,' and Christian privilege does a lot to cover up voluntourism."

Jamie Wright, one of Corey's early co-hosts, is a former long-term missionary and author of the 2018 memoir *The Very Worst Missionary*. In her book, she explores the concept of Christian privilege, especially how it relates to the assumption that wanting to do something is a qualification to do so. "God doesn't call the equipped; He equips the called" is a common saying in the missionary sphere. This mentality encourages a culture in which all you have to do is want to be a missionary to become one. "If you raise your hand," Jamie says, "someone will send you out."[32]

On God's Guidance

According to the Center for the Study of Global Christianity, approximately 440,000 Christian missionaries served abroad in 2018.[33] Around 130,000 of them were Americans, more than double the 57,000 Americans who served in 1970.[34] Travel is more accessible than it has ever been, which makes organizing trips easier. Evangelicalism has boomed as a result.

Even when short-term missionaries, or religious voluntourists, truly believe that delivering Christianity will simultaneously deliver hope, happiness, and greater fulfillment to people in need, faith can quickly become an excuse for imposing Western superiority.[35] And yet, Jamie Wright writes in her memoir, "nobody wants to tell anyone they shouldn't be a missionary. . . . It's practically against the rules."[36]

In November 2018 American John Allen Chau was killed by members of an isolated tribe on North Sentinel Island, in the Andaman Sea, off the coast of India. Travel to the island is prohibited, and the inhabitants of the island have a history of not being enthusiastic about visitors.[37]

Chau grew up in Vancouver, Washington. He idolized famous American evangelical missionaries like Jim Elliot, who was killed while carrying out the Great Commission in Ecuador, and, at twenty-six, his goal was to follow in Elliot's path by bringing Christ to people who had not had the chance for

Christian salvation.[38] His training was his faith, his tool was scripture, and his purpose was to carry the word of the Lord.

He also had some practical preparation. Chau trained with All Nations at their headquarters in Kansas City, Missouri. All Nations has links to YWAM, and a key piece of All Nations trainings are village simulations designed to prepare missionaries for evangelism against all the odds.[39]

Missionary-focused village simulations are what they sound like, but still strange enough that it is worth illustrating one. Imagine being blindfolded, driven around for a while, and unceremoniously dumped on a dirt road. First, you must find the village. Then, the "villagers" run at you with spears and scream in a language you do not recognize. You need to figure out how to look completely unthreatening while politely requesting that they change their entire belief system to the one tucked under your arm. If the dirt road is in Kansas and the village is a set, the villagers are wearing costumes, and the language they are speaking in is not a language at all, you may be in a missionary training village simulation.[40]

Chau's attempt to contact the residents of North Sentinel Island appears to have been earnest and good-hearted. Even so, the idea driving his mission, that because you believe something you have the right and the duty to push it onto others, is at the core of colonial imperialism. It takes an enormous sense of privilege to presume you have the power—and the right—to attempt to influence a population that wants nothing to do with you. And yet, convictions like Chau's are at the center of the short-term missionary fervor.

On November 15, 2018, he landed on the island by kayak. He was greeted with arrow fire and quickly left. The next day, he paid fishermen to take him again. When the fishermen returned the following day to check on him, they reported seeing island residents dragging his body along the beach.[41]

Faith as Foundation

When Nick Cocalis co-founded Next Step, a nonprofit, short-term mission trip provider, with Andrew Atwell and Todd Gehrmann in 2007, he was just a senior in college. "Our lives," Nick said when discussing the origins of the organization, "were personally changed by short-term mission experiences and, ultimately, what God was doing in our lives, and we wanted to create that experience for people that we cared about most."[42] Today, Next Step sends thousands of young people on short-term mission trips each year. They have programs in Haiti and Guatemala, but their focus is mostly on destinations that are omitted from the majority of voluntourism statistics and rounds-ups: those within the United States, including Los Angeles, Colorado Springs, the Navajo Nation and Pine Ridge Reservation, and Fairbanks, Alaska.

Nick left his full-time role at Next Step in January 2018, but he was still the person appointed to speak with me on behalf of the organization when I reached out hoping to discuss the organization later that same year. He estimated that, at the time, 90 percent of Next Step trip participants registered with Next Step through a faith-based organization such as a church, youth group, Christian school, or sports team. However, he said, "about 50 percent of our trip participants would not identify as Christians or Christ-followers when they go on our trips." They may not start the trips as Christians, but it is hard to imagine a committed atheist going along with twice-daily devotionals and nightly worship services, even when the worship is designed to look like a rock concert.[43]

Into 2020, Next Step's mission statement was clear. The organization strives "to provide opportunities for students to explore their faith, experience God, and extend service to others, all in the name of Jesus Christ."[44] Next Step even developed an app that can help. MyStep, the Next Step app for iOS and Android, provides participants with inspirational videos, devotional stories, and a live prayer wall.[45]

Yet, when asked about the role of religion in the Next Step experience, Nick sidestepped in a way that has become typical of short-term mission programs that are trying to distance themselves from programming like YWAM and missionaries like John Allen Chau. "I don't think [religion] plays any part," Nick said; "I think that you have a group of people that are followers of Jesus trying to live and act as Jesus did, and the repercussion of that is others following Jesus." His statement is confusing. If you enter into an experience to follow Jesus and hope others will follow, religion is, at minimum, present in the experience.

Nick's statements also contradict how Next Step describes trip products to potential customers, revealing a disconnect between the messaging used to market their trips to buyers and the messaging used to explain those same trips to those—like me—suspected of being skeptical. In the majority-Mayan town of Sumpango, Guatemala, Next Step participants were, according to the trip description available for summer 2019, helping to "win this community over for Christ." They would "make disciples" within the community while working on a church construction project, helping at the Vacation Bible School, building additions on local homes, or volunteering at an orphanage.[46] Also in 2019 the Next Step website described trips to Fairbanks, Alaska, as an opportunity to aid local ministries "in their battle to spread the love of Christ throughout the beautiful wilderness state." Hands-on work included assisting in the construction and maintenance of Christian retreats.[47]

But, Nick had insisted, "I wouldn't say that there are any religious goals. I hesitate to even use the word *religious*." "We don't," he said, "go out with any sort of, quote, unquote, 'religious agenda' into a community or on a trip." The dissonance between Nick's assertions on behalf of the organization and its marketing are painfully obvious.

Even Nick will admit that Next Step's commitment to providing their participants with a transformative religious experience has, at times, interfered with the impacts they are trying to initiate on the ground. "When we started Next Step," Nick said, "we were focused on the ministry opportunity for the participants. We cared about the communities, but we didn't know how to care about the communities."

Nick points to one example of this mismatch between caring for the participant and caring for the community in particular: the aftermath of Hurricane Sandy. In 2012, while Nick was still the missions director at Next Step, Hurricane Sandy hit New York. Next Step jumped into action. Nick now identifies the move as one of the organization's biggest failures. They sent more than a thousand voluntourists to New York over eight weeks to help with recovery. Nick admits that the driving force for the trips was what they felt "God could do in the students' lives" in a post-disaster setting. In the process, they lost any pretense that the program was for the communities they were ostensibly helping. The experience was for the paying participants.

After some reflection, the three founders published an apology video in which they recognized that they had been operating on misaligned priorities. "Our student participant experience was the thing that was driving our income, our profits, our growth, our jobs," Nick remembered—so that was what they, like most trip providers, had been putting first. In the mea culpa video, the founders state they are committed to changing this way of thinking and holding communities equal to participants. Next Step even issued a new vision statement: "to be a platform where short-term mission trips collide with long-term community development."[48]

Collide is an appropriate word. The expression of privilege and power, especially through faith, is never peaceful, just as a collision is never subtle. When trip fees account for 93 percent of your revenue, as they did for Next Step in 2016 ($2,572,233 of $2,754,220), it is not surprising that managing the relationship between trip participants and the places they visit can quickly result in a nasty collision.[49] Alternatively, a trip provider could forgo attempts at a balance altogether. Following the release of the apology video, the worship and programming section of the Next Step website, still read: "Although we are committed to the communities we serve with and the work projects we invest in—our primary focus has always been on people and their personal relationship with Christ." This contradicts Nick's remarks, the organization's apology video, and the vision statement.[50]

Partnerships with local churches and religious groups in host communities have been crucial to Next Step's growth. All trip providers rely on some version of such partnerships. The word *partnership* suggests active community support and engagement, and something at least approximating a fair exchange. But when voluntourists' wants are at the core of the experiences, the question will always remain: Is the community simply playing host to someone else's life-changing experience?

8 | The Development Conundrum

In the western mountains of the Dominican Republic, outside of the small town of Río Limpio, there is a greenhouse graveyard. In the summer of 2015, the massive wooden skeletons draped with tattered sheets of white plastic were overrun with vines and bushes. Young trees stretch upward where trellises used to provide support for beans, peppers, and okra. Somehow, despite the thick overgrowth of weeds, there was still produce ready for harvest in the bellies of the shredded beasts. The aid-project-gone-wrong—a gift to the people of Río Limpio—was still trying to give.

A few years before, the greenhouse project had been spearheaded by a group of NGO and development organizations. The groups, collectively referred to locally as Frontera Futuro, the name of one of the largest participants, had worked in Río Limpio for some time before proposing the greenhouse project. They knew the town reasonably well, and they believed they knew the surrounding environment.[1] They were especially inspired by the nearby Nalga de Maco National Park, a tradition of organic farming in the town, and local interest in ecotourism development. With the greenhouses, Río

Limpio residents would be able to grow large amounts of produce organically and without exacerbating deforestation. It seemed a strong foundation for a successful development project, and it was, at first, a very welcome one.

The development groups trucked in materials and labor, picked an open spot, and started building, but not long after the greenhouses were completed, a storm ripped through the spindly structures. Unbeknownst to them, there was a good reason arable land in the middle of an agricultural area had been left vacant. Without the funds to start over, the greenhouse graveyard was left to rot.

The shredded greenhouses were not the town's first failed development project. In 2015 Río Limpio had concrete sidewalks and impressive power poles, but the power poles were misleading. They connected nobody to anything. They had been installed, but they had not been connected to the grid. Once again, Río Limpio had received a gift it could not use and was left trying to figure out what to do with it.

Río Limpio isn't unique. Despite the United Nations touting tourism as a path toward sustainable development, voluntourism has not worked as a means of reliable and ongoing growth.[2] And yet, the dream outcome—a community with everything it needs, all built for free by foreigners—is still being sold as an attainable future.[3] All the community has to do is to say yes. All the voluntourists need to do is to try.

They do try.[4] Like ME to WE co-founder Craig Kielburger yelling, "You can change the world!" to eight hundred students from the middle of a high school gym, hopeful travelers swivel their heads toward the calls to greater purpose and meaning.[5] Communities buy into the idea of a particular type of progress, while voluntourists are sold on the chance to find themselves on a developing-world construction site. The results are rarely what either party was hoping for.[6]

The Money

While voluntourism is a money-driven business, the proliferation of for-profit trip providers complicates the process of tracking down where dollars flow.

When the money trail is legible, it provides a clear illustration of why framing voluntourism as a development initiative is little more than a sales pitch.

In tourism a higher price typically suggests a better-quality product. A hotel room that costs $500 per night is generally assumed to be nicer than one that costs $150 per night. In voluntourism, this expectation flips. Most people are looking for a steal, not necessarily because they are on a tight budget, but because a high price tag has come to signal inauthenticity. Potential voluntourists tell themselves that if a trip is less expensive, it must be more altruistic.[7]

Global Crossroad, the company that facilitated my trip to Tanzania in 2009, emphasizes that it offers programs at bargain prices, sometimes, the website boasted in May 2020, as much as "200 percent less than prices charged by a number of major US-based, non-profit, volunteer abroad organizations."[8] This is the company's primary selling point, and it counts on it to explain why 25 percent of the low price each of its thousands of travelers pays has historically gone toward marketing trips to other aspiring travelers. Global Crossroad openly admits that only a "limited amount" of each program fee reaches the voluntourism project and host family. Based on its estimates, even a "limited amount" is a gross overstatement:

GLOBAL CROSSROAD TRIP FEE BREAKDOWN (2020):
Marketing and advertising: 25 percent
Staff salaries: 20 percent
Operating expenses: 10 percent
Research and development of programs: 10 percent
Airport pickups, accommodations, meals, paying in-country staff:
    20–40 percent
Profit: 10–15 percent[9]

Add these items up, and it's unsurprising that Global Crossroad has little left to contribute toward the projects its customers are assigned to undertake. It also helps to illuminate why so many trip providers encourage or even require customers to fundraise on top of their trip fees to cover project costs like materials and local labor.

Projects Abroad, another trip provider, also provides a breakdown that shows where trip fees go.

PROJECTS ABROAD TRIP FEE BREAKDOWN (2020):

Direct costs (housing, food, donations to placements, airport transfers, materials, individual insurance): 32 percent

Indirect costs (office rent at destination, local staff salaries, business expenses, predeparture staff salaries/office/expenses): 24 percent

Organizational costs (admin, HR, bookkeeping, insurance, IT): 13 percent

Recruitment and communication (marketing, events, PR): 24 percent

Taxes: 4 percent

Excess (profit): 3 percent[10]

Unlike Global Crossroad, Projects Abroad does include donations to placements in their breakdown. However, they lump it in with other on-the-ground costs, doing little to illuminate how much they are passing along to host organizations. Thanks to the work of journalist Juliana Ruhfus, we know that in 2012 the "donation to placement" for one Projects Abroad orphanage partner was less than $13 per volunteer per week.[11]

A four-week Projects Abroad trip will run a traveler around $3,000. Projects Abroad no longer offers orphanage experiences but has replaced them with similarly priced nonresidential childcare volunteer opportunities. If the $13-per-week donation remains standard, it accounts for less than 2 percent of the total trip fee. In a study of voluntourism opportunities and impacts in Rwanda, 5 percent of each volunteer fee to a leading locally run trip provider was allocated to the community through cash and in-kind donations. It's a better ratio than Projects Abroad or Global Crossroad, but still not a robust one.[12]

Trip providers have to maintain a robust bottom line—so it's in their best interest to hold on to as much of the cash that comes through their pipeline as possible. To do this, they construct opportunities that offer the most adventure possible at the price voluntourists are willing to pay. The first to feel the brunt of cost cutting are the very people trip providers market as the beneficiaries of voluntourists' good intentions: community members. Donations are dropped, fewer local workers are hired to oversee projects, and it is not unheard of for families to be expected to host paying volunteers without compensation or support.[13]

It is worth reinforcing that the status of Projects Abroad, Global Crossroad, and so many other trip providers as for-profits is not itself the problem. If the goal of a trip is to improve a community through sustainable development, voluntourism is an entirely inefficient system, whether the trip provider is a for-profit or not. For development to be sustainable, it requires a multigenerational timeline, long-term commitment, and the prioritization of a place and its people above external motivators. Voluntourism provides little of that. It's a short-term commodity that changes tactics, offerings, and destinations in response to market forces. The deeper one looks, the clearer it becomes that voluntourism and sustainability do not mix.[14]

The Impacts

The oil-and-water relationship between sustainable development and voluntourism *could* be proven through data—the sort that is essential for robust annual reporting, transparent business practices, and external evaluations. Throughout the voluntourism industry, however, rigorous data is in terrifyingly short supply.[15] However, there is a qualitative equation for measuring impact that can be applied even with limited information:

Outputs + Outcomes = Impacts

Outputs are the things that are created by development projects—wells, school buildings, energy efficient stoves, and so on.

Outcomes are the observed results of those outputs. These may include a decrease in waterborne illnesses among those who now have access to clean water, an increase in the number of children with access to education, or a reduction in firewood use among families that have more efficient stoves.

Impacts result from the outputs and outcomes, and they take time to reveal themselves. They are the ripples that spread outwards *and* the roots that run deep. Is a family able to make more money and invest it back into their farm because they spend less of their day looking for firewood or sick from waterborne illnesses? Are students staying in their communities after graduation and using their skills to start businesses? Impacts address big questions over long periods of time. The reports trip providers publish are, by and large, overflowing with outputs. Instead of offering systematic long-term assessments, they boast of schools built and wells drilled. They call these things "impacts" when, in reality, they are only a means toward possible future impacts that have yet to be realized.[16] And sometimes they aren't even that.

Author and human geographer Mary Mostafanezhad was in Chiang Mai, Thailand, when she discovered that Borderless Volunteers, the small nonprofit arm of a Thai for-profit travel company, had figured out how to maximize outputs while bypassing outcomes and impacts entirely. Once one Borderless Volunteers group finished building bathrooms at a local school and left for home, the structures were demolished to make way for a new project, built by a fresh set of volunteers.[17]

Stories of trip providers assigning many groups to teach the same lessons or paint the same walls circulate frequently, but it is rare for a trip provider to get caught in the act. Due to the short-term nature of voluntourism, a voluntourist or researcher may have an inkling that something is up, but they are rarely around long enough to see their suspicions come true.

With trip providers prioritizing outputs over impacts, it is no wonder voluntourists have become known for biting off more than they can chew. They want to solve big problems, not the small and mundane things that may actually be attainable in a school vacation.[18] When that proves impossible, they are disappointed and frustrated. Instead of questioning the system and their place within it, they lash out at the trip provider or even the host community.[19]

True development—deep development that moves communities forward in whatever direction they believe forward to be—is rooted in investment (capital) and talent generation (capacity). When voluntourists try to build a wall, they take capital and capacity from a local worker. When voluntourists try to teach a class, they take capital and capacity away from a local teacher. When voluntourists hand out school supplies they brought with them on the plane, they are undermining local businesses, robbing them of capital and capacity development.

And yet, somehow, even the senseless repetition witnessed in Thailand can be more attractive to communities than the alternative—nothing. It is not uncommon for places to be passed over for assistance if they cannot (or will not) provide a project that volunteers want to do. If they do not want volunteers teaching their children or if they wish to use skilled local labor, trip providers skip over them. There is always a less demanding community willing to accept the help trip providers want to give, even if it isn't helpful.[20]

At the same time, voluntourists want access to a comfortable bed, good food, and clean water, but they also want to be surrounded by the types of poverty they have seen on television. Even modest status symbols—pillows, new cookpots, a nice cellphone—can make a destination unpalatable to voluntourists by not appearing poor enough. If a place is not poor enough to meet voluntourists' standards of what the developing world should look like, they (and trip providers) find what they are looking for elsewhere.[21]

Through these behaviors—voluntourists' poverty-seeking, and trip providers' poverty maintenance—any arguments for voluntourism as development fall apart. If voluntourism were a reliable form of development, the needs it purports to be addressing would be declining. Instead, they are multiplying to accommodate more voluntourists. Trip providers would be sprinting toward self-obsolescence. Instead, they are being bought up by investors who see an easy way to make big money. Communities would be celebrated for advocating for what they want to develop toward. Instead, they are punished for progressing.[22]

Dame ("Dah-may")

One of the worst outcomes of voluntourism as a development practice is *dame culture*. I first heard of dame culture when I was working alongside a few former Peace Corps volunteers on a sustainable tourism initiative in the Dominican Republic. The phrase was part of their daily vocabulary and was used to refer to areas that have been so saturated with short-term aid that they have lost the contours of a healthy community. *Dame* means "give me" in Spanish. It is a command, not a request.

When a friend described the concept of dame culture to me, she illustrated it with a story that has been passed around by Peace Corps volunteers at Dominican bars and breakfast tables for years. In the Dominican Republic, it is common for agricultural workers to live in *bateyes*—ramshackle communities with limited resources and poor living conditions that are close to the sugar mill or other processing plant at which the residents work. Once upon a time, a mill or a factory (depending on who is telling the story) announced that it was shutting down, and everyone in the batey would have to relocate. When a nonprofit heard what was happening, they decided to build a new home for the community. They erected a compound with houses and streets, and ultimately moved the workers and their families to this new village.

In the story, the problems started almost immediately. The town was isolated, and it was hard to find jobs nearby. At the same time, volunteer groups began to arrive, bringing food, books, clothing, and even mattresses. You had to be home to receive the gifts, so families faced a decision: leave to find work and potentially miss a freebie worth more than a day's wages, or stay and wait? As the story goes, many people picked the logical choice. They stopped working in favor of more time with their families and free stuff. They were a dame community with no apparent way out.

The term *dame* is Spanish, but the problem is global.[23]

It is critically important that we address immediate need when and where it arises. Healthcare is a human right. So is nutritious food and access to education. But when these things are given without significant community buy-in, and no attention is paid to transitioning toward sustainability, communities disintegrate. Instead of helping, dependence is manufactured and replicated in ways that are irresponsible and cruel.[24]

Eventually, voluntourists become frustrated with a community for having "too much" or for asking for more or not acting grateful enough. Ingenuity is interpreted as entitlement, and they label them spoiled, like fruit going to rot—something they were expecting to be sweet but that can no longer hide the complexities beneath its skin.[25] Kids see their parents' creativity and, in striving to replicate it, are stripped of agency as well. It is not empowering to be given everything you need to survive in exchange for a video of you looking sad and downtrodden until someone hands you a stuffed animal.[26] This does not add up to the development promised, but to exploitation, and when the things stop coming, those who are presumably being helped have nothing to keep them from falling even harder than they did before.[27]

When the fountain of freebies eventually and inevitably cuts off, communities collapse, the support system that once existed becoming victim to the erosion of blind generosity.[28]

Social Development

A leading argument for why voluntourism as development is okay, even when evidence points to it as inefficient and often harmful, is that it serves as a form of *social development*. Some say that by exposing voluntourists to developing communities, voluntourists become better people, and that by exposing developing communities to voluntourists, community members learn about the world. It has even been argued that proximity to whiteness raises community members' status, giving those who work with white voluntourists a social boost among their peers without white "friends."[29] It has been argued that, together, a shared humanity is unlocked. In reality, voluntourism relies on the maintenance of difference, not the dissolution of it.

Voluntourists may find a sense of greater understanding through their experiences, but a reciprocal connection remains elusive—even of the artificially manufactured sort.[30] Just as Heddwyn Kyambadde watched orphanage residents rub dirt on themselves before running toward arriving volunteers, communities are forced to play a part so that voluntourists can leave with the feeling that they have changed inside. This artificial intimacy encourages voluntourists to spread items and ideas that are not necessarily welcome in their host communities. Cultural belief systems and westernization are pushed, often subconsciously, toward communities that may want to go in a different direction, one that bypasses the West's worst habits.[31]

White Elephants

Development is a process that does not follow borders drawn on maps. It is personal, it is local, and that is why successful development is complicated. Even when a project is well executed and results in long-term sustainable positive change that does not require continuous reinvestment, it is unequal and unevenly distributed. If you need proof, look to the United States of America. One of the most developed countries in the world has millions of homeless and hungry children and an abysmal healthcare system. Entire swaths of the country are decades behind the richest regions. Development is unfair no matter where you live, but particularly in places where short-term aid is passed off as long-term development.[32]

The local people of Río Limpio were still nervous to talk about the project that led to the greenhouse graveyard years after the project sponsors packed up and left. They have heard that if you criticize a volunteer group, the groups stop coming—and they don't want them to stop coming; they simply want them to do better work.

The only person willing to speak openly about the greenhouse debacle required the protection of anonymity.[33] He knew that, while his opinions were widely shared in local living rooms and around dinner tables, they weren't something you talk about in the open, and especially not to outsiders.

The business owner shared that the problems started at the very beginning of the project. From the get-go, the coordination was sloppy. The organizations brought in volunteers and materials but did not consult with community members about project logistics, despite their having generations of expertise on local weather, geography, and successful agricultural practices. As a result, the organizations picked ground that was available for the output they wanted to build but that was uniquely poorly suited for the outcomes and impacts they hoped to see manifested. They used low-quality wood for the greenhouse frames and cheap plastic covers that ripped off in strong winds.

The organizations and volunteers left soon after building the greenhouses. They did not see what happened next. They did not know there was a good reason for why a large swath of level, arable land was not already being farmed. It was in the midst of a wind tunnel.

Had they been executed properly, the greenhouses in Río Limpio could have been a phenomenal community asset and the business owner made it clear that he would love to see them rebuilt better. By August 2016 the community had begun to clean up the mess the development groups had left in their wake. The land would get a second shot, but this time the people of Río Limpio would have control of their future.

The greenhouse graveyard is a particularly visually arresting example of a failed aid project, but it isn't unique. A national organization, foreign donors, and the Dominican government chose to operate upon their community, but without them—and it went spectacularly awry.

Projects such as the greenhouse graveyard highlight how outsider input is routinely prioritized over local know-how. When governments rely on outside investors for aid dollars, they tend to stop listening to the voices of those they are supposed to be serving.[34] When they do eventually tune in, they tend to act too quickly in adjusting for their mistakes, creating layers of harm as they ricochet between being out of touch and overly enthusiastic.[35] What results are *white elephants*—aid projects that are more taxing than they are generative. White elephants look good in presentations and promotional videos but go to rot on the ground.

Millions of voluntourists are booking trips based on what they want to do and where they want to go, not what skills they have or what communities really need. When they fail, they make the situation even worse.[36] Unreliable work done by outsiders will never create positive change and doing work poorly that locals can do well is not development. What communities need are self-directed systems, not flimsy handouts.[37]

Sustainable community development is often frustrating because it tends to be slow. When the focus shifts to raising the standard of living for entire communities, not solely individuals, it takes longer to see a payoff. Across voluntourism, the emphasis has been on quick payoffs and singular projects. Organizations build schools without thinking about what an education requires. Donors support projects without asking questions or considering advisability. Voluntourists build greenhouses without local expertise or buy-in. In the process, power structures replicate, divisions multiply, and people are stripped of agency.

Ultimately, communities lose the ability to chart their own futures and then are labeled as entitled when they ask for a leg up.[38]

9 | Playing Doctor

A young woman in scrubs is assisting a doctor. The sounds of metal scraping on bone fill the small operating room. The patient groans in pain. Exhausted, hungry, and sweating under the lights, the young woman says she needs to step away for a moment to clear her head. She sits on a stool in the corner, and another volunteer slides into her place beside the doctor. Moments later, the young woman on the stool crashes to the ground, unconscious. Chaos ensues.

This moment was the shock point of *Volunteers Unleashed*, a 2015 CBC DocZone documentary that I also appeared in. In the documentary, Larsa Al-Omaishi, the volunteer who fainted, was presented as the embodiment of the voluntourism problem. When she watched the film for the first time, she was infuriated. What had happened was more complex than the simple story of a silly young volunteer biting off more than she could chew. She wanted to share the real story by revealing the whole story.

Larsa graduated from Duke University in 2011 with a degree in neuroscience. Shortly after graduation, she started working in brain trauma research through the Barrow Neurological Institute in Phoenix, Arizona. "Where I was working, I kept getting told, 'no, you can't do that unless you're a doctor.'" So she resolved to become one. She was accepted to medical school at the University of Queensland with a start date of January 2014.[1]

The spring before starting medical school, Larsa had no significant obligations and did not feel like staying in her job just to fill the time before hitting the books. "I just thought about how easy it would be to sell everything I had," she says, "and then just leave for a few months. Could I do that?"

She did the math and decided that yes, she could. "Which was actually wrong," she laughs, "I should have noticed that." But she didn't, so she started looking into programs that could potentially jumpstart a career in international health.

First, she tallied up what she could offer. She was a certified EMT, so she had practical skills. She had gone through extensive ethics training for her research work, which had required her to spend time in the trauma ward, so she knew she could handle a stressful environment. The daughter of Iraqi refugees, she also spoke Arabic.

But she had already been to the Middle East and wanted a new experience. Africa would be new, but she was advised that her Arabic would not be very helpful in Morocco or Egypt. While looking for other options, a program in Tanzania caught her eye. The application said applicants must be enrolled in medical or nursing school to be a medical volunteer. Larsa decided to apply anyway. Maybe with her EMT certification, they would give her a shot.

When International Volunteer HQ (IVHQ), a for-profit voluntourism provider that has sent more than one hundred thousand volunteers around the globe since 2007, notified her of her acceptance to a four-month program with two months at an orphanage and two months at a local clinic, she was elated.[2] She quit her job, booked her flights, and was off to Tanzania.

When Larsa arrived in Arusha on June 25, 2013, her first assignment was eight weeks of volunteering at the Save Africa Orphanage, a home for children ages three to eighteen in Usa River, just outside of Arusha, a popular hub for safari outfitters.[3] It's the same place my school group traveled to for our safari in 2009, and Arusha's popularity as a gateway to Tanzania's parks has spawned a parallel business linking tourists (often the same ones also booking sightseeing trips) with opportunities to make their vacations more altruistic.

"When I signed up," Larsa remembers, "what I understood of orphanage [volunteering] was that you went to an orphanage, and your purpose was to hold the children so that they got that human connection because they don't have enough hands to do that and if you have children who are infants living in cradles who are not taught human touch it becomes a developmental handicap." What she expected was not what she was met with.

Soon after Larsa and another voluntourist started working at the orphanage, the teacher at the orphanage's school stopped showing up. Larsa is not sure why she left. It could have been that the teacher was told not to come because volunteers were willing to attempt her job for free. Or, maybe, she was still receiving pay but didn't feel like showing up because the volunteers were there to fill her role. Perhaps she didn't like having volunteers around and her absence was a silent protest. Whatever the reason, the two volunteers with no teaching experience suddenly became responsible for instructing a room full of young children—and they didn't speak the same language.

Each day, Larsa would take a *dala dala*, or local taxi bus, from the shared volunteer house to the stop nearest to the orphanage. The kids always seemed short on food, so as she walked the rest of the way, she would stop to buy two loaves of bread. Once they arrived at the orphanage, Larsa and the other volunteer tried to maintain controlled chaos. It was not what she had signed up for, and it was not something she felt comfortable doing.

After a few weeks of trying to make it work, she quit.

Larsa did not quit the IVHQ program entirely, though. She decided that she still wanted to participate in the second half of her placement, the clinic portion. There, she would be able to do the things she had trained for. There would be translators and a doctor to guide her. Success was not guaranteed, but it was possible to imagine.

When Larsa arrived at her new housing a few days early, the previous cycle of volunteers was still there. It was a Thursday night—social night. Everyone was awake, excited, and getting ready to go out. When they asked if she wanted to go to a nightclub with them, it took her a moment to process the question.

"I had to wrap my mind around the fact that I was in Tanzania, and we were going to a nightclub. I hadn't put the two ideas together in my head," she says. Once she overcame the cognitive dissonance, she joined them for a night out on the town. Energized, she was confident that this time, this placement, was going to be amazing.

The next morning, the volunteers invited her to join them at the clinic. She could shadow the clinic's medical director, Dr. Robert Byemba, and have a chance to meet him before the other volunteers in her cohort arrived. Larsa agreed enthusiastically, pulling on her scrubs before rushing out the door.

The Olorien Community Clinic is a project of New Hope Initiative, a faith-based nonprofit with medical, orphanage, and education projects in India, Kenya, Nicaragua, and Sierra Leone in addition to Tanzania. In Arusha the clinic operates in partnership with the Olorien Bible Baptist Church and American donors.[4] On paper, it sounds slick and professional. What greeted Larsa at the clinic was sobering.

"I remember seeing a lot of sick people—a lot of really sick people," and painfully limited resources. She remembers one child in particular, probably three or four years old, who had come in with a bad burn. "The doctor, using no electricity, had managed to successfully create a skin graft from her stomach onto the burn on her thighs. That was the first time that it dawned on me that this wasn't your typical Western medical clinic. This was going to be really hard. I realized, 'I'm going to see a lot of sick people that I'm not going to be able to do anything for.'"

She was asking herself, "what am I doing here?" before she had even started.

Experiential Learning

Larsa had been surprised when IVHQ accepted her as a medical volunteer. Yes, she had her EMT certification, which required two hundred hours of study, a written test, a practical test, and shadowing, but she had not started medical school—apparently one of the requirements of the program. When the cohort of volunteers she would be working alongside arrived, she realized how low the bar for entry really was.

Many were only volunteering for a week or two, barely enough time to learn the ropes. Some had not been accepted to medical or nursing school, yet. A number were premed students still pursuing their undergraduate degrees, eighteen- and nineteen-year-olds who had taken a few biology courses and wanted a hands-on experience for their medical school applications. Most had no bedside manner training, no medical training, and no ethics training. Larsa watched them take pictures of patients' wounds and infections without permission and complain when they weren't allowed to hold a scalpel or take the lead.

Larsa had a basic idea of how the body works and a broad understanding of potential traumatic injuries. As an EMT she had learned how to stabilize patients, but she did not know what to do after splinting a break or stopping a bleed. "I definitely overestimated my abilities," she says, looking back. "At the end of the day, I was not a doctor. I had not even started medical school." And yet, somehow, she was one of the most experienced volunteers.

Soon, Larsa learned to watch out for the premed students. Unlike her, they didn't know what they didn't know. They were eager and wanted to learn, but they didn't know their limitations. Some of their errors were funny, like when a student put a stethoscope in their ears backward. Other errors were less humorous. No, they should not be begging nurses to let them try drawing blood. No, this was not the place to practice stitches, even if the doctor would reluctantly coach them through it. No, patients are not canvases for students' learning curves. The clinic personnel seemed reluctant to tell volunteers when they'd gone too far, so Larsa tried to help keep them in check when they wanted to get hands-on by explaining why they couldn't just try cutting someone open.

It was exhausting, and it was only a matter of time until she'd hit a wall.

Trauma

When an older woman came into the clinic with a machete wound on her leg, Larsa recognized her. She had been in a few days earlier after slicing into her shin while chopping wood. Larsa had been shadowing Dr. Byemba when they tried to suture the wound back together. Now that it had reopened, they would have to act fast to avoid further infection.

It had already been a long day. A filmmaker and cinematographer were collecting footage for a documentary on voluntourism, and they needed certain shots to frame the story that would become *Volunteers Unleashed.* "They wanted to get footage of us getting on the public transportation, and they wanted to get footage of us arriving," she remembers, "so that meant we needed to leave a little bit earlier. Not much, maybe ten or fifteen minutes." It was enough that she didn't get breakfast—which was typically sparse and often ran out anyway.[5]

The clinic staff quickly transferred the patient to a private operating suite the size of a modest utility closest. With the table and sterilized equipment, the room already felt full. On a typical day, Dr. Byemba, a second doctor, and a voluntourist or two would squeeze in around the table. But, Larsa says, the second doctor, a Canadian woman, did not want to be on camera, and the filmmakers were adamant about capturing the procedure.

Losing the second doctor would open up some space for the camera crew, but Dr. Byemba would need more assistance from voluntourists than usual, so he pulled two others into the room in addition to Larsa. She was the most qualified of the three, and she had seen the patient before, so she volunteered to be the doctor's lead assistant.

Before they could start, the ragtag medical team needed to sedate the patient. In a Western hospital, that would be the job of an anesthesiologist. But anesthesia is dangerous and far too risky to use without reliable electricity to run monitoring equipment. Instead, the clinic used a cocktail of drugs calibrated to make the patient more comfortable without putting her in danger.

Larsa remembers the cocktail as a mix of Valium and ketamine. Valium would help the patient relax, and ketamine would cause them to disassociate from the pain. Instead of relying on expensive equipment, they just needed to make sure she kept breathing. That was Larsa's job. She would watch the blood as it oozed out of the wound. Bright red meant things were going well. If it started to look darker, though, that would be a sign that the patient was not oxygenating properly. Without an oxygen saturation monitor, blood pressure monitor, or an arterial line, it was up to Larsa, Dr. Byemba, and the other volunteers to keep the woman alive without modern safeguards.

As they started to work, the temperature in the room inched upward. Between the doctor, the three voluntourists, the filmmaker, the camera operator, a member of the clinic administration, and the patient, there was barely room to move. Soon, Larsa began to feel lightheaded. The sound of the metal tools scraping against the patient's bone was not helping.

When Larsa alerted Dr. Byemba that she was feeling ill, he encouraged her to go outside. One of the less experienced voluntourists would step in to fill her spot at the table. Whether out of hubris or disorientation, Larsa did not follow instructions. Instead of leaving, she sat down on a stool and hoped that her head would stop spinning. Soon after, she crumpled to the ground.

Larsa does not remember exactly what happened next, but she can piece it together from fragments of memory and the scene in *Volunteers Unleashed*. Dr. Byemba left the patient to rush to her side and began to use a bag valve mask to ensure she was getting oxygen. While he did this, the two other voluntourists tried to maintain the patient.

When the patient started to struggle, a half-lucid Larsa ended up at the woman's head performing a head-tilt/chin-lift, a technique for maintaining an airway taught in the most basic CPR and first aid classes—including my health class when I was in eighth grade. But then one of the other voluntourists butted in. He told her she needed to move the patient's tongue out of the way and to turn her head to the side. "I shouldn't have been at the head. I should not have been trying to maintain her airway. That should have been someone else's job," Larsa admits, especially since she had passed out only moments before. But, in a state of confusion, she took the advice. In the film, turning the patient's head to the side is presented as a solution to Larsa's incompetence. In reality, the change could have caused more harm. But, she admits, "it made for really good footage."

Larsa knew the situation was on tape, but she did not know what they would choose to include and how they would contextualize it until she watched the documentary a few months after the 2015 release. They had caught her in a terrible moment on an awful day, and then, as she flipped into muscle memory and tried to get back to work, she looked even more clumsy (at best) and irresponsible (at worst).

In the end the patient was fine, and Larsa understands why the filmmakers chose to use such compelling footage. She should have left the room when Dr. Byemba told her to. She should not have passed out. She knows that she probably shouldn't have been there at all, yet Larsa still wishes she had a chance to explain herself on camera. The film does not mention her qualifications and experience prior to the trip, and she believes she ended up looking like one of the teenagers taking selfies with wounds or hounding the doctors into letting them practice doing stitches.

Once again, she decided the best thing she could do was to quit. Larsa left her placement early, spent a week in Zanzibar trying to decompress, and flew out on October 25, 2013. She had planned to be in Tanzania for four months; she left within three.

Months later, Larsa communicated her concerns to IVHQ. In response to a post-placement survey, she wrote that she had watched "someone who had never drawn blood before try to learn on a patient. I watched someone who had never done stitches before learn on a patient." "This is," she continued, "unethical, as these patients are not aware of the volunteers' lack of experience or qualifications." "I realize," she wrote, "that this is Tanzania and that any help is better than nothing, but I think that some students go there with the mentality that if they screw up, it doesn't matter."[6]

In the years since Larsa's placement, IVHQ appears to have raised its standards for medical volunteers in Tanzania to a minimum of two years of nursing or medical school. No proof of this is required to apply. However, applicants are warned that they will need to supply certificates, résumés, and two letters of recommendation to local personnel at least three weeks before their program start date—presumably after they have purchased their flights, applied for any necessary visas, and perhaps even started packing.[7]

IVHQ has also altered its orphanage offerings. After vigorously defending orphanage volunteering programs, IVHQ began quietly phasing them out in 2017.[8] The organization has replaced orphanage volunteering with opportunities to volunteer in "childcare centers" and continues to offer teacher placements for nonteachers, including with special needs students, as well as placements with HIV/AIDS patients for volunteers not trained in supporting vulnerable individuals. All of these opportunities are open to volunteers under the age of eighteen with parental or guardian consent and character references.

Babysitting

About nine months before Larsa arrived in Arusha, Emily Scott was at a different clinic in the same city helping deliver a baby.

Emily had left Kenya in 2006, wondering, in her words, "WTF?"[9] Even so, she returned to Kenya the next summer, where she met a group of nurses on a medical mission. "A light went on," she remembers, "I was like, 'oh, they have a skill.'" When she returned home, she started looking into nursing schools. If she were a nurse, she could still travel to volunteer, "but," she says, "actually make a difference."

Since going to nursing school, Emily has regularly participated in medical missions. Along the way, she's learned that her perfect fix for her voluntourism problem, becoming a nurse, is not foolproof. "Every time I went" on a trip, she remembers, "I said, 'next time I'll do it better, next time I'll do it better, next time I'll do it better,' just to process it."

In 2012 Emily and her husband, Aaron Reddecliffe, decided that one way to do it better would be to stay longer. They agreed on four months in Tanzania and signed up through the same program Larsa would later use— IVHQ—because it was cheap.

Emily would work in the labor ward of the Ngarenaro Health Centre, a women's reproductive health clinic, and Aaron, a certified teacher, was placed at a local school. They would both be addressing immediate needs, but their deeper shared goal was to use the four months to build local capacity along with their own skillsets. Aaron could share some of his teaching expertise while learning from the local educators, and Emily could do the same at the clinic.

As a new(ish) nurse with only a few years of experience, Emily was fully aware that she was not an expert. From her past voluntourism experiences, she also suspected that there would be other volunteers not as experienced or prepared as she was. What she did not expect were students still in their prerequisites for medical school delivering babies because they had paid for the opportunity to do so. Either no one thought it was a bad idea or no one was empowered to speak out against it. More than nine months before Larsa arrived at the Olorien Community Clinic, Emily was experiencing the same shock at another facility in the same city.

Emily and Aaron had chosen a homestay over the volunteer house, but they saw how the voluntourists who did live at the house spent their free time. "There were kids," Emily remembers, "who paid their few hundred bucks and stayed at the volunteer house and bought cheap drugs and had a blast." The morning after a party, the young voluntourists would arrive at their placements late or would not show up at all, and no one seemed to care. Throughout their stay, Emily and Aaron couldn't shake the feeling that, for many, the experience was focused more on cheap feel-good vacations than anything reminiscent of transferring skills or expertise.

Outside of the clinic, Emily could shrug off the lack of commitment and skill, but inside the Ngarenaro Health Centre she had to confront it head-on. One girl is lodged permanently in her memory. She was American, like Emily, young, and was working through her prerequisites for medical school. She had gone on safari and, Emily remembers, she "was upset because she didn't get to touch the animals."

One day at the clinic, Emily and the girl had to deliver a child together. Typically, Emily did not deliver babies unless it was so busy that there was no one else to do it. It was simply not her specialty. "In this situation," she recalls, "there were enough volunteers that the local nurses would just pull up a cot and go to sleep and let the volunteers do it." So, while she was not the only nurse present, she was the only one on hand.

In a delivery, there should be at least one person to assist the mother and one person to assist the baby at all times in case both need immediate close attention. Emily put the safari-loving volunteer in charge of the seemingly healthy baby. While she was focused on the new mom, Emily heard a loud gasp from the side of the room. In fractions of a second, every possibility rushed through her head. She jumped toward the child, but the voluntourist was confused by her alarm. She had only been reacting to how cute the baby was. A gasp that caused no harm may seem like a small thing, but it could have been disastrous.

"Everybody wants to hold a newborn baby," Emily says, echoing Larsa's frustration over medical establishments catering to voluntourists. "You can go to any developing country and volunteer in a labor ward and catch babies, and people love to do that because it's a great story." No experience necessary.[10]

Sometimes, a volunteer will even have a child named after them. "I've gone ten rounds with people," Emily says apologetically; "maybe people get the sense that volunteers love it." Foreigners come in, and they provide a service. However suspect the performance, it is not surprising that community members try to find ways to thank them. For all of recorded history, we have named children after their saviors. "But why," Emily asks, "is [the voluntourist] your savior?" Why is someone who traveled across the world to practice on your body and take pictures with your babies worth naming your child after?

The Social Contract

Child Family Health International (CFHI) is a nonprofit medical education trip provider with more than thirty programs in more than ten countries and dozens of academic partnerships. Founded in 1992 as a response to medical voluntourism, CFHI provides students with experiences calibrated to participant expertise and with a focus on shadowing and cultural education.[11]

CFHI Executive Director Dr. Jessica Evert has personal reasons for keeping scalpels out of the hands of voluntourists.

After her first year of medical school, she decided to take a year off to volunteer. Studying anthropology and human biology as an undergrad had amplified her interest in not just being a doctor but also using medicine to address systemic inequities in healthcare. East Africa, with its poor healthcare system, seemed like the perfect place to continue to learn, and the organization she signed up with sounded like the ideal program.

Jessica probably wouldn't have significantly questioned her voluntourism experience if it wasn't for one needle, on one day. The local doctor who handed her the needle had done hundreds of successful lumbar punctures and invited her to give it a try. She was shaking as she prepared to attempt to insert the needle between vertebrae and into the spinal canal. The patient was a seven-year-old Kenyan child. There was no anesthesia.

As the child writhed in pain, he defecated and urinated on himself, screaming and pushing against the people holding him down. Jessica did not even get the lumbar puncture. They had to do it again. By the end, she was disgusted with both herself and with the program that would let her cause such immense suffering under the guise of learning. Her trial and error hurt someone. "Since that moment," she says, "I have been on a quest to change the understanding around these activities and to expose them for what they are."

As she finished medical school, progressed to a residency at the University of California, San Francisco, and became Dr. Jessica Evert, she saw how it was not just trip providers who were promoting unethical programs. The educational institutions committed to training the next generation of medical professionals were in on it too. "At the highest level," she says, "I started to see how institutions are motivated by their own self-preservation, status and reputation, and financial gain."

As many as a quarter of all medical students in the United States participate in health-related programs internationally, including voluntourism. Universities have learned that offering global health-themed voluntourism programs is a way of boosting their profile, attracting students and faculty, and making money from organizing and brokering trips. By 2009 nearly half of all dental schools were marketing volunteering abroad to their students.[12]

As medical schools are building their profiles and filling their bank accounts with voluntourism, they are dismantling a long-standing *social contract*. Understanding what the medical social contract is and how voluntourism breaks it is critical to understanding why letting students play doctor abroad is destructive.

Dr. Jessica Evert describes it like this: "In the U.S., we have to have a steady flow of nurses, doctors, physical therapists, et cetera. So we have a system of teaching hospitals and clinics where students are doing part of the clinical care in a way that is safe, with redundancies, and with accountability for licensed practitioners." Students are allowed to learn, but they are not acting independently. Even with oversight, there are risks and inconveniences. Routine appointments take longer when a student's work needs to be double-checked, and it is a factual reality that surgeries are more dangerous when less-skilled hands are in the room. As a society, we have decided that these risks and inconveniences are worth it. We need a constant flow of new doctors and nurses. Providing spaces where people can learn is required to maintain that flow.

The catch, as she tells it, is that the social contract is just that: social. It is held between people and institutions with social ties and community bonds, and there is an understanding that the students who are practicing on patients will, someday, become experts in the community—ideally, the one they learned in. When people travel outside of their community, whether it be local or national, to practice on other people for short periods of time, that accountability and trust break down.

"For anyone to say that it's okay for westerners to learn on the backs of vulnerable patients in lower-resource settings is ridiculous," she says, "we have too much information to make that a valid argument." "Once you have enough evidence to know that something isn't ok and is harmful," she insists, "you don't just let those harmful things keep happening."

"Fundamentally," she adds, "there is a lot of racism and colonialism that dominates this." The idea that everyone has to learn somehow, so it might as well be in resource-poor communities, is, she emphasizes, "racist, and it is colonialist, and it is sexist, and it is classist. It is basically saying that poor people are disposable."[13]

Crisis Response

Emily Scott hoped to continue doing medical work abroad as a registered nurse after leaving Tanzania, but she needed to get out of the clinics full of unskilled and dangerously empowered voluntourists. She shifted her focus toward joining a crisis response team—teams of doctors and nurses who are deployed in areas after disasters. However, she found that every well-respected crisis response team required applicants to have experience as a member of such a team already. Before they would consider her, she needed to pay her dues with a less prestigious program.

Her chance came in 2015. On April 25 of that year, a 7.8-magnitude earthquake rocked Nepal, killing thousands.[14] When Global Outreach Doctors, a medical relief organization that provides care in developing areas and crisis zones, invited Emily to assist in the initial response, she said yes, booked her flights, and packed her bags.[15] She knew that the situation in Nepal would be chaotic. What she did not expect was how the organization itself would contribute to the problems she witnessed.

When the trip organizers and participants arrived in Nepal, they bought supplies directly from local hospitals, carving into local resources. In contrast, Emily remembers other groups brought enough supplies to augment what was available, not deplete it. Whenever they ventured to villages to provide medical care, Emily says, "the director was much more concerned about stopping and getting photos than he was about actually doing anything helpful." He even insisted they drive past people asking for help because they did not look bad enough to make for a good photo op.

Just as premed students use voluntourism to pad their medical school applications and medical students use voluntourism to attempt skills they are not allowed to practice at home, even medical professionals can find themselves in unethical situations when they look to practice outside of their community. Emily would love to someday work with Doctors without Borders but, she says, the experience they expect to see often requires working with shadier programs. "You have to go with whoever will take you," she says. When mistakes happen they are called learning opportunities.

10 | Teaching Children

The uneven power dynamics and lack of expertise that Larsa Al-Omaishi and Emily Scott experienced in clinics in Arusha, Tanzania, are replicated in classrooms in developing communities around the world. Just as foreigners in scrubs practice on patients, sometimes resulting in dangerous situations, voluntourists with bundles of pencils are play-acting teachers, frequently stunting educational outcomes. What Emily Scott saw in her clinical work, her husband, Aaron Reddecliffe, experienced as he tried to teach in a local Arusha school.

Aaron comes from a family of teachers. When it came time for him to pick a career path, he initially refused to become a teacher. He started coaching swimming, then found himself working at a preschool, and, despite his best efforts, by the time Aaron and Emily arrived in Tanzania in 2012, he was a certified teacher focused on early childhood education. Aaron had the skills for the job, and he had planned ahead. While he knew he would probably be leading some classes, he hoped to focus on building teaching skills locally, buttressing local teachers' methods while learning from them in the process. More than anything, he wanted to do a good job.

When he arrived at the school in Arusha, Tanzania, Aaron met with the other long-term volunteer, an Australian teacher, to create a plan of action for the coming months. The school already had teachers—local teachers—who had their own teaching methods, so the two volunteers decided to spend the first week, or more if needed, just listening and watching.

What Aaron observed concerned him. There were few learning resources available to students, and the ones they had were oppressive. The textbooks were outdated and written from an unabashedly colonialist perspective that did not reflect current realities nor make room for local history.

A well-trained teacher can accommodate for out-of-date materials, but the students were not being encouraged to ask questions nor prompted to connect the dots between topics. This was an issue of training, not commitment. The teaching staff said they did not have many (if any) opportunities for professional development. They were not using ineffective teaching methods because they believed them to be superior—they simply had not had the chance to learn about and employ other styles.

Foreign teachers such as Aaron often hit another roadblock stemming from outdated materials: What should they be teaching? And have they ever learned it? What a person can teach is limited by their educational background. You can't teach what you don't know, and, typically, a volun-tourist's previous educational experience does not include the local history, social context, tradition, nor culture of their host community. Just as out-dated textbooks reinforce colonial dynamics, the bounds of foreigners' own knowledge reinforce the idea that knowing your history is unimportant compared to the history of the places voluntourists come from—typically, more economically powerful nations.[1]

Reframing how to teach is a tremendous task, especially coming from someone who is attempting to navigate the line between team member and intruder. It felt easy, however, when compared to the challenges presented by the revolving door of voluntourists.

"The entire time we're doing this," Aaron remembers, "we have other 'volunteers' coming through the organization." They would come in for a day or two and want to play and hand out snacks and teach the same 1-2-3, A-B-C lesson because that was all they were equipped to teach. Their intentions were good, but every day that short-term voluntourists came in was a day lost. The kids had no interest in focusing on their actual lessons when there were balloons to keep in the air and novelty erasers to collect. "With the teachers, we were making baby steps," Aaron says, "but with the kids, it was all undone."[2]

The voluntourists left feeling inspired by all that they had accomplished, but the real outcomes were quite the opposite. Emily remembers Aaron coming home defeated after days filled with distraction. The voluntourists left before they were able to see how their presence negatively impacted the steady flow of classwork, the rhythm of lessons, and the culture of focus all of the teachers were trying to build. As the customer, the voluntourists had gotten what they had paid for—affirmation, immersion, and the appearance of impact.[3] The students had paid the price.

The damage of the disruption they caused goes deeper than a missed history lesson. Years later, as a teacher in the Pacific Northwest, Aaron had interns in his classroom who were there to observe, learn, and assist. The minimum internship length was three months. Rapid turnover in teachers, or any adults in a role model or caregiver position, can have negative psychological consequences on students, even his "white kids in Seattle."

Aaron couldn't stop the flow of voluntourists, so he doubled down on his work with the teachers. If the kids could not focus, at least he could help their teachers develop new skills and techniques that may maintain students' attention despite distractions.

Responsibility

"In retrospect," Aaron says, "I was trying to do the right thing, and I'm in correspondence with some of the teachers still, but at the same time, even that feels yucky to me at times because how do I know that I know better? It's that pervasive attitude that needs to change. The 'I know better.'"

Aaron could see the "I know better" attitude in the voluntourists who came and went over his months at the school. He was surprised, however, that the teachers were not pushing back, especially against those who hijacked their lesson plans. "White people," he says, using the predominant race of voluntourists as a catchall for all voluntourists, "are 99.9 percent at fault." Still, there is something happening on the other side—the local side—that is absorbing the pressure voluntourists are applying instead of pushing back against it. The "white man [is] coming in, talking a big game, and the teacher steps back because [the white man] says he knows what he is doing," Aaron says, frustrated, "but that is a product of a broken system, not of an individual person."

TMS Ruge, a Ugandan entrepreneur, raised in East Africa and the United States, recipient of a 2012 Champion of Change award from the White House, and CEO of Raintree Farms, a medicinal crop company in his hometown of Masindi, agrees with Aaron's assessment.[4] When he runs programs in African communities, he is regularly asked, "When are the white people coming?" "As someone who is local and who is trying to build systems and build agency," he says, "it cuts you to the core."[5]

TMS says short-term injections of hands-on assistance can be helpful immediately following a crisis, but aid agencies and trip providers often use crises as windows of opportunity. Once they are established on the ground, they look for ways to reinvent themselves to continue capitalizing on the location. That is when the problems take root. The longer the trip providers stay, the greater the loss of local agency. TMS points to generations of Africans who are "abdicating our responsibilities," which leads, he says, to kids "who know that the first thing you say to a white person is 'mzungu give me money.'" The children have learned that if they look needy enough and say it sweetly enough, they probably will get it.

In many host communities, locals are aware that they are on the losing side of an unequal relationship. Their expertise is undermined by foreign confidence, and, as TMS has observed, they do not seem to have the energy to stand up against the onslaught.[6] Maybe they are worn out. Enduring hundreds of years of being told they are capable of less and know less because of where they were born and the color of their skin would sap the morale of any community. But TMS is frustrated by how this continues to manifest, even as they can see it happening. "This process wouldn't go on," he insists, "if we were free-thinking people and able to say 'you know what, we don't need you. Even if we stumble, we are going to be able to stand up on our own.'"

TMS's work has hit a nerve with many people, but he insists that all he is asking is that his people reclaim agency. He is one of a growing number of activists who are not only calling out voluntourists but also calling on their own communities to stand up against the pressures of trip providers. "When you are so colonialized," TMS says, "you cede control of the future." If locals started asking, "what is the benefit to us to do it your way?" and demanding answers, he believes there would be less harm done to the bodies and minds of local residents of voluntourism destinations.

Perhaps ironically, voluntourists' good intentions are one of the biggest roadblocks to greater local control. Voluntourists feel they have a responsibility to care for those who appear to have less, and giving money isn't enough. They want to have their hands in the mix, whether writing on a blackboard or stitching up a machete wound.[7] Pushback from locals might not be enough to get them to stop entirely, but it could, TMS hopes, lead voluntourists to ask themselves why they feel so entitled to and responsible for communities that are not their own.

For now, communities continue to face pressure to be more open, authentic, welcoming, and—most importantly—thankful for days or weeks of education-less schooling and bruised bodies from poorly executed blood draws. It is not uncommon to thank a doctor for doing a good job, but what if the "doctor" is a nineteen-year-old who was handed the scalpel despite having no business being in the room? What if you were told that the nineteen-year-old was there to save you, that whatever he does is the best care you could ever get? And, worse, that you should be grateful for it?

The unequal dynamic that appears in medical and educational voluntourism vividly illustrates how power plays out when one party is composed of self-elected saviors, and the other is cast as helpless. But how do we address these failures while not removing the needed care and assistance that does sometimes drip from the leaky faucet? If voluntourists dollars are paying for the gauze and the pencils that real doctors and real teachers need, is that trade-off worth it?

"Would it be better," Emily Scott asks, pausing to wrestle through her thoughts, "to have nobody come at all? There are situations where, if you're having volunteers come who have minimal medical training and know nothing about infectious diseases or tropical medicine, that is worse than nothing." Yet, as clear as that is to Emily, she still does not know if ending all voluntourism in medical settings would fix the problem. "None of us do," she says. When it comes to potentially removing underqualified care, "either you sound cruel, or you sound naïve."

In 2017 Emily and Aaron launched *Two Dusty Travelers*, a travel blog and resource for ethically minded tourists and travelers. Aaron does not want to call the blog penance, but they are sharing what they have gleaned from their mistakes. "To be honest," he says, "we've done, unintentionally, terrible things volunteering, and we share it to make ourselves feel less guilty."

Every human deserves access to high-quality medical care. Getting to that point should not include teenagers practicing on patients. The same is true for education. But, in voluntourism, the people with power are those with privilege, and the privileged get to call all the shots.

11 | Orphanages

In 2012, the same year Emily Scott and Aaron Reddecliffe were in Arusha, Catherine Cottam booked a trip to Kenya inspired by Paul Wesley. She had heard that the actor, who played broody vampire Stefan Salvatore on the television drama *Vampire Diaries*, would be leading a voluntourism trip open to fans, and she jumped at the opportunity. When the trip provider tried to pull money out of her bank account early, she got cold feet. Hanging out with Wesley *and* volunteering would be a dream, but she would have to settle with satiating only the voluntourism bug.

Eventually, she found a trip provider she felt she could trust: A Broader View Volunteers, a nonprofit that offers orphanage placements for voluntourists ages twelve to sixteen if traveling with parents and over seventeen for solo travelers.[1] The A Broader View trip to an orphanage in the northeast of Nairobi matched the mix of volunteering and adventure Catherine was looking for and would fit into her schedule perfectly. She was working on a master's degree in school counseling at Western Carolina University, and the July 5–18, 2012, trip, with a short break in the middle for a safari, would be a well-earned respite from schoolwork.[2]

The orphanage director met Catherine when she landed in Kenya, and they stopped along the way to the orphanage northeast of Nairobi to buy paint. Catherine later journaled that it was the first time she could remember being the only white person in a public space. When they arrived at the orphanage, she met the dozens of children who lived there along with the handful of other voluntourists she'd be working with. After she received a tour of the facility, they walked to a nearby village to get sweets. Catherine immediately felt wanted, she felt needed, and she was ready to contribute. Less than twenty-four hours after her plane landed on Kenyan soil, the experience was already better than she had dreamed it could be.

Soon, though, Catherine started to get the feeling that things on the ground were not lining up with how the orphanage represented itself online. The amount of deferred maintenance was appalling, and the locals managing the orphanage were ignoring even simple inexpensive repairs. "It was winter," she remembers, "and the glass window in one of the dormitories was broken." When she asked about it, the kids said it had been like that for a long time.

She had paid around a thousand dollars for the trip, and there were four other voluntourists also paying to be there. She didn't know how much of her trip fee went to A Broader View and how much went to the orphanage, but finding paying volunteers and generous donors didn't seem to be an issue. She couldn't fathom why things like the window were going unaddressed.

There was also the issue of donated supplies and toys disappearing. Catherine had arrived with a bag full of toys, and she was not unique. A few days into her trip, a group came specifically to donate items for the children. After they left, Catherine saw the orphanage director load much of what they had brought into his car and drive away. He came back, but the toys and supplies did not. While she was cleaning, she found more items secreted away—locked rooms packed with donated toys that the kids were not able to access. Pulling extras aside would have made sense if the orphanage were overflowing with toys, but it was not. The kids had nearly nothing.

The only explanation she could come up with was that the orphanage director was reselling the donated items. Hopefully, some of that money was getting back to the kids in the form of food or medical care, but the condition of the orphanage made this seem unlikely.

Unlocked Gates

Orphanage voluntourism is one of the most popular forms of voluntourism. It is also the most critiqued. The evidence showing that institutional care harms children is mountainous, and orphanages are not a preferred form of childcare in the world's most developed countries.[3] This raises two questions:

1. What are the reasons for moving away from the institutionalization of children in orphanages and similar facilities?
2. Given those reasons, why are so many people furthering the existence of orphanages as donors and voluntourists?

The first hurdle to understanding the orphanage crisis is an issue of terminology. The common understanding is that orphans do not have parents because their biological parents have died. However, the United Nations defines an orphan as any child that has lost at least one parent. Not two.[4]

The discrepancy between the commonly accepted meaning of *orphan* and the term as defined by the UN is highly visible in sub-Saharan Africa. According to researchers Linda Richter and Amy Norman, there were approximately twelve million children categorized as orphans in sub-Saharan Africa in 2004. More than 80 percent of those children had a surviving parent. Having a surviving parent does not necessarily mean that the parent is capable of being a caregiver. Still, it contradicts the popular understanding of what it means to be an orphan. Additionally, not every child categorized as a single or double orphan lives in an orphanage, and not every child who lives in an orphanage is a single or double orphan.[5]

A lack of awareness of the definition of what constitutes an orphan and who orphans are has led to an anemic understanding of the social safety nets that should be working to keep the vast majority of children in families.

Raising a child costs money—money for food, for clothing, for medical care, school, and for daycare or a sitter if both parents work and there isn't a friend or family member able or willing to help out. Sometimes, these costs are too much to handle, especially if a child is one of many, is born into a family without resources, or has additional medical needs.

Sending a child to an orphanage is most often considered only when resources are scarce and the need is great. It becomes more enticing when families are promised that their child or children will have access to the tools needed for a "better" life, especially opportunities for education. Parents in orphanage-laden countries are frequently coerced into sending their children into institutions with promises of care and even cash payments. They do not know that their children will rarely receive the education promised, will rarely be allowed to return home, and, depending on the nation, could be adopted by another, often foreign, family without the knowledge of their biological family.[6]

Keeping a child with their parents (biological or adopted), a single parent, or in the home of a relative or community member is less expensive than raising them in an orphanage. More importantly, it is also better for the child.[7] But funding for home-based care isn't flowing into communities. Instead, money is poured into a style of institution that, even in its most ethical and well-funded form, doctors, psychologists, social workers, educators, and parents can all agree is not conducive to long-term positive outcomes for children.

Wherever there are orphanages, there are voluntourists and visitors willing to pay to spend time with the children in their care. Most of these voluntourists and visitors do not know that the majority of the children they are purchasing access to have families. In a survey of one hundred prospective orphanage volunteers in Siem Reap, 75 percent had no idea that the majority of children in residential care centers in Cambodia have living parents.[8]

Business-savvy (and morally corrupt) entrepreneurs take advantage of this gap in awareness when they build orphanages to meet the demands of Western donors and stock them with trafficked children trained to act happy and not say too much.[9] As Cottam experienced in Kenya, the money visitors bring in to orphanages all too often seems to end up in the pockets of orphanage administrators.[10]

There are many children globally who need to be cared for by someone other than a biological family member. The need for a care safety net is real and will never disappear. Orphanages, however, are an archaic system of warehousing children that has transformed from a stopgap measure into a full-blown industry.

Orphanages are incentivized to maintain low standards of living because voluntourists and visitors want to see poverty. They often employ a small staff because voluntourists want to feel needed. This also serves to maintain a reliance on paying voluntourists who, if an orphanage appears too well run, feel less compelled to donate generously. If the kids have "too much," voluntourists leave. If they do not feel needed, they leave. Orphanage directors meet voluntourists' demands by neglecting the children they are supposed to be caring for. And yet millions of voluntourists want to work with kids, especially in orphanage environments.

Actively and visibly caring for others carries status. The cuter the people a voluntourist cares for, the more attention they receive for their work. Black and brown babies who are "poor but happy," preferably with holes in their clothes and dirt on their faces, garner the most positive reactions.[11]

There is also a biblical imperative for volunteering at orphanages. In the Bible, James 1:27 states, "Pure religion and undefiled before God and the Father is this: To visit the fatherless and widows in their affliction, and to keep himself unspotted from the world."[12] This verse is frequently cited in the Christian community when encouraging and defending orphanage volunteer work and adoption and even founding orphanages.[13]

However, one simple thing supersedes all other explanations for the orphanage voluntourism industry—it feels good. Seeing a baby smile triggers the same emotional response as hearing your favorite music or even having sex.[14] Academic studies in voluntourism tend to be small, but a 2012 study of sixteen Canadian voluntourists in Saint Lucia, South Africa, showed what is known to be widespread: voluntourists seek out opportunities to engage with young kids.[15] The most reliable way of accessing children is by going to places that have a high concentration of them, such as orphanages.[16]

Roots in Tragedy

When Peter K. Muthui was six weeks old, a storm rolled in while his mother was out fetching firewood in rural Kenya. She sheltered in a building while waiting for it to pass. Lightning struck the building, and she died in the collapse. Not long after, when Peter was just over a year old, his father died from depression-related causes linked to his wife's tragic death.

Peter and his five siblings were left with no one to care for them. His relatives were scared of taking on six more mouths to feed, so the responsibility for the children fell on a group of women from their local church. The situation lasted for a few months, but it was not sustainable. The strain of caring for six kids was simply too much, and the community decided to forward the case to the authorities.[17]

Unable or unwilling to place all six children together, the court split the siblings up between three institutions. Peter's two elder brothers were sent to a reformatory school, his two elder sisters to a similar institution for girls. Peter and his youngest sister, Joyce, were sent to an orphanage for children with physical challenges, despite neither of them meeting that criterion. For two years, the siblings were unable to visit each other, or even to write letters.

In 1984 they were miraculously reunited at an orphanage in Nairobi. "This became our 'home' for the rest of our childhood years," Peter says, although they couldn't live as a family. The siblings were housed based on age, not origin, so their interactions were limited. At least they were together.

The orphanage itself was not a miracle. Today, Peter is emphatic that "these places, even when run by well-meaning care providers, can never replace a family." He recalls that most of the attention and affection he and the other kids received was not from reliable adult role models but from voluntourists and visitors. He would run toward people when they first arrived, excited for attention and treats, but, he says, addressing voluntourists directly, "Once you left, feelings of loneliness, rejection, and isolation kicked in."

Peter also saw how voluntourists played favorites. They tended to focus on the children who were the cutest, picking up and playing with the ones who were the most conventionally attractive and giving less attention to those who were less photogenic. The favoritism was likely inadvertent, but, Peter says, the long-term effects of voluntourists' behavior on him and other care leavers (those who have left institutionalized care) include low self-esteem and feeling "unworthy, rejected, and alone."

When voluntourists left, or simply when they were not looking, physical abuse kicked in. "To make matters worse," he remembers, "after you left, we would get a beating from our house mothers for our clingy behavior."

Peter watched his siblings leave him one-by-one as they aged out of the orphanage and had to figure out how to fend for themselves. When he was released, he too struggled to find footing in a world he was unprepared to navigate. He had never had to take care of his own needs, so necessary life skills, such as cooking or creating a budget, felt like insurmountable hurdles. He had limited social skills and struggled to form relationships.

Eventually, through force of will and formidable faith, he managed to find stability, finish high school, and attend university, where he studied sociology and communication. When he graduated, he returned to the orphanage he grew up in as the social programs manager. For nine years, he tried to make it a better place for kids like him.

Having seen orphanages from both sides, as a resident and as an administrator, Peter knows how they function and why they fail. "Institutional care for large groups of children," he says, "often treats every child the same, irrespective of their age, gender, abilities, or needs. Children in institutions are typically isolated from their community of origin, separated from their siblings, and unable to maintain a relationship with their parents and extended families." This results, he says, in children who "lack a sense of identity." So, along with not knowing how to cook or budget or build relationships, they do not know who they are. They are vulnerable to exploitation and abuse, and to repeating the pattern. "Their children," Peter has observed, "are more likely to be placed in an institution, creating a devastating inter-generational cycle."

Today, Peter lives in Nairobi, where he is a founding partner and the director of Child in Family Focus–Kenya, a nonprofit that works to reform Kenya's childcare system.

The Love You Give

In 2019 Peter starred in *The Love You Give*, a documentary short aimed at raising awareness about the realities of orphanages and the damage they cause.[18] The film was produced by the Better Care Network and ReThink Orphanages. ReThink Orphanages is a coalition of organizations working to sever the orphanage pipeline and decrease the institutionalization of children. The coalition strives to spread greater understanding of what is going on in residential care centers and the role of voluntourism in propping them up while also pushing for stronger child protection laws.

Leigh Mathews is a co-founder of ReThink Orphanages and founder of ALTO Global Consulting. Through ReThink, Leigh raises social consciousness and pressures governments. Through ALTO, she helps from the business side by guiding her clients toward protecting, rather than exploiting, children. In recent years she has been guiding big-name voluntourism trip providers out of the business of orphanages. World Challenge, a veteran student travel company, relied on Leigh's direction as they phased orphanages out of their lineup of options offered to the more than eight thousand students that travel with them to more than thirty countries annually.[19] It is a tricky process, especially when orphanages have become reliant on the income and assistance that voluntourism trip providers, like World Challenge, provide. Pulling voluntourists out without proper planning can, Leigh says, amplify the same issues the trip providers are trying to disentangle themselves from.

Most of the published numbers related to orphanages and residential childcare come from the United Nations, specifically UNICEF, but UNICEF is limited by which countries choose to self-report and how accurately they choose to do so. At a minimum, this leaves children in unregistered orphanages out of the final tally.

Despite the fishy math, far and away the most frequently referenced statistic in the orphanage debate is that eight million children are living in orphanages globally. This number was most recently popularized by Lumos, the child welfare nonprofit founded by author J.K. Rowling that is committed to moving children into family-based care.[20] However, Leigh argues that the eight million number is outdated and deflated. "When you dig back into the figure of eight million [children in orphanages]," that everyone cites, she says, "it's a 35-year-old statistic." Today, it is probably significantly higher, "but we don't know," she insists, "because governments don't allow information to be collected."[21]

The money that fuels the orphanage industry is also not being tracked properly. Leigh points to her native Australia, a leading voluntourist-sending country. "The Australian government doesn't track the flow of money to orphanages out of Australia," she says, "and the Cambodian and Nepali and Haitian governments"—a noncomprehensive sampling of three popular destinations for orphanage tourism—"don't track the flow of money in" to orphanages. As a result, critics of the industry are themselves vulnerable to criticism. They are told they do not have enough evidence or that they are operating on anecdotes.

The passage of the Modern Slavery Act in November 2018 helped to solidify the platform of Australian anti-orphanage campaigners. Key language in the act affirms that human trafficking is slavery and that orphanage trafficking, the placement of children in and movement between illegal or unlawful orphanages, is a form of modern slavery that falls under that umbrella.[22] The legislation was a massive move for a country where an estimated 57 percent of universities advertise orphanage volunteering as an opportunity for their students and, by recognizing their nation's role in driving the demand for orphanages, the Australian government accomplished something no other nation had—implicating themselves as part of the problem.[23]

The next step, Leigh says, is to build deeper understanding of the damage orphanages cause, even ones that operate legally or that look "okay." Calling orphanages "bad" is one thing, but understanding *why* they are abusive and exploitative is critical to moving toward family-based forms of childcare.

Attachment Disorders

Orphanage voluntourists and visitors tend to speak fondly of the unbridled affection the children show them. The stereotype is that orphanage residents run to be hugged, want to be carried, and will pout if their feet hit the floor. This desire for closeness can appear cute in person and pictures, but it's terrifying. Children raised in healthy environments with strong adult role models approach outsiders with caution. They rarely have an insatiable internal urge to please and entertain strangers. If a stranger asks them into their car, they say no. They go back to where they feel safe and secure. But if there is not a place where they feel safe and secure, and when there are no positive adult role models that are constant and supportive, what reason do they have to keep their feet on the ground?[24]

Orphanages and other residential care centers that prioritize the wants of a revolving cast of voluntourists over the needs of the children in their care contribute to the manifestation of attachment disorders. Attachment, with much of the foundational research explored by Mary Ainsworth and John Bowlby in the 1960s and 1970s, refers to an enduring and deep bond that connects children to their caretakers. While established in infancy, attachment is flexible across time and circumstances. One of the lasting effects of volunteer-based staffing on children in orphanages is a lack of continuity in attachment. A healthy attachment between a child and a caregiver results when caregivers are reliable and capable of providing for a child before they need to ask for help. When a child's caregivers rotate and are unreliable, and sometimes do not even speak the child's language, this can contribute to the development of an attachment disorder, or most specifically, disinhibited social engagement disorder.[25]

Disinhibited social engagement disorder is characterized by unrestrained openness and affection, combined with an inability to form and maintain relationships. What makes children with attachment disorders adorable will impede their ability to function outside of the orphanage walls. As Peter K. Muthui experienced, the psychological damage orphanages inflict can cause issues with building and maintaining relationships and romantic connections and increases the likelihood that children of individuals who grew up in orphanages will eventually end up in the same type of care situation.[26]

A kid running up to a stranger for a hug is not cute. Whether they are doing it because they are playing a role or because they have lost sight of boundaries, it is not real warmth. Rather, their behavior is the result of trauma, and indiscriminate affection is a sign of the psychological damage.

Physical and Emotional Abuse

Orphanages only attract donations, voluntourists, and visitors if they look like they need help. This has resulted in rundown compounds full of kids with dirty faces, ripped shirts, skinny wrists, and dirty sheets even if an orphanage is bringing in enough money to address these issues. Many orphanages generate additional income by putting kids to work. Children often work, beg, or, most frequently, perform, to earn their keep. Telling a child that they will not get dinner if they do not sing and dance for a room full of strangers is abuse, even if the audience is smiling and clapping along.[27]

A few times during Catherine Cottam's stay at the orphanage northeast of Nairobi, the children put on a singing performance. The kids never seemed to sing for fun, or when there were not white guests or voluntourists within earshot, but they'd put on a show when instructed. "I got the impression," Catherine says cautiously, "that they didn't have much of a choice. That if they didn't [perform], they probably wouldn't get to eat." She never saw what the consequences were, but she is certain that anyone who refused to take part in the performances would undoubtedly have experienced repercussions.

There was something else that benefited visitors, but that put children in harm's way, at the orphanage where she was volunteering. The voluntourists were living and working in close proximity to vulnerable children without safeguards for their welfare, yet neither the trip provider nor the orphanage administrators conducted background checks. Catherine thinks that she had to turn in a résumé when she first applied for the trip, but that was it. "Had we been bad people," she says, "it would have been easy to have gone into the dorms anytime we wanted."

While problematic orphanages dot the globe, Cambodia has gained particular notoriety for the proliferation of orphanages that cater to voluntourists. By 2017 the problem had become so severe that both the number of orphanages and the number of children living in them was rising even as poverty and the number of children who fit the definition of an orphan was declining.[28]

Examples of exploitation in Cambodian orphanages abound, but perhaps the most upsetting are those rooted in religion. In the spring of 2013, Cambodian authorities raided a Christian orphanage run by Ruth Golder, an Australian septuagenarian. Golder was frantic. She had run the foreign-funded facility illegally for years. Now she was caught. Orphanage residents—children—had tipped authorities off to vicious beatings and the withholding of food. Other children who had been kicked out by Golder for pushing back against her abuse also reported vicious and exploitative behavior.

Cambodian authorities removed the children, but the process of placing them into foster care or reuniting them with the families who had given them up for the promise of a better future was long and painful. The damage will be lasting, and this was one just one orphanage run by one smiling woman who managed to convince donors, predominately churches and Christian organizations, to give her the money she needed to illegally acquire, abuse, and profit off of children.[29]

Sexual Abuse

As Catherine Cottam experienced, housing voluntourists close to orphanage residents is common in orphanage voluntourism. When I was in Tanzania in 2009, the volunteer bunkhouse was no more than one hundred feet from the nearest residents' rooms, and nothing was keeping me from wandering beyond my own moral compass. Minimal oversight of voluntourist behavior and little to no vetting before arrival is also common. This, combined with the fact that voluntourists who stay on the grounds of an orphanage often have twenty-four-seven access to the children should they wish to exploit the setup, should be terrifying to anyone even remotely concerned about child welfare.

Most voluntourists are like Catherine Cottam. The relaxed rules may raise some concern, but they wouldn't think of taking advantage of them. Well-meaning voluntourists do not imagine the worst. A small minority of voluntourists, however, sign up *because* of the lack of hurdles, the averted eyes, and the unlocked doors.

In 2012 journalist Juliana Ruhfus and a colleague decided to put orphanages' boundaries (or lack thereof) to the test. Undercover and without verifying their identities and intentions, they asked the director of the Children's Umbrella Centre Organization orphanage in Phnom Penh, Cambodia, whether they could take a few kids on a field trip. He quickly organized a group of children into a lineup. The unknown visitors could take their pick. Cambodia has become notorious as a hub for sex tourism and child sex trafficking, and orphanages are a link in the chain. In this case, the orphanage director facilitated strangers' driving out of the gates with handpicked kids he was supposed to be protecting. The journalists were there to prove a point on camera—at orphanages, you can get away with almost anything if you are Western and willing to pay.[30]

In 2016 twenty-one-year-old Oklahoman Matthew Durham was sentenced to forty years in prison for abusing children at the Upendo Children's Home in Nairobi, Kenya, while he was volunteering there two years earlier. Like most orphanage voluntourists, there was no vetting process before he was given nearly unrestricted access to young children. Unlike most voluntourists, he took advantage of it, abusing at least seven residents during his time at the orphanage.[31]

That same year, British Airways made an undisclosed payment to a group of young girls who were molested at orphanages in Kenya, Uganda, and Tanzania between 2003 and 2013 by pilot Simon Wood while he was on stopovers. The girls were between five and thirteen at the time of the abuse.[32]

In 2008 Gregory and Mary Rose Dow moved from Pennsylvania to Boito, Kenya, to start a government-licensed orphanage. They had never run a similar operation, but they said they felt called by their faith to try and quickly filled a compound with more than eighty children. It took almost nine years for the truth of what they were doing at the Dow Children's Home to come to light.

In 2017 Gregory was caught raping a young girl who lived in the orphanage. He fled the country. Mary Rose was imprisoned in Kenya for five months before being fined for having taken a group of girls to a local clinic to have implants inserted. The girls were unaware of the purpose of the procedure, but they later discovered that they were birth control implants. Gregory, who had a previous conviction for molesting a child in the United States in 1996, did not have to worry about impregnating them when he raped them.

After the orphanage was finally shut down, the challenge of integrating the children back into their communities began. Many were able to return to family members who had given them up after the Dows' promised they would have access to education and a higher quality of life under their care. Those without families, or with families unable to take them, were placed at other orphanages. Three children died between 2008 and 2017 as a result of the Dows' abuse and neglect.

According NTV Kenya, when Gregory and Mary Rose Dow reunited in Lancaster, Pennsylvania, they continued to deny the allegations, insisting they were lies fabricated by a former neighbor.[33] A few months later, in July 2019, Gregory Dow was arrested and indicted on four counts of engaging in illicit sexual conduct in a foreign place.[34] Nearly a year later, in the summer of 2020, Dow, formerly idolized for his concern for the most vulnerable, pleaded guilty to all counts. The victims were between eleven and thirteen.[35]

These events are not anomalies. They are frequent, they are recent, and they continue today.

Financial Exploitation

Not every orphanage is a petri dish of physical child abuse. Still, the performance of poverty through dirty faces and broken windows that Catherine Cottam experienced is nearly universal at orphanages that accept volunteers. It can also be an early warning sign that additional levels of harm are taking place.

Soon after voluntourists at Happy Home Orphanage in Kathmandu, Nepal, discovered that the orphanage director, Bishwa Archarya (also spelled Acharya), was exploiting children for financial gain, the stories of abuse and neglect began pouring in. The director had even hidden children from their families to continue cashing in on donors' generosity. In 2014 he and his wife were convicted of abusing children in their care. A few years later, they were back in business.[36]

Despite the poor conditions orphanage residents are often forced to live in, it is typical for orphanages that host voluntourists on-site to have more upgraded housing for their paying guests. Voluntourists may have tile floors while the children have cement. They may have running water while the children have to bathe with buckets. They may have electricity or even internet access while the children have neither.

While tiles, Wi-Fi, and running water are not necessary for a child to thrive, orphanage residents do not have these small conveniences because they are a money sink.[37] Giving the children more does not ultimately result in more income for the orphanage. Giving voluntourists more might. Using donated funds to improve living conditions may result in lower donations in the future. Using donated funds to, say, buy a new car, benefits the orphanage owner without undermining their means of making money.[38]

Sometimes financial exploitation is even more flagrant. In Siem Reap, Cambodia, for example, orphanage residents have regularly been spotted parading through the streets carrying flags, banners, and posters advertising their homes as entertainment destinations, turning vulnerable children into tourist attractions.[39]

Illegitimate Adoptions

Adoption is another profitable orphanage monetization strategy. International adoptions have been popularized by high-profile celebrities who have collected children from around the globe into families that resemble United Colors of Benetton ads. Simultaneously, Christian leaders in the United States have latched onto James 1:27—the same passage cited in support of volunteering at and founding orphanages—and are using it to promote a gospel of adoption, especially of foreign children.

The gospel of adoption is especially prevalent in the evangelical church.[40] Bethany Christian Services is a faith-based adoption and foster agency that operates in more than thirty states and a dozen countries and that works with more than fifty thousand people annually. In 2010 Bethany reported a 26 percent increase in adoptions. Many have linked this jump to increased interest in adoption among Christians in the West.[41]

The adoption process is expensive. Using the Bethany Christian Services fee calculator, the estimated cost for someone in New York to adopt a child from South Africa in 2019 added up to $43,151 to $51,828, including an $18,850 to $21,450 payment to Bethany. This is within the standard range across the countries in which Bethany brokers international adoptions.[42]

The massive increase in demand for children has resulted in a bottleneck in the eligible orphan pipeline. As the number of people looking to adopt has skyrocketed, the number of children up for adoption has decreased—especially healthy babies without special needs. The shortage can lead to fraud and trafficking as less-scrupulous agencies and orphanages work to maintain a stock of healthy kids for prospective parents to pick from.[43]

On January 12, 2010—the first month of the same year Bethany reported a surge in adoptions—a massive 7.0-magnitude earthquake rocked Haiti. The initial earthquake and subsequent aftershocks resulted in the deaths of as many as 316,000 people, depending on who is doing the counting.[44] For those seeking babies to adopt, the crisis represented a perfect opportunity.[45]

Laura Silsby, leader of the New Life Children's Refuge, arrived in the Dominican Republic with a team of voluntourists ranging from eighteen to fifty-five years old, soon after the earthquake. Most were members of Baptist churches in Idaho, and they were operating on the belief that their faith called them to help. Laura and the voluntourists crossed the border into Haiti before illegally rounding up thirty-three children, loading them onto a bus, and trying to take them back to the Dominican Republic without legal permission, paperwork, or even proof that the children were in need of care. In court, Laura would argue that she was doing what was best for the kids. She would, she said, have founded an orphanage and given them a stable home. Her website advertised a different future. It suggested that the children would be made available to American families for adoption, at a price. Whether the children were going to be shopped around for adoption or not, it was child trafficking.[46]

Haitian officials were outraged but not surprised. They had seen this coming. Images of seemingly helpless and abandoned Haitian children had spread across the globe. Haiti is only a two-hour flight from Miami, and the market for adoption was hot. Laura Silsby and the voluntourists were arrested on January 29, 2010, and subsequently charged with child abduction. The group's Dominican adviser, Jorge Torres Puello, was also arrested for his role in the crime. He was already wanted for trafficking charges in both the United States and El Salvador.[47]

Most of the voluntourists in Laura Silsby's group were released in the month following the arrest, but Laura wasn't released until May 2010. By that time, many of the children she had tried to abduct were reunited with family members or placed in other, hopefully safer, group homes.[48]

Orphanages often offer child sponsorship in place of, or in addition to, adoption. Donors who purchase child sponsorships are led to believe that, for a small monthly or annual donation, a child will be fed and educated. As a thank you, the donor will get a letter, photo, or maybe a drawing or keepsake from the child. I still have the green string bracelet a young health-compromised boy—now a man—in the Dominican Republic made me after my mother began sponsoring his education more than ten years ago. We, and he, were lucky. We knew him before we sponsored him. We knew his medical caregivers, his support network, and we had ways of keeping tabs on him that were only possible because we had been involved with the clinic that served him for many years. Today, we're still friends on Facebook, and the bracelet has sat in the pencil holder on my desk for over a decade.

This outcome is what many sponsors dream of, but it is rare enough to be an anomaly. Child sponsorship may seem innocuous, but it is a method of commodifying children by turning them into items to which access can be purchased. By buying into this system, donors are affirming that the market is ripe for further exploitation, empowering those with the worst intentions to keep going.

Disruption of Progress

The more financially successful orphanages are, the harder it is to replace them with more ethical, humane, and sustainable childcare options, such as home-based care and family support programs. If the money is in orphanages, there is not much incentive for those leading them to try something less personally lucrative.[49]

A handful of governments are trying to stop abuse despite industry resistance. However, the nature of where orphanages thrive makes it hard for disempowered, dysfunctional, or corrupt governments to make a dent.[50] The fact that orphanages are often being financially supported by individuals and institutions outside of their country of operation through voluntourist fees and donations further complicates the situation. Cash and goods move across borders with little regard for local child welfare legislation, ferried along by voluntourists. The focus follows the money, and there is more of it going to orphanages than to better alternatives.[51]

Responsibility

Throughout the orphanage voluntourism industry, voluntourists enjoy feeling necessary without processing the dark realities of a system of care that is, in actuality, a type of tourist attraction. Even when the exploitation is clear and visible, privilege offers the opportunity to avert one's eyes. Choosing not to see is a game only the powerful get to play.[52]

Next Step Ministries, the medium-sized-but-mighty Wisconsin-based short-term mission provider, has offered low-cost trips to orphanages in Guatemala and Haiti for years. When asked whether they knew about the controversy surrounding orphanages, the dangers they pose to the psychological and physical well-being of children, and the campaigns to stop orphanage voluntourism, Nick Cocalis, one of the three co-founders of Next Step, responded on behalf of the organization with the following rousing endorsement of their due diligence and commitment to child welfare:

> Um, yes. And forgive me I'm going to take a second here. I want to be careful how I answer this one. I guess what I would share is yes, Next Step is aware of different, you know, philosophical, spiritual, and relational thought processes on orphan care and what that looks like. Um, I think that from our standpoint, because of the sensitivity of some of our current partnerships, um, I don't think we have a public comment on what we think is best in orphan care other than to say that we are continually careful and considerate of our current and future partnerships and, um, some of the things that you mention definitely go into our strategy and planning and so, I'm going to avoid the question a little. I don't think it's our place to comment on the overall methodology of orphan care. We're not necessarily, although we support some of that realm, we're not necessarily experts in that realm.[53]

Peter K. Muthui challenges Next Step, and all other voluntourism trip providers, to rethink their lack of culpability. His eventual success, he says, should not be shown as a shining example of why orphanages can be okay, just as my family's experience in the Dominican Republic is not conclusive evidence that sponsorship is an ethical way of caring for children. Peter got lucky; others do not. His brother killed himself. His sisters, he says, married young, had children young, and without support could easily fall into a generational pattern.

"Know that your kind act," he says, "may be perpetuating the unnecessary institutionalization of children—since many unscrupulous orphanages continue to recruit children from vulnerable families and keep their doors open so you can have a place to visit and work during your short stay overseas."[54]

Some big trip providers have taken a stand against orphanage volunteering and the institutionalization of children and are encouraging others in the space to follow suit. In 2017 World Challenge ceased offering trips to orphanages with the help of consultant and activist Leigh Mathews, and they are encouraging competitors to follow their lead. Other large trip providers, like International Volunteer HQ, have left the space less enthusiastically, arguing in defense of their work before letting their history with orphanages fade into the background.[55] It is still a win in Leigh Mathews's books, albeit an imperfect one.

Leigh is quick to reinforce that a trip provider pulling out of an orphanage does not guarantee the orphanage will disappear. In most cases, they find other people willing to volunteer either through less ethically concerned trip providers or by coordinating volunteer programming themselves. Sometimes, they change the way they talk about their work, painting an ethical patina over the same old product—a sort of orphanage greenwashing. "They say, 'we're not an orphanage,'" Leigh says, but, as Next Step has shown, changing the words in a mission statement is not like waving a magic wand. True change takes time, energy, money, an admission that whatever was happening before wasn't good enough, and the moral courage to actually start doing things differently, even if it isn't in your own best interest. Most orphanages, and the trip providers who work with them, aren't willing to go down that route. So, when it is convenient to be an orphanage, they are. When it is not, they become residential care centers, homes for children, children's villages, or something else that excises the unpopular lingo while not changing anything on the ground.

Journal Entries

After years of mulling over her experience in Kenya, Catherine Cottam knows that memory is profoundly fallible, and she is careful to be precise.

"It's really interesting," she says, pausing in her historical analysis of her past actions, "because even, at one point, I say in [my journal] that my concern is that I'm unsure what skill I could teach them to help them after I leave. So, even while I was there, I had some notion of 'what is this really doing to help?'"[56] One of the ways she tried to help was by buying two milking goats for the orphanage. "I wonder how many times those specific two goats had been purchased by volunteers," she says, "and if [the orphanage director] was getting half the money from it every time."

When Catherine started as an orphanage volunteer, she let empathy lead her. She made decisions based on what felt good to her, and what she thought would feel good to those she was trying to help. But empathy becomes a problem when there are not also deeper veins of pragmaticism and self-awareness.[57]

Four years before Catherine arrived at the orphanage in Kenya, Michelle Oliel was there. A young corporate lawyer based in Toronto, she wanted an adventure. So in 2008 she booked a trip to the same orphanage. Unlike Catherine, Michelle loved her experience, and it influenced her decision to switch to human rights law.

Years later, Michelle reconnected with a fellow former voluntourist at the same Kenyan orphanage. Michelle had not returned to the orphanage, but her friend had. What Michelle learned from her friend's return visit, and from others who had volunteered there, was gut-wrenching. She couldn't believe she hadn't seen through the façade. Soon, Michelle was part of a group of former voluntourists struggling to sort out precisely what was going on. They created a Facebook page to collect stories, compare experiences, and try to make sense of how their transformative adventure matched up with the new revelations.

Children at the orphanage were being forced to work and were denied food. All the while, the orphanage leadership was stealing money meant to improve the quality of life of their charges. Kids with injuries were denied access to medical care, and a young boy had his femur shattered for wetting the bed— voluntourists had heard his screams. The kids, Michelle learned, were punished for saying things that might discourage a visitor from making monetary donations. "They were not allowed to say they had a family," she learned, "because people won't donate to pay your school fees if you have a family."[58]

"Everybody who went there has the same story," Michelle says, "When they found out, they said, 'I knew something wasn't right.'" As a human, and a human rights lawyer, she couldn't let it go. She had to do something.

Shut Down

At the same time as Catherine Cottam was volunteering at the orphanage, Michelle Oliel was working to find a way to shut it down. She had inadvertently supported abuse, mistreatment, and corruption by visiting and financially supporting the orphanage through trip fees and fundraising. She could not change how she had contributed to an institution that was causing harm, but she could help shape its future.[59]

Michelle and the community of former voluntourists and activists that had grown from their shared revelations considered trying to take the orphanage over. They'd run it themselves—but better. It quickly became apparent, however, that a takeover would be neither ethical nor feasible. Orphanages are not suitable for kids, so keeping them in a "better" orphanage would not actually fix the problem, even with physical abuse off the table. Instead, they decided to start by cutting off the cash flow. They alerted donors that their dollars were fueling abuse and neglect, and then they started raising some money of their own. They were going to carefully, thoughtfully, and lovingly rip the orphanage to shreds.

"Ripping" sounds harsh, but it is illustrative. The group did not have the luxury of time. The orphanage director would undoubtedly figure out that he was cornered. They could only guess what would happen then, and they did not want to exacerbate the situation. So, they built relationships with local community members who knew critical information about where the kids were from (sometimes right down the road). As they compiled this information, they laid plans to use it.

The first group of children were pulled out of the orphanage toward the end of 2011. A few more were reunited with their families soon after. Those were the easy matches, though. They were the local, or nearly local, kids with families able and willing to support them now that they knew that the orphanage had not been delivering on the promises of education and a better life.

While the orphanage was operating without interference, each child had utility and value. The utility was to look cute and entertain guests. The value came from that utility. If the kids did their jobs right, voluntourism fees, monetary donations, and items would continue to pour in. As kids were rehomed, the cost began to rise above the value of the utility and the danger of the government catching wind of what was going on skyrocketed. Orphanages are not illegal in Kenya, but entrapping, abusing, and exploiting children is.

The risks suddenly outweighed the rewards, and the orphanage director started kicking kids out faster than Michelle and the other former voluntourists could find homes for them—whether with their biological families or other ethical caregiver options. Most of the children were located quickly, but some slipped through the cracks.

In December 2013 an update appeared in the Facebook group for former voluntourists at the orphanage. The director had closed the institution for good, but he wasn't done with the orphanage business. He had moved his operation to another orphanage about two and a half hours south.[60] Orphanages are fairly easy to set up and even easier to fill, and he was on to his next.

Michelle's experience shuttering the orphanage became the genesis of the Stahili Foundation—a nonprofit dedicated to improving the safety nets around vulnerable children, decreasing institutionalization, and increasing access to education. As co-founder and executive director, Michelle has many projects on her plate, but where it all started is frequently on her mind.

A feeling of frustration is central to many voluntourism experiences—frustration that one cannot communicate easily, frustration at cultural differences, frustration at one's discomfort, and frustration that one is not as helpful as they thought they might be.[61] Michelle Oliel transformed that frustration into a powerful force for change. It started with one orphanage in one town, but the ripples have manifested, and Stahili has become an important voice in the anti-orphanage and anti-voluntourism movements.

But there are still loose ends. Michelle's phone buzzed while she was on her honeymoon in 2018. The message included a photo of a boy she hardly recognized. Another former orphanage resident had spotted him on the street. He brought the boy clothes and offered assistance. Hopefully, with time, they could help him find the stability all children deserve.

As of early 2020, the orphanage director had not been prosecuted and remains involved in orphanages. Stahili hopes to catch him in a way that can hold up in court and break his pattern of exploitation and abuse for good. For now, they are tracking his movements, along with those of the leadership of nearly two dozen other orphanages.

Today, Michelle hates driving past the rusted blue gate of the orphanage northeast of Nairobi. But the rust is progress. There, they won.

12 | An Indictment

On December 9, 1868, the *Manchester Guardian* published Sorabsha Dadabhai's open letter to Mary Carpenter. The secretary to the Philanthropic Association in Broach (now Bharuch) in Gujarat, India, had seen an earlier letter to the paper by the British activist and knew of her work on the ground. Unimpressed, Dadabhai felt it was time to set the record straight.[1]

After thanking Carpenter for her good intentions and agreeing that greater access to education would benefit the women of India, Dadabhai got to the point. "I can never persuade myself to believe that such transient visits could leave any durable trace behind them." Carpenter was playing hopscotch across India and missing all of it in the process. She had been attempting to assess and "reform" India with only surface-level awareness. She had fixated on how India differed from England, without taking the time or even having the capacity to understand why that was, and how it wasn't necessarily a bad thing. As for the things that should be addressed, such as expanding educational opportunities for women, there were cultural hurdles that would take years to overcome—years that Carpenter wouldn't be there.

"Even a bare knowledge of letters in a female is looked upon here by nine tenths of the population as tantamount to arming a child with a deadly weapon," Dadabhai wrote, "being unacquainted with the use of which, there is every risk of the child either cutting its own throat or that of somebody else." Cultural shifts needed to be encouraged, gradual progress set in motion, and the barriers dismantled, but Carpenter's pushy methods, Dadabhai argued, could bring catastrophic harm to the entire mission of advancing women in India. Dadabhai hoped that providing a public warning would lead Mary to question her methods. "Every backward move is not necessarily a degenerate one," Dadabhai wrote. Mary could step back and move forward if only she were willing to listen.

Dadabhai's letter is not a masterwork of contemporary activism. It is ethically complicated and uses language that is bigoted and classist. Yet it still represents a community trying to speak for itself. When Dadabhai wrote, "I should not undertake an experiment the failure of which may have a tendency to foreclose effectually all future opportunities of success," they are not saying that progress is unimportant. Rather, Dadabhai is asking Carpenter to slow down. The way Carpenter was going about things could have terrible consequences. Dadabhai asks Carpenter to pause, pivot, ask questions, listen, and then reconsider.

In the end, Carpenter did not do any of the things Dadabhai requested. Pathological altruism, the same pathology that is pervasive in voluntourism today, drove her forward. What happened to the communities left in her wake did not seem to matter to her unless it resulted in accolades.

Contemporary Colonialism

Some have called voluntourism a form of *neocolonialist engagement*.[2] To call it something *neo*, or *new*, risks divorcing it from its past, contrasting it against the colonialism of old and severing the direct line from Thomas Cook and Mary Carpenter, through expansionism, wars, and innovations, straight on until today. To do such a thing would be false.

The colonialism of today, as practiced in voluntourism, is not recent nor new. The players have changed and the costumes have been updated, but trip providers, voluntourists, development agencies, and international aid programs have taken up the roles set down by colonial militaries and governments. "All colonialism is the same," TMS Ruge insists, what is playing out in voluntourism is "just another shade."[3] This makes voluntourism a form of *contemporary colonialism*—colonialism, but an iteration for the current era.[4]

Unlike the colonialism in our history books, contemporary colonialism is most often expressed through many small actions and seemingly unimportant decisions. Many qualify as *microaggressions*. The term microaggression refers to typically small, sometimes nearly invisible, and often unintentional discriminatory actions toward marginalized people and racial minorities. They are not limited to interactions between white people and people of color. Microaggressions can take place between any people who are separated by a dividing line. This includes interactions between people of different genders, people of different sexual orientations, the conventionally abled and the disabled, and interethnic interactions. When compounded, these microaggressions can cause tremendous damage.[5]

Voluntourism adds another characteristic to microaggressions: *micro-exploitation*. Through millions of seemingly positive or innocuous actions, from handing out shoes to painting a wall, voluntourists of every gender, age, race, and religion perform acts of micro-exploitation that are largely unintended, unseen, and unrecognized by the voluntourist. The cumulative impact of this endless onslaught undermines personal agency, disempowers communities, and creates cycles of dependency that stunt economic development.

Years before Aaron Reddecliffe and Emily Scott traveled to Tanzania in 2012, they arrived in a slum in Nairobi, Kenya. It was 2007, and they planned to spend two weeks volunteering at a local school. One of their projects was to repaint the school building, and they invited the kids to chip in.

Aaron remembers it quickly turning into a splatter war, with paint flying everywhere. It was fun, and Aaron and Emily were excited to see the kids let loose and enjoy themselves. It wasn't until it had died down and they were surveying the damage that they registered that their clothes were drenched in paint. For Aaron and Emily, this was not a big deal. They had access to clean shirts and pants in their bags and through their wallets. For the kids, it was not as simple. "Once Emily and I started talking about the problems with voluntourism," Aaron remembers, "we realized we probably wrecked their only set of school clothes." Living in the slums, surrounded by poverty and hardship, they almost certainly did not have another set of clothing ready to wear to school the next day. "And we just laughed and had fun wrecking them."

On the global scale of harm exacted on communities through voluntourism, the splatter paint situation was a tiny event, but it still weighs heavy on Aaron more than a decade later. "We left there thinking we were great and had made a difference," he says, "but, looking back, what we did was super super shitty."[6]

He is not wrong. It was stupid, thoughtless, and probably very upsetting for the children's caregivers, who had to figure out how to salvage or replace clothing covered in heavy-duty industrial paint. The money that went toward the paint could also almost certainly have been better applied somewhere else. Walls can hold up a roof without fresh paint, but, as Aaron would later learn, a school is just a building without the right teachers, books, and supplies.

Neither Emily nor Aaron acted out of malice. However, they've come to recognize that their behavior was rooted in a series of naïve and hierarchical assumptions that likely would not have been possible if not for the manifestation of contemporary colonialism in voluntourism.

Contemporary colonialism looks different from the colonialism of old. There are fewer severed hands, fewer overtly enslaved laborers, and fewer forced conversions, but the demands for performances of authenticity and access in exchange for often-unhelpful aid is just a new way of asserting dominance. In the past, nations made self-interested decisions that ignored the disastrous impacts on less politically and financially powerful places. Today, the priorities remain the same. Disguised as a benevolent desire to do good, the damage continues.

Slow Violence

Many travelers assume that greater cultural understanding, and thus more egalitarian engagement, are natural byproducts of voluntourism experiences. The reality is that voluntourism is prone to produce the opposite. By reinforcing stereotypes, voluntourism encourages those who take part in and organize experiences to think of issues of development, particularly systemic poverty, as matters of chance. The only way to be okay with having more, dropping in, giving some, and then heading home is by telling yourself that it's bad luck that others have less.[7]

The idea that poverty is the result of being dealt a bad hand, not the fault of a rigged deck, is at the core of voluntourism. It is a noxious idea that masks the real and complicated conflicts that drive global inequity, and it gives those with more power permission to look away from the parts of their privilege that make them uncomfortable. Instead, voluntourists focus on what is easy to fall in love with: smiling faces, simple projects, and photogenic poverty.[8] By labeling structural violence, resource exploitation, centuries of political manipulation, and contemporary colonialism as bad luck, voluntourists are empowered to continue to treat the communities they work in as development playgrounds.

To excuse the subjugation of the many for the entertainment of the few, the voluntourism industry has created an evolving vocabulary that cements a hierarchy where voluntourists are always at the top. Whether we use the terms *First World* and *Third World* or *developed* and *developing*, the evolving lingo distracts from a universal truth that has held constant: the West is always setting the standard for success. Voluntourists are the Us, and the rest are the Other.[9]

The voluntourism industry relies on this binary of difference while simultaneously branding it as "old history" that we should rush past without a second look. The past goes unspoken, context goes unrecognized, and our repetitions of previous failed practices are celebrated as heroic solutions.[10] Voluntourists may not look like the khaki-clad conquerors we have read about in history textbooks, but extracting personal gratification from a community while ignoring the history, sociology, and psychology of a place is an imperialistic endeavor worthy of a pith helmet.

In author Rob Nixon's 2011 book *Slow Violence and the Environmentalism of the Poor*, the author reveals how the worst of climate change is being ignored or overlooked because it takes place in areas that people in power tend to pretend do not exist. The damage in these areas is not characterized by sudden, photogenic crises that reveal a Western hero—it is leaching, it fuels social unrest, and it is killing people slowly. He calls it *slow violence*.[11]

Voluntourism is another form of slow violence. Slow violence exacerbates vulnerabilities and thrives on instability. Similarly, voluntourism relies on communities that are hurting enough to accept any help they can get and disempowered enough to not advocate for themselves when things don't proceed as expected.[12]

For former voluntourists, accepting the violence of voluntourism can be excruciating. They intended on doing good, even when they did not know what good might look like.[13] Learning that they participated in a practice that caused harm is understandably painful, and many choose to simply ignore the signs.

Pantomiming Progress

The existence of pathological altruism hinges on two things appearing at the same time: 1) a desire to do good and 2) good not resulting from an action or set of actions pursued in response to number 1.[14] From there, it loops. Number 2 does not inform number 1. Rather than spurring adjustment or reform, negative results may even reinforce one's conviction to keep trying. People and communities are left hurting, and the pathological altruist gets to feel good about having wanted to do good—even if the positive change they envisioned didn't manifest in reality.[15]

Wanting to do good is a beautiful thing but looking away from discomfort and blindly following altruistic intentions has led to half-built libraries, shredded greenhouses, exploitative orphanages, ruined school uniforms, and traumatized patients. However, the answer to pathological altruism is not to squash out the desire to help. Putting a permanent ban on giving back would be silly, futile, and damaging in new and unique ways of its own.

So could voluntourism still be worth it? Could this damage be secondary to a greater good: both for the voluntourists and for those they seek to help?

The residue of hundreds of years of resource extraction overlapped with a century and a half of tourism, both done to fulfill the insatiable consumption demands of richer and more developed societies, has yet to alleviate poverty in developing areas. Now, the West sends voluntourists in to fix the problems that stem directly from damage wrought by colonialism. Instead of questioning why these issues exist, trip providers sell the opportunity to plug the holes with freshly painted walls, basketball courts, and cheap handouts pulled from duffel bags that still have the airport tags flapping from the handles.

As a culture, we call these experiences educational—for the voluntourists, at least—but the lessons learned through forced interactions are only a semblance of an understanding. Host communities have become staged shows running on loop for audience members who demand to feel as if they are the first to see the performance. The actors cannot learn their lines *too* well, and they cannot make things *too* nice, because when life becomes more comfortable, the show falls apart. In the photographs voluntourists take home, the walls of a cage are invisible, but they are still present.[16]

Trip providers serve as the ticket collectors for this pantomime of progress, the modern incarnation of the trading companies that exerted control in the colonialism of old. Where once they dumped cheap goods and collected valuable commodities, they now chaperone voluntourists, extracting them when their time is up.

Both voluntourists and trip providers are culpable in this exchange, even if they are oblivious to the larger systems at work.

In *medical voluntourism*, voluntourists with minimal or no medical training are allowed to practice on patients because they want to, and they can pay for the opportunity, breaking the social contract that undergirds our health systems and prioritizing their experience over patient outcomes.

In *orphanage voluntourism*, voluntourists engage in an activity linked to human trafficking, child abuse, and the child sex trade. In the best cases, orphanage voluntourism leads to community and family dissolution and psychological damage.

In *development voluntourism*, voluntourists crowd out local labor and tackle projects that are often poorly executed, unneeded, or redundant. Schools stand empty or unfinished, wells break down, walls are painted over and over, and greenhouses are ripped to shreds. In the process, local capacity is crushed, and local agency is destroyed.

On *short-term missions*, voluntourists project their beliefs onto communities and use their faith as an excuse for behavior that is irresponsible and self-centered.

In *teaching placements*, trip providers undermine educational objectives by empowering untrained voluntourists without local expertise to bumble through slapdash lesson plans and hand out novelty erasers.

In *voluntourism of every form and style*, voluntourists build the narratives of the places they visit through images that are snapped quickly and shared globally. The constructed stories become glue traps: alluring, sticky, and nearly impossible to get free of. Through the types of images Erin Schrode refused to help create and Emily Worrall fights against as Barbie Savior, voluntourists conquer communities in person, and online.[17]

If voluntourism is good at anything, it is good at priming cultures and communities for this colonialist consumption. Made into one homogenous mass of poverty, beauty, simplicity, and need, the Other is perpetually, unalterably, for sale.[18] It is a messy transaction from the start, and what the voluntourist gets is the host's loss. In the meantime, trip providers get to play judge and executioner for entire communities.

Mary Carpenter traveled to India four times between 1866 and 1876 in pursuit of her vision of civilizing the country by providing a particular type of education to its women. When she was questioned, she refused to listen. All that challenged her beliefs, she refused to see.

Today, voluntourism providers continue to expand the market that Thomas Cook opened up. Likewise, voluntourists continue to pursue "making a difference" and "doing good" with the zealousness of an addict.[19] As critiques of voluntourism have gained traction, some from within the multibillion-dollar voluntourism industry have been willing to call out the system as complicated and occasionally corrupt. Individuals have not gotten quite so good at implicating themselves just yet. Only what affirms has been embraced.

Heddwyn Kyambadde, the Ugandan filmmaker who grew up watching kids rub dirt on their faces and later attended Biola University, remembers cautioning people about going on mission trips. After giving a presentation where he shared his perspective on how voluntourism can be less than good, a parent called him out: "How dare you ruin this experience for my child?" This has become a frequent objection to the voluntourism debate, but Heddwyn has two questions of his own: "Is your fear being called out? Or is your fear that you will be wrong?"[20]

13 | Turning Tide

In 2016 Scottish actress Louise Linton self-published *In Congo's Shadow*, a memoir about her experience volunteering in Zambia as a teenager. Some thought it was a parody along the lines of Barbie Savior. Others thought it was a bad joke. It was neither.[1]

The actress wrote about hiding from rebels who never entered Zambia as fighters and of a monsoon season that does not exist in the country.[2] After publishing a book peppered with incorrect assertions, problematic parallels, and wording seemingly picked out of a colonialist playbook, Louise became the unwitting poster child of the white savior complex. The outcry against *In Congo's Shadow* gained further momentum when the press reported that she was in a relationship with Steven Mnuchin, Donald Trump's national finance chair, top fundraiser, and secretary of the treasury.[3] She was not simply a clueless C-list actress who had written a deeply problematic book and was now having to face the music. She was entrenched in the establishment that made her privilege and wealth and profound naïvety possible.

Shortly after Louise Linton's memoir was first vivisected in triplicate on social media, activist and entrepreneur TMS Ruge wrote a piece that took a different angle on the issue. Instead of further eviscerating the author, he turned his gaze toward his fellow Africans. In "Dear Africa, Louise Linton Is on Us," TMS calls out native Africans for their role in allowing people like Louise to exist. The white savior complex is not going to fizzle out on its own, he says. Colonialism is going to continue to evolve for as long as it is allowed to survive. Africans have agency, TMS wrote, but they need to claim it.[4]

In his piece TMS names his fellow Africans and the governments that are supposed to represent and defend them as participants in the problem. They let voluntourists through the borders and then empower them to disempower others. They open their hotels and cruise ship ports to multinational tourism brands and let them run roughshod over entire communities in the name of personal growth and global understanding. They extol the benefits of repaired roads, free schools, and access to clinics—even when the services are subpar or tantamount to endangerment.

"We are so colonized," TMS said to me in an interview two years after publishing his Linton-inspired piece, "that I could sell anything that says 'Made in America,' or 'Made in England,' but if it says 'Made in Uganda' [Ugandans] won't buy it."[5] What point is there in tweeting and posting and sharing memes if there is no pride nor agency, and when people are happy complaining about white saviorism but do not want to—or do not know how to—stop it? "How do we celebrate independence every year," he asks, "when we don't actually have it?"[6]

White People Stuff

Zion Amanda Kente offers a perspective that bridges an ocean. Born to Rwandan parents in Kinshasa, Democratic Republic of the Congo, in 1993, she moved to Rwanda and then to Tanzania before relocating to the United States at the age of twelve. Zion spent the second half of her childhood in

Pennsylvania before she moved back to Tanzania in 2016. In 2017 she moved again, this time to Uganda, to pursue a master's degree.

Before moving to the United States, she knew little about her continent's history. "A lot of school systems here," she explains, speaking from Uganda, "are based on the American and European school systems." The funding for teachers, books, and other supplies comes from foreign aid, so there are "certain things they need to teach, like European history."[7] As Aaron Reddecliffe observed while teaching in Tanzania, African history gets squeezed out of the curriculum, especially when the books are outdated and the foreign "teachers" don't know what they're talking about. "You can never know your potential if you don't know your history," Zion insists.

Growing up in Pennsylvania, Zion was confused when she heard people talking about voluntourism trips delivering hope, change, and a résumé boost. She knew that the countries she had lived in were works in progress, but so was the United States. Yes, poverty was a problem, but there were people in Tanzania, Rwanda, and across Africa that were working to create change. Zion's American classmates did not have to fly over to make it happen.

"The fact is that this is white people stuff." Black people, especially Black women, Zion says, have been "screaming about this for years" but are not being heard because their voices do not carry weight in Western society. "The only way to make it stop is to make white people stop, and, unfortunately, a lot of white people only listen to people who are white."

"Even then," she adds, "sometimes they will not listen."

Zion does not think that countries overrun with voluntourists should completely shut their borders to philanthropy. Isolationism is not an answer to the voluntourism problem, but aid "has to be done in a way that is mutual, respectful, and certainly sustainable." And voluntourists need a severe wake-up call. "Imagine how many feelings you are hurting," she says, "and you're not just hurting feelings, you're destroying lives."

If those of racial, financial, educational, geographic, and myriad other privileges, and who seek to improve the world, truly want to see the places they visit become healthier, more vibrant, and more prosperous, they need to reimagine how they cultivate change. They need to accept that moral convictions can be wrong and that assumptions may be incorrect. They need to absorb that the ways giving-minded travelers have engaged globally for nearly two hundred years have been hurtful and harmful. They need to understand that voluntourism, despite being lauded as the "future" of tourism, is grounded in ideologies that strip communities of the very traits and characteristics prospective voluntourists hope to cultivate in themselves—resilience, strength, leadership, and self-reliance.[8] The colonialistic ideas voluntourism is built upon today are no better at facilitating a better future for communities than the imperialism of the past was, often in the very same places.[9]

No White Saviors

Two years after *In Congo's Shadow*, in the summer of 2018, many of the individuals I was interviewing for this book started asking me if I had seen a new anti-voluntourism Instagram account. The buzz reminded me of when Barbie Savior first started—everyone wanted to talk about it, but no one wanted to share their opinion first. Instead, we would each take turns edging toward the brink of saying what we were thinking, hoping someone else would jump. What everyone could agree on was that the @NoWhiteSaviors account was bold. Whoever was behind it had a serious bone to pick.

Barbie Savior entered the voluntourism debate with satire and humor, pushing people off balance with dramatized dioramas and sarcastic captions. No White Saviors was taking a more aggressive approach.

The first post was a simple image featuring a quote, attributed to Teju Cole, and a sprig of greenery: "The White Savior Industrial Complex is not about justice. It is about having a big emotional experience that validates privilege."[10] The account did not provide any further explanation, leaving it to the reader to establish their own response.

The location tag for the first post was Haiti, but the team behind the No White Saviors account is actually based in Uganda. At first, they kept their identities under wraps, not necessarily anonymous but intentionally half-buried. As they gained traction, they slowly increased their visibility. According to No White Saviors, the team includes a mix of native Ugandans and Kenyans, many of whom remain anonymous, but from the start, Olivia Alaso, a Ugandan, and Kelsey Nielsen, an American, were doing most of the talking.

Kelsey describes herself as a "reformed white savior." She grew up in an evangelical church and left home for Uganda at the age of twenty-three to set up a family center. Her experiences in Uganda triggered a transformation that led her to advocate against the global white saviorism that had originally inspired her, albeit subconsciously. As the No White Saviors account picked up steam, she could be spotted in the comments section of posts calling out celebrities, influencers, Louise Lintons, and nobodies alike for colonialist, racist, imperialist, and unethical behaviors including the medical abuse of children, "poverty porn" photography, and imprecisely worded questions.

Some returned her volley with their own criticism, saying she was using her whiteness to seize power in a space that wasn't hers to control. Her outspokenness is not about power, she has countered, but about carrying a burden which her fellow No White Saviors team members should not have to bear. Taking on the emotional labor of engaging in tough conversations may sound like speaking the loudest. But, Kelsey has insisted, her goal is to educate people, predominately white people, without harming people of color in the process.

The women behind Barbie Savior, Emily Worrall and Jackie Kramlich, think of their work as an art project. For those behind No White Saviors, their work is an advocacy project. The difference is not a minor one. Barbie Savior looks inward, whereas No White Saviors screams to the nosebleeds.

Historically, if people who have been marginalized, oppressed, or discriminated against do not speak loudly, they are drowned out. No White Saviors has offered those affected by voluntourism and the White Savior Complex a protected platform from which to air their grievances, providing community members with the opportunity to be heard through an enormous global megaphone while retaining the protection of anonymity if they choose. This protection is vital for people in voluntourism host communities who want to say something but don't feel safe speaking out. For a small business owner, saying no to taking selfies with camera-toting voluntourists may result in lost business. Saying no to the entire apparatus that brought the voluntourist there could have far more significant repercussions.

No White Saviors argues that calling on those looking to give back and the entities that empower them, such as trip providers, to question themselves should start a conversation—not shut it down. They've received mixed responses. As their audience has grown, so too has the range of reactions, from the affirming and encouraging to the vitriolic and even threatening.

"Behind closed doors," they shared in October 2018, "we are being called extreme, hateful, racist, and it has even been suggested that Satan himself is using us to come against the 'good work' missionaries are here doing."[11]

As their platform has surpassed half a million on Instagram, the core messaging has stayed the same. Privileged people need to recognize their privilege. White people need to wake up to the reality of internalized racism and help to dismantle it. Both groups need to stop trying to save the world. Instead, they need to start working on themselves by confronting the internalized biases and beliefs that are subjugating those without the same privileges. With thousands of people chiming in on each post, the messaging can sometimes get tongue-tied, but even when wires get crossed, the spotlight No White Saviors has shined on the ideologies and mental processes that allow for voluntourism and missionary work to happen has been arresting, unsettling, and remarkable.

The No White Saviors lens has laid voluntourism bare as a groomed, sanitized, and prepackaged experience that sells intimate access to communities with less to people with more. Voluntourism is tourism in its most contrived form and, while the branding may be more burlap than Bellini, it still reeks. As the traveler is handed a simplified experience with no room for nuance, the complexity that makes life fascinating and the world beautiful is stripped away. People are erased, communities are turned into caricatures, and cultures are given a fresh coat of whitewash for paying visitors who roam at will and leave feeling fulfilled. Question this, and critics will say you work for the devil.

The No White Saviors team is not surprised by the responses, though. Millions of voluntourists have internalized the message that their heart is in the right place, their hands can change the world, their body is a vessel for grace, their mind can move mountains, their presence is a gift, and that they can will goodness into being. All they have to do is to show up. To have this logic questioned may feel like an attack, but it is one that is long overdue.

Thomas Cook was not wrong in believing that travel can be transformative, but he was wrong when he forced Western expectations onto the places he popularized. Mary Carpenter was not wrong in thinking that the women of India deserve access to education, but she was wrong when she assumed that she was the one to deliver it. Likewise, today, voluntourists are not wrong for wanting communities to have clean water, reliable healthcare, good schools, and full bellies. They, and the entire voluntourism industry, misstep when they presume that being able to book a trip, purchase a plane ticket, and fill a few duffel bags with items to give away, is the same as being qualified to deliver that assistance.

In the words of No White Saviors, "Accountability feels a lot like bullying when you're used to being praised for your harmful behavior."[12] But once the sting wears off, there's work to be done toward truly making a difference.

14 | The Future of Voluntourism

In 2015 a new cruise brand entered the crowded field and decided to carve out a niche by making the criticisms of voluntourism work in their favor. They would offer a product that would fulfill voluntourists' dreams while mollifying critics.

The Fathom brand was presented as a small and scrappy upstart, obscuring the parent company—Carnival Corporation & PLC—and the big money behind what appeared to be a boutique operation. They would serve the apparently untapped market of millennials who liked the idea of all-inclusive leisure cruising but who also wanted the endorphin rush of giving back.

I reached out to Fathom in 2015 after I heard about them from Dominican locals while traveling in the area where they were beginning to operate. When Tara Russell, the president of Fathom, told me that the trip development had "taken some long-term relationship development and investment," with people in the Dominican Republic, I knew that to be true because I had heard about it firsthand from Dominicans themselves. How it was going to pan out, though, was as yet unclear.[1]

Fathom had promised local partner organizations that it would invest in the community, give back sustainability, and minimize its footprint on the ground. Before the first ship left port, these promises were already beginning to give way to the usual easy route of simple projects done quickly and without long-term planning. At least one organization that had been excited to work with Fathom was starting to feel queasy after learning that the volunteer excursions would not be in-depth nor require training. Projects that organizations had spent months designing would be simplified down to their most basic components so that any Fathom traveler could take part. Customer satisfaction was already more important than community needs, and the trips hadn't even started yet.

If the plan for large-scale voluntourism in a small community did not work, Fathom President Tara Russell had a plan. "If we are not demonstrating genuine positive impact outcomes in what we're doing," Tara said, "then we're going to have to go back to our travelers and say, since we learned that this is not the most positive way for us to engage, here's an alternative.' We would not just continue doing it if it wasn't creating a positive outcome, right?"

In the end, Fathom skipped that stage. When journalist Lucas Peterson booked a seven-night Fathom cruise to the Dominican Republic for the all-inclusive price of $249 plus taxes and fees, the now-former *New York Times* Frugal Traveler columnist knew he had found a bargain. The trips were just getting started, but they had already been discounted heavily.

Lucas Peterson reported that his trip with Fathom appeared to be at half-capacity despite the deal, and the voluntourism angle wasn't landing well with travelers. A reforestation project was canceled due to a lack of interest. The English tutoring opportunity went on as scheduled, but the reporter's ninety-minute session with an eleven-year-old girl did not make it past numbers and the basic alphabet. Before his September 2016 column was published, the price for the same week-long trip he had taken would drop to $199.[2]

Less than two months after the Frugal Traveler column ran, Carnival announced that Fathom would cease operations by the following summer.

The company's social good darling would only make a few more loops of the Caribbean before docking for good.[3]

For those critical of voluntourism, Fathom's failure was an exciting outcome. Customers had been offered low-cost, no-effort, easy-access voluntourism on a platter and turned it down. It was too commercial, too transactional, and too cheesy. There was, finally, it seemed, a line, and once you have a line you can start trying to move it.

Changing the voluntourism industry will never be easy, but Fathom's failure made it easier. To riff on the words of Anaïs Nin, the twentieth-century French-Cuban American writer (Cuba was another proposed Fathom destination): *not changing has to become more dangerous than changing ever could be.*

A New Vocabulary

Reforming voluntourism will not require a reinvention but a renovation. The intention to give is good and should remain. The desire to travel is not going to disappear spontaneously. Renovating voluntourism means stripping it down to its bones. We need to put all the bad stuff in a dumpster (including, in the vast majority of cases, any type of volunteering at all) and transform the skeleton into something that is informed and community-centric, supports small-scale development, encourages sustainable business models, and probably runs under a different name.

Some may say that such severe measures are premature, particularly in light of how little data there is on the impacts of voluntourism long-term. It is true that we cannot see the full picture yet. That is partly because repercussions play out over generations. It is also because colonizing entities have rarely invested resources into surveying communities on the negative impacts of their empires. However, we can see where the origins of voluntourism have brought us to today. We know that voluntourism has increased global mobility but does not seem to have markedly increased global understanding. We know that it has benefited voluntourists socially, academically, and professionally, yet there is little evidence that it has significantly improved local lives or economies. Where voluntourism has succeeded, the work of volunteers has not been the reason why.

Some trip providers and educational institutions are beginning to hold themselves to a higher standard. They are more aware that the activity their students and clients love to do has a dark side. They may not be ready to stop running trips, but many are willing to begin to address the issues apparent in their programming. This is progress, and progress is good, even if it is slower than one might like. It is better to have millions of voluntourists who are aware of the issues inherent in their chosen activity and open to further information than to have the same number remain stubbornly closed off to the realities right in front of them.

Trip providers who are ready to do things differently, or who are already holding their travelers to high, skills-based standards, need to construct a new vocabulary. According to Dr. Jessica Evert, executive director of Child Family Health International, greenwashing has blended things that are vastly different into one muddled morass of "ethical" and "authentic." Someone who is searching for an ethical medical education opportunity, like those CFHI offers, and someone who is looking for a pay-to-play chance to wield a scalpel, are probably using the same keywords when they Google. That might be good for the less-than-ethical traveler, as it could accidentally push them in a better direction. However, it can make it hard for the traveler who is ethically minded—but may not necessarily know what to look out for—to tell the difference between the good, the bad, and the ugly.

One solution to this problem would be the creation of a certification system with a strict set of enforceable guidelines for truly ethical travel opportunities, some of which could include targeted, qualified, and thoughtful volunteering. Implementing such a certification system is not a new idea.

Tourism Concern spent three decades studying, reporting on, and calling out unethical behavior in tourism.[4] They published materials designed to help voluntourists make more ethical decisions, but when it came to creating a certification, they balked.[5] When faced with the challenge of defining what ethical tourism is, they recognized that they would never be able to come to a consensus. What is ethical is ever changing and often subjective.[6] Tourism Concern shut down in 2018.

Irish development organization Comhlámh, UK-based association the Year Out Group, and Fair Trade Volunteering, among others, have succeeded where Tourism Concern stalled. By creating certifications and codes of conduct for ethical voluntourism, with varying levels of specificity and transparency, they have drawn lines in the sand. None of them go far enough in stripping the volunteering out of voluntourism, but at least they exist as evolving representations of what is currently considered best practice.[7]

Brandon Blache-Cohen, Cody Paris, and Eric Hartman created another standard for ethical voluntourism in 2014 because, they believed, the existing best practice guidelines were neither rigorous enough to make activists happy nor accessible enough to get trip provider buy-in.[8] They called their criteria the Fair Trade Learning Standards. All three of these men have connections to Amizade, a "fair trade learning" or "service learning" nonprofit voluntourism trip provider. Brandon Blache-Cohen is the executive director of Amizade, Cody Paris serves on the board of directors, and Eric Hartman has long-running ties to the nonprofit trip provider. This highlights an issue throughout attempts to reform voluntourism: the foxes are running the henhouse.

Historically, certification systems (organic, fair trade, etc.), if widely embraced, can result in shifts in personal behavior and reforms to institutional norms.[9] The problem is that a community is not a banana. This comparison may seem absurd, but it's important. Whether a banana is organic is a binary; it either is an organic banana or it is not an organic banana. The impacts of voluntourism on communities cannot be judged by the simple binary by which we judge bananas.

This tension is apparent in the Fair Trade Learning Standards. There is no measurement or assessment protocol, and there is no actual badge or certificate to reward programs that meet their standards. Should they start stamping their approval on programs, just about any trip provider could find a way to fit the mold with the help of the right spin doctor. A list of good practices does not spontaneously manifest good actions, and having no means of measuring success empowers unethical programs to twist their language—incentivizing even more of the greenwashing that already plagues the sector.

Based on the records Amizade has made publicly available, the organization doesn't even have a history of following the criteria created by three people with intimate knowledge of it. Amplifying community voices, especially as part of the decision-making process, is a key piece of the Fair Trade Learning Standards. From 2016 to 2019, the Amizade Annual Report Infographic, the form of the annual report that Amizade makes easily accessible online, has not included any community voices, perspectives, impacts, or even outcomes.[10] Amizade reported over $2.3 million in income in 2019, 84 percent of which came from program fees.[11]

Oversight and certification could be helpful in corralling voluntourism, but standards and stamps created from within the industry are not going to fix the problems the industry thrives on.

The Placement Paradigm

Willy Oppenheim believes that the core of the voluntourism problem isn't defining what is ethical or creating a set of standards that pressure providers into behaving differently. Instead, he points to something he calls the *Placement Paradigm*.[12]

A *placement* is where a voluntourist is assigned to work. Placements are the result of a process that is fairly uniform across voluntourism trip providers regardless of how many ethical buzzwords are on their website. A potential traveler goes to a website and searches for trips by country, by activity, or both—not by organization nor by required skills. Then, they apply (a formality) to a trip. If accepted (which they will be), they are given a placement at a project site or with a host organization. Some trip providers allow voluntourists to connect with their host before they arrive, but this is a formality. Once they apply, the voluntourist has the "job."

This system exists because it is the best way for trip providers, the middlemen, to make money. If potential voluntourists were encouraged to connect directly with hosts to arrange trips, the trip provider would quickly become irrelevant. If hosts could approve or deny potential voluntourists, it would slow down the placement process and force trip providers to say no to potential customers. Trip providers succeed by saying yes to everyone.

The word *placement* is particularly important because it helps to illustrate the passivity of the voluntourist in planning their own experiences. As Larsa Al-Omaishi learned when she applied for a medical trip to Tanzania without any medical school experience, the application process she had taken so seriously did not matter. Voluntourists do not have to earn a position. So long as they meet the minimum qualifications (age and ability to pay are the two most important ones), they will be placed somewhere. "I really feel sometimes like the Emperor has no clothes," Willy Oppenheim says. "It is such a glaring issue, but no one wants to talk about it because their hands are dirty."[13]

More precise placements would not solve all of the ethical issues in voluntourism, but ensuring that voluntourists have something necessary or valuable to provide would go a considerable way toward guaranteeing the potential of something good coming out of an inherently unequal situation.[14]

Willy Oppenheim founded Omprakash, a nonprofit that helps host organizations recruit qualified volunteers, in 2004, because he saw the potential for improvement in the placement process. Unlike conventional nonprofit trip providers, Omprakash does not charge travelers a fee for using its platform. It does not sell placements, and it has no financial incentives for creating a voluntourist pipeline. "We are not about putting a price tag on relationships," Willy insists; "as soon as I start selling [trips], I'm participating in the same complicated value exchange."

Omprakash does sell a tool that is helping to address another weak spot in the voluntourism equation: education. Many trip providers, especially educational institutions, claim to provide cultural awareness training before and during trips. Unfortunately, this typically adds up to a few handouts and a half-day seminar. "Very few companies in this space," Willy says, "want to take the visionary step to tell their customers that there is some homework."

What currently passes for a curriculum tends toward what he calls "How to Not Offend or Get Yourself Killed."

EdGE (Education through Global Engagement) online programs are designed to educate anyone before they go away to give back—especially short-term voluntourists. The platform does not solve for voluntourism as a form of contemporary colonialism. However, the courses do press students to become more aware of the web of assumptions and biases they may be taking into their voluntourism experiences and how those beliefs may harm communities in which they hope to work.

Willy says that some of his professional peers have argued that there is no difference between selling an online course for voluntourists, like EdGE, and a voluntourism trip. Both are products that profit from people who want to travel to "give back." Willy laughs at this. To him, it is like comparing selling broccoli to selling guns. Trip providers are selling something that has the potential to do profound harm. You could theoretically give someone some sizeable bruises if you beat them with a head of broccoli, but it is more likely to fortify than it is to cause lasting damage. Omprakash does help people find voluntourism opportunities, but by serving a side of broccoli to their travelers through EdGE, they are trying to pack a different kind of punch. The program is not a perfect solution, but it may represent progress.

Slow but Steady

When Leigh Mathews helped World Challenge ease out of orphanage voluntourism in 2017, they proved that change doesn't have to come from the young upstarts of the voluntourism industry, like Omprakash. The behemoths can press reform forward if they are willing to pay a price. World Challenge is more than thirty years old and has facilitated trips for more than 150,000 students. Orphanage programs were some of their most popular trips, but they decided the cash wasn't worth the cost.

Two years after transitioning away from orphanage voluntourism, World Challenge was still struggling to explain their decision to customers eager for opportunities to spend time with vulnerable children. At an Ethical

Student Travel Forum event World Challenge organized for teachers and school administrators in Atlanta, Georgia, team members Pete Fletcher and Dan Porter and consultant Leigh Mathews talked through why they moved away from orphanage options. They were open about their mistakes, honest about their missteps, and transparent about the progress they have made toward addressing the past and moving toward a better future. The audience, however, was not entirely sold on the changes. After over an hour of information on why orphanages cause harm, a teacher insisted that his orphanage trip was different. He had no intention of stopping.

There were undoubtedly other factors at play for the adamant teacher besides concern for the welfare of children in residential care. He led the trip. He fundraised for the trip. His students probably loved him for the trip. To give something up that had made him and his students feel so good and so full of purpose would likely feel like giving up a piece of himself. I have encountered the same response at schools and universities around the United States. Administrators will readily admit that there are problems with specific activities, such as orphanage voluntourism or unqualified disaster response, but quickly find ways to exempt their offerings from the critiques. They can see what is wrong with the system, but they refuse to implicate themselves.

This reticence to follow World Challenge's example highlights how trip providers who are trying to do better can be stymied in their reform efforts by clients who are unwilling to see why change is necessary. The orphanages World Challenge used to visit will have quickly found new sources of financial support, and many of the groups that traveled to them with World Challenge will likely turn to different providers to get what they want. It appears to be easier for schools and community groups to change vendors than it is to explain to students and parents why they will no longer be offering the profoundly problematic trips that have become beloved cornerstones of their community service programming. Leigh Mathews holds trip providers that cave to this sort of client pressure accountable. If you say you are going to try to do better but refuse to rise to the occasion, you are, she says, "just going to cause a different kind of harm."[15]

Since phasing out orphanage trips, World Challenge has continued to reduce the role of volunteering in their offerings. The company's eight thousand annual student travelers can pick from trips centered on engaging in local communities and learning from local leaders, and World Challenge has increased the amount of time student travelers spend learning about local initiatives and customs. The options for volunteering are focused primarily on conservation, including sea turtle conservation in Costa Rica, orangutan habitat protection in Borneo, and rhino breeding in Botswana.[16]

Trip providers that want to move toward more ethical voluntourism options would do well to look to World Challenge as an example of how incremental changes can be rolled out and paired with client re-education to make transformative growth productive and profitable. Some clients may be stubborn, but it is possible to do better without going broke.

There are other steps trip providers should be taking that can be implemented slowly, thoughtfully, and without having to go out of business.

Commit to honesty, respect, and transparency internally and in all marketing. Remove images of children and other vulnerable individuals from websites and brochures, replace traveler-oriented language with community perspectives, and clearly lay out where travelers' dollars are ending up.[17]

Implement frequent community needs assessments in partnership with both third-party subject experts and community members.[18] If something isn't needed, don't do it. If something can't be done professionally and sustainably, don't do it. If you're considering doing something just because travelers ask for it, don't do it.

Require pretrip education programs and schedule opportunities for self-critical reflection during and posttrip.[19] These can be integrated into coursework or through alternative platforms, such as Omprakash's EdGE program.

Move toward true sustainability. Trip providers should be facilitating local employment and local skills development. When a local workforce is not available for a particular project, training programs should be set up to address that gap.[20]

Thoroughly vet volunteers, and be prepared to say no. Background checks, interviews, and rigorous applications should be required of all potential travelers.

Ideally, the final bullet on this list would be to shut down. Unfortunately, that is unrealistic. A multibillion-dollar industry is not going to disappear overnight in response to ethical concerns—even if the industry is rooted in the idea of doing good. However, even if we accept that voluntourism is not going to die out anytime soon, it is still possible to reduce the harm that voluntourism causes through thoughtful trip provider reforms.[21]

The Traveler's Potential

Faster reform is possible from the travelers' side of the equation than from trip providers. The voluntourism industry developed because people wanted to go somewhere exotic and do good—but they needed someone to sort out the logistics. Now, technology is shaking this up. With an ounce of adventurism and a basic understanding of how search engines work, potential travelers may bypass trip providers and take control of creating a more ethical experience.

Travelers choose voluntourism because they want a different list of outcomes than they can achieve from a beach lounger at an all-inclusive resort. Voluntourists often seek status in their community and a résumé boost—although voluntourism is no longer the boon to college and job applications that it once was.[22] Voluntourists hope to return feeling more connected to the issues in their hometown, and more motivated to help—despite little evidence that voluntourism leads to long-term community service at home.[23] Voluntourists want to feel close to people who they have only seen in the pages of *National Geographic*, in documentaries, or on social media.[24] Voluntourists want to grow and develop into better versions of themselves, and they want to feel good about what they have done and the impact they have had.[25]

Voluntourism falls short of most of these aims. Voluntourism neither boosts us up nor makes us engage more. It does not manifest good, nor does it bring us closer to locals than other forms of travel could. It does not fulfill its promises, and it puts the participant at risk of forming a pathological need to save the world.

Just as there is a list of actions trip providers can take to begin to do better, we as travelers have options for how to manifest better outcomes by redirecting our attention to more ethical forms of travel.

Swap out service for engagement by embracing the role of a visitor. Practice respect and deference. Let the hosts direct conversations and activities. Do not assume your right to be in any space. You are a guest.[26]

Be a student of the world. Take the time to sit, observe, and think before consuming. Being conscious of ignorance opens us up to new cultures and new ideas. Learning comes from encountering the unknown in an uncomfortable enough environment that you are set slightly off balance but a safe enough environment that you can absorb what you encounter.[27]

Pay attention to the moral metadata. Every image has a package of data associated with it called metadata, which includes the exposure settings, GPS location, and date. But there is another set of data: *moral metadata.* The moral metadata is written by the photographer and the subject together. It should guide the creation and distribution of every image. Photos can be disempowering and anonymous, taking away the agency of the subject through quick snaps pushed to social media platforms.[28] Alternatively, they can be empowering, serving as evidence of one's existence. The person with the camera decides which kind of moral metadata they manifest. Go in with your camera down. Take pictures carefully. Avoid selfies and staged set-ups. Consider what an image says about the place and the people in it before you share it with anyone else.

Safeguard children. Stop traveling to or supporting orphanages. Do not try to be a teacher, childcare provider, or healthcare professional if you are not qualified to practice in those fields in your home community. Traveler's actions, especially those of voluntourists, are impacting the present and futures for millions of children, leaving marks that can last generations. Absorb this, as it is heavy; act accordingly.[29]

Think globally and act locally. Engaging with issues is good, as is wanting to improve communities. Focus on your own. Learn about how critical issues—hunger, lack of access to healthcare, inadequate education, homelessness, joblessness, pollution, disenfranchisement—impact your hometown. There are no communities on earth that do not face one or more of these challenges. When you travel, be an ethical, thoughtful, and economically impactful tourist. When you are at home, listen, learn, and find ways to dig in.[30]

Although identifying opportunities can sometimes prove challenging, there are places and times when volunteers can be helpful outside of their home communities. The best volunteer outcomes result when a needed skill is applied in a targeted way: high-quality medical care while better, more permanent, systems are being built, engineering and infrastructure development projects, reciprocal teacher training, finance management education, the unsexy stuff. An accountant or grant writer can do more for a local nonprofit than a high schooler with a shovel will ever be able to. If you aspire to create good in the world, pursue a career that will serve you in the scenarios you wish to be in. Emily Scott became a nurse. Larsa Al-Omaishi became a doctor. Michelle Oliel became a human rights lawyer. Aaron Reddecliffe continues to work as a teacher.

If you are impatient, there are conservation and agriculture projects that benefit from the labor voluntourists provide without many of the negative impacts voluntourism typically manifests. Conservation volunteers tend to have a strong grasp of the issues they are trying to combat, both before going on their trips and after returning, and the focus on fieldwork removes much of the community friction and fallout.[31]

Learning to Do Better

In September 2017 Hurricane Maria slammed into Puerto Rico. Two years before, Erin Schrode had gone viral for an image of her carrying a refugee child out of the water of Molyvos Harbor on the island of Lesvos. A lot had happened since then. She had advocated for refugee rights on a global stage. She had been hit by a rubber bullet while protesting the Dakota Access Pipeline at Standing Rock. She had even run for Congress in 2016. Her campaign did not make much headway in her home district, but it did garner nationwide media attention.[32]

Erin had also built a relationship with José Andrés, the world-renowned chef and founder of World Central Kitchen, a nonprofit that provides immediate emergency relief, education, jobs, and opportunities for social enterprises in areas during and after crises.[33] When Hurricane Maria hit Puerto Rico, World Central Kitchen mobilized, and Erin Schrode received a call. The chef wanted her as part of the team. Soon, she was appointed chief operational officer of #ChefsForPuertoRico, an operation that would serve more than 3.6 million meals with the help of more than nineteen thousand volunteers—mostly, Erin says, locals who were themselves grappling with the devastation inflicted on the island.[34]

For the first time in a while, Erin was not the face of the conversation. While she was doing lots of press coordination, it was in the name of the initiative. "It didn't matter to me that the article didn't say my name," she says, reflecting on the experience. "It was a really interesting reminder of why I do what I do. I always knew it, but to not talk about it on social media and to not have my ego or name attached" was eye-opening. She was focused on the job: "When I have the opportunity to do the work or to talk about the work, I am going to do the work."[35]

In the aftermath of the hurricane, all people off of the island saw of Puerto Rico was devastation. Through press and social media, the world witnessed beaches strewn with debris and resorts that looked like King Kong had gone on a rampage. Much of the island went without power for months, and stories of food and water shortages dominated headlines. The portrayal was accurate, but it didn't make for good tourism marketing. So when Puerto Rico was ready to reboot tourism—an industry that forms a foundational piece of the local economy—tourists didn't jump at the opportunity.

"A lot of families and corporations felt guilty about going to Puerto Rico and not contributing," Erin remembers, so they abstained from booking trips. But Puerto Rico needed them. "What we were able to do," she says, "was to offer people meaningful opportunities to volunteer and give back while they were coming to Puerto Rico. . . . We had a lot of vegetables that needed to be chopped."

Puerto Rico did not need voluntourists, but it could use them to get tourists back into the country. The voluntourists would see that the beaches were still beautiful, the food was still delicious, and the people were still welcoming. When they got home, they would spread the word and hopefully inspire others to book vacations sans vegetable chopping. "Disaster porn does not help bring people to an island that is safe, and that is stable," Erin emphasizes. She had learned that voluntourism was often antithetical to sustainable development. Still, in that place, and in that case, voluntourists could begin to rewrite the narrative of Puerto Rico's tourism industry.

Erin's path toward making a positive impact is not one I would recommend to aspiring altruists, but neither is it a dark cautionary tale. It is a true story, a human story. She has been a voluntourist, an activist, and an advocate around the world. After her first trip to Lesvos, she returned to the Mediterranean to continue to bring awareness and aid to people in crisis, and each time she tried to do better by decentering herself and putting the spotlight on others. She is the first to admit that some of her work has been inefficient or has played into stereotypes of white people saving the day in places that could—if empowered—lift themselves off the ground. Like many a former voluntourist, she has learned to do better by making mistakes, but she does not encourage others to treat causing harm as an opportunity for growth.

The realizations that activists like Erin Schrode and Emily Worrall, doctors like Larsa Al-Omaishi, nurses like Emily Scott, teachers like Aaron Reddecliffe, child welfare advocates like Michelle Oliel and Catherine Cottam, and I have had as we have tried and failed to do good have been critical to our

he ways we have stumbled are crucial to a broader understand-
can misstep when empathy runs roughshod over evidence.
es, our mistakes, and our realizations serve best as cautionary
e have erred, others can do better. What we have learned,
others can build upon. What results, I hope, are better ways of engaging,
more productive ways of aiding, and a better world.

It is time to do as we have learned to do better, not as we have done.

15 | On to an End

A more ethical and sustainable future for tourism does exist. It resides somewhere between all-inclusive resorts and boutique safaris, small local hotels and guide companies that may be more scrappy than swanky. Many businesses are already thriving in that middle and are ready to provide exceptional vacation experiences while bringing money to where it needs to be—local communities. This way of traveling is not as easy as paying a flat fee for everything you could possibly need, but it is more fulfilling and certainly more sustainable.

The outputs of sustainable tourism development are often less visually impressive than those of mass tourism. A resort will not spring from the ground in six months. Thousands of people will not cascade out of a cruise ship on any single day. When and where sustainable tourism works, it should build solidarity, promote understanding, support self-sufficiency and sustainability, and maximize local social, cultural, and economic benefits.[1]

To accomplish this, visitor numbers and actions must be managed not just in nature preserves, but in any place that is vulnerable to touristic predation.

Aid needs to be limited to skilled providers and crisis responders. Decisions need to be grounded in local needs, not investor incentives.[2]

The visual impacts of this gradual, thoughtful, and measured development may be slower to materialize, but true progress is a compounding variable, and the positive impacts will always be deeper because they have had time to grow roots. And roots are particularly helpful when things are uncertain and unsteady.

Before the COVID-19 pandemic, the tourism industry was growing practically uninterrupted, from the big multinationals to mom-and-pops.[3] In 2018 more than one in every ten jobs worldwide were related to the tourism industry, and developing economies continued to see rapid growth.[4] This rapid development posed a challenge for developing areas aiming for sustainability even before a global pandemic forced travelers to press pause.[5] If sustainability is a simmer, then what was happening was a rolling boil, and the water was threatening to boil over. In 2019 one pot did. After more than 170 years, Thomas Cook collapsed, stranding thousands of travelers and employees.[6] It has yet to be seen how many airlines, hotels, restaurants, and small businesses COVID-19 takes down, but voluntourism will not be one of the casualties. It's too well suited to crises to be taken out by one. And, of course, when things are uncertain, people want to give back. New York City experienced a 288 percent increase in volunteer applications in March 2020, just as the city was shutting down.[7]

Inequality is systemic not surface.[8] It cannot be solved by building playgrounds, painting walls, distributing pencils, or even drilling wells, but rather through economic engagement, political advocacy, and truly egalitarian exchanges that take place on terms set by host communities. "So much needs to be shifted in the entire way we approach activism, voluntourism, service, and giving back in its entirety," Erin Schrode said while reflecting on her journey from the shores of Lesvos to Puerto Rico, "but the fundamental desire to do good and to collectively better our world is a beautiful notion."[9]

Since 2014, I have spent hundreds of hours in conference halls and classrooms speaking to students (and their teachers and parents) about how to do better at giving back. It has never felt comfortable. Writer Nicholas Kristof uses the term *bridge character* to describe someone like me.[10] I am a palatable white woman whose very appearance neuters "Third-World" narratives so that people can swallow their medicine without feeling threatened. This position has given me a double privilege. When I was younger and a voluntourist, I was celebrated by my community for my selflessness. Now I get to rip apart the very same activity and be celebrated by a different community for my self-awareness. Neither is the full story, and both make me uneasy.

I might be more confident in this role if I had definitive answers, but tourism is personal, so you're going to have to decide what works for you. Read, watch, absorb, act at home, and, yes, travel. But travel as a student of the world, not someone hell-bent on saving it.

Walking away from voluntourism did not magically transform me into the perfect tourist, and I continue to feel a pull toward new places. As I daydream about exploring them, I am still coming to terms with the fact that I will make mistakes, and I will undoubtedly, inadvertently cause harm. Hopefully, the harm will be less than before, the good will be greater than before, and a cosmic scale somewhere in the universe will tip a little more toward equilibrium.

From Thomas Cook and Mary Carpenter to every single traveler today who wishes to leave only positive footprints, the question has rarely been whether our actions come from a place of goodness, but if those good intentions guarantee that lasting good will come of them. Whether you see yourself as an adventurer, a nomad, a traveler, a volunteer, or a tourist, if you itch to explore and your feet always seem to point in a new direction, you are changing the world. The only question left is what kind of change you will choose to make.

ACKNOWLEDGMENTS

Thank you to the friends and family who provided critical notes and feedback throughout this process, especially Ed and Ridgely Biddle, Martha and Candice Bautista-Biddle, Matt Davidson, Ty Tashiro, Caroline Koppelman, Adam Beal, Becca Goldstein, Susan Goldstein, Montana Ortel, and Gillian Stoddard.

Thank you, Paige Abernathy, my first, best, and only research intern. When we first spoke, you said that one of the reasons you wanted to work with me was that you didn't entirely agree with what I had to say. You were intrigued yet skeptical. Your perspective was a gift, and I am so lucky to have had your help early in this project.

Thank you, Neda Bolourchi, for helping me get my citations in order. Thank you, Bridget Barry, my editor at the University of Nebraska Press, for taking a chance on a first-time author. Thank you, Emily Wendell, Tish Fobben, Haley Mendlik, Jackson Adams, and the entire team at the University of Nebraska Press and Potomac Books, for your support, and thank you to Sarah C. Smith from Arbuckle Editorial for catching my spelling mistakes.

Thank you to my agent, Jeff Ourvan. After declining to represent the proposal for this book, you made a proposal of your own. If I were willing to tackle a formidably long list of structural, style, and content changes, you would consider reconsidering. Every item on that list was something that I had wanted to do but was too scared to try. Thank you for challenging me from the start.

Thank you to the instructors at Columbia University who watched this limp along in undergraduate writing workshops, especially Elizabeth Greenwood, Meehan Crist, Michelle Orange, and Kate Zambreno.

Thank you to my teachers at Miss Porter's School who balked at my creative use of commas and enthusiasm for passive voice, especially Jamie Perry, Rick Abrams, and Sarah Dalton Quinn.

Thank you to Jane Goodall and the team at Jane Goodall's Roots & Shoots and the Jane Goodall Institute for giving me a platform when I was eighteen and daring me to use it. A portion of any royalties I receive for this book will be donated to Roots & Shoots, a global movement that empowers and educates young people to make a difference in *their communities*.

On-the-ground experiences form the core of this book, and I have many people to thank for sharing their stories. I am fully aware that not everyone will love how I have portrayed them, but I have striven to retain empathy while prioritizing the truth. Thank you especially to Erin Schrode, Larsa Al-Omaishi, Aaron Reddecliffe, Emily Scott, Catherine Cottam, Corey Pigg, Emily Worrall, Heddwyn Kyambadde, Zion Amanda Kente, Willy Oppenheim, Benjamin Lough, Eric Hartman, Jessica Evert, Leah Missik, Nick Cocalis, Leigh Mathews, Michelle Oliel, Kelsey Nielsen, Olivia Alaso, Peter K. Muthui, Rob Oliver, TMS Ruge, Jamie Wright, Rachel Goble, Ajayi Scott-Robinson, Alexia Honegger, Ali Solomon, Bethany Young, Claire Bennett, Claire Ferguson, Daniela Papi-Thornton, Elana Rabinowitz, Gillian Stoddard, Jacob Taddy, Jamie Sweeting, Justine Abigail Yu, Lauren Biegler, Lonny Grafman, Madara Žgutė, Ruth Wacuka, Stacey Cooper, and the many others who chose to speak anonymously.

If stories have been the core of this project, research has been the scaffolding that holds it all in place. I have relied heavily on the work of talented minds from around the world, especially when writing about places I have not had the chance to visit. The work of the following people has been particularly vital to this project: Mary Mostafanezhad (née Conran), Alexandra Knott, Andrew W. Bailey, Keith C. Russell, Alexandra Coghlan, Andrea Freidus, Carlos M. Palacios, Harng Luh Sin, Victoria Louise Smith, Xavier Font, Martin Mowforth, Ian Munt, Barbara Vodopivec, Rivke Jaffe, Stephen Wearing, and Nancy Gard McGehee.

And then there is Benjamin Quittner Davidson. You are my first editor for every project and my best editor without a shadow of a doubt. Nearly every sentence in this book has you somewhere within it. Thank you.

NOTES

PREFACE

1. I refer to the orphanage and school that we stayed and worked at as Bethsaida. The center is, officially, the outreach arm of the Bethsaida Orphans Education Centre, formerly known as the Olof Palme Orphans Education Centre. While the name change took place in 2005, the names were used interchangeably when I was there in 2009.

1. 1866

1. Carpenter, *Six Months in India*, 153; Mullens, *London and Calcutta*, 38–39.
2. Mullens, *London and Calcutta*, 35–43.
3. Carpenter, *Six Months in India*, 153.
4. Mullens, *London and Calcutta*, 49; "Scenes in British India," *Ballou's Monthly Magazine*, May 1866, 351.
5. Carpenter, *Six Months in India*, 194.
6. Carpenter, *Six Months in India*, 1–4; Ghose, *Women Travellers*; Carpenter, *Life and Work*, 31, 272.
7. Carpenter, *Life and Work*, 8, 29.
8. Carpenter, *Life and Work*, 29, 44–47.
9. Carpenter, *Life and Work*, 51.
10. Carpenter, *Life and Work*, 101, 110.

11. Carpenter, *Life and Work*, 143–47.

12. Carpenter, *Life and Work*, 157–58.

13. "A Lady's Mission to India," *Irish Times and Daily Advertiser*, October 26, 1866.

14. Carpenter, *Six Months in India*, 15.

15. Carpenter, *Six Months in India*, 19.

16. Ghose, *Women Travellers*, 116.

17. "Miss Mary Carpenter in India," *Irish Times and Daily Advertiser*, January 26, 1867; "Miss Carpenter's Interview," *Friends' Intelligencer*, May 16, 1868.

18. "Miss Mary Carpenter in India"; Carpenter, *Six Months in India*, 265.

19. Carpenter, *Six Months in India*, 182.

20. Sorabsha Dadabhai, "Female Education in India," *Manchester Guardian*, December 9, 1868.

21. Dadabhai, "Female Education in India."

2. A CERTAIN KIND OF TOURISM

1. Brendon, *Thomas Cook*, 5; Swinglehurst, *Cook's Tours*.

2. Brendon, *Thomas Cook*, 5, 21–24, 31; Newmeyer, "'Under the Wing of Mr. Cook,'" 243–67.

3. Brendon, *Thomas Cook*, 19–23; Piers Brendon, "Cook, Thomas (1808–1892), Travel Agent," *Oxford Dictionary of National Biography*, https://www.oxforddnb.com/view/10.1093/ref:odnb/9780198614128.001.0001/odnb-9780198614128-e-6152.

4. Brendon, *Thomas Cook*, 23–24.

5. Brendon, *Thomas Cook*, 25.

6. Brendon, *Thomas Cook*, 12.

7. Dickens, *Oliver Twist*.

8. Swinglehurst, *Cook's Tours*, 17.

9. Ghose, *Women Travellers*, 109.

10. Ghose, *Women Travellers*, 110, 124.

11. Bornstein, "Impulse of Philanthropy," 622–51.

12. Brendon, *Thomas Cook*, 6; Swinglehurst, *Cook's Tours*, 8.

13. Brendon, *Thomas Cook*, 6–7; Newmeyer, "'Under the Wing of Mr. Cook,'" 243–67.

14. Brendon, *Thomas Cook*, 32–36.

15. Brendon, *Thomas Cook*, 35–39; Newmeyer, "'Under the Wing of Mr. Cook,'" 243–67.

16. Brendon, *Thomas Cook*, 40–43.

17. Swinglehurst, *Cook's Tours*, 62.

18. Brendon, *Thomas Cook*, 3, 52; Swinglehurst, *Cook's Tours*, 35.

19. Brendon, *Thomas Cook*, 90–92; Auerbach, *Great Exhibition of 1851*, 137.

20. Auerbach, *Great Exhibition of 1851*, 137–38; "Thomas Cook's Revolution," *New York Times*, August 5, 1892.

21. Auerbach, *Great Exhibition of 1851*, 138; Swinglehurst, *Cook's Tours*, 25.

22. Auerbach, *Great Exhibition of 1851*, 137.

23. Auerbach, *Great Exhibition of 1851*; Spicer Brothers, *Official Catalogue of the Great Exhibition*; King, "The Crystal Palace and Great Exhibition of 1851."

24. Brendon, *Thomas Cook*, 57; Auerbach, *Great Exhibition of 1851*, 138.

25. Newmeyer, "'Under the Wing of Mr. Cook'"; Swinglehurst, *Cook's Tours*, 85; Brendon, *Thomas Cook*, 48.

26. Brendon, *Thomas Cook*, 50, 71.

27. Brendon, *Thomas Cook*, 54, 73, 79.

28. Brendon, *Thomas Cook*, 55, 70, 99; Newmeyer, "'Under the Wing of Mr. Cook.'"

29. "Mr. Cook and the Kaiser: Triumphant End of a 'Personally Conducted' Career," *Nashville American*, March 7, 1899; "Death of Mr. John M. Cook: A Remarkable Life History," *Times of India*, March 8, 1899.

30. Swinglehurst, *Cook's Tours*, 82; Brendon, *Thomas Cook*, 100–115.

31. Swinglehurst, *Cook's Tours*, 53; Brendon, *Thomas Cook*, 105.

32. Brendon, *Thomas Cook*, 107–8, 120; Becker, *Overbooked*, 10; Hazbun, "East as an Exhibit," 3–33; "Death of Mr. John M. Cook."

33. Hazbun, "East as an Exhibit," 4.

34. "Recollections of a Tour in Lower Egypt, Palestine and Syria." *Friends' Intelligencer*, April 29, 1876.

35. "Recollections of a Tour"; Smith, *Correspondence of Palestine Tourists*, 198.

36. "Recollections of a Tour"; William W. Patton, "Travels in the Holy Land: The Ride from Beirut to Baalbek and Damascus; Hardship of Tourists: The Cost and the Discomfort of a Trip to Palestine," *Chicago Tribune*, January 13, 1867.

37. Rogers, *Domestic Life in Palestine*, 51; Smith, *Correspondence of Palestine Tourists*, 222; Hazbun, "East as an Exhibit," 8.

38. Smith, *Correspondence of Palestine Tourists*, 200.

39. Brendon, *Thomas Cook*, 134; Rogers, *Domestic Life in Palestine*, 43, 82, 242.

40. "Death of Mr. John M. Cook"; Brendon, *Thomas Cook*, 122; Hazbun, "East as an Exhibit," 6–8, 19; Budge, *Cook's Handbook*.

41. Smith, *Correspondence of Palestine Tourists*, 198; Patton, "Travels in the Holy Land"; Brendon, *Thomas Cook*, 134.

42. Brendon, *Thomas Cook*, 227; Hazbun, "East as an Exhibit," 18; "Death of Mr. John M. Cook"; Swinglehurst, *Cook's Tours*, 88–89, 95, 97.

43. Swinglehurst, *Cook's Tours*, 68.

44. Carpenter, *Six Months in India*, 262; Brendon, *Thomas Cook*, 146–47.

45. Mullens, *London and Calcutta*, 51.

46. Brendon, *Thomas Cook*, 147.

47. Brendon, *Thomas Cook*, 119, 97; Swinglehurst, *Cook's Tours*, 143.

48. "Thomas Cook's Revolution."

49. Brendon, *Thomas Cook*, 155–56, 243, 315.

50. Hazbun, "East as an Exhibit," 11.

51. "Thomas Cook Collapses as Last-Ditch Rescue Talks Fail," BBC *News*, September 23, 2019, https://www.bbc.com/news/business-49791249.

52. Brendon, *Thomas Cook*, 81, 92, 156, 243, 315; Swinglehurst, *Cook's Tours*, 117; Newmeyer, "'Under the Wing of Mr. Cook'"; Hazbun, "East as an Exhibit," 3, 5, 11.

3. CARS, PLANES, AND RESORTS

1. Teo, "Femininity, Modernity, and Colonial Discourse," 173–90; Perkins, "Compagnie Générale," 51; Hazbun, "East as an Exhibit," 3–33.

2. Brendon, *Thomas Cook*, 107–8, 167, 178; Becker, *Overbooked*, 349.

3. Mary Adams Abbott Travel Papers (1920–1927), "Journals and Letters of a Trip Around the World—July 1920 to February 1927," Journals of Mary Adams Abbott, Arthur and Elizabeth Schlesinger Library on the History of Women in America, Radcliffe Institute for Advanced Study, Harvard University, https://iiif.lib.harvard.edu/manifests/view/drs:10472616$1i.

4. Journal Entry, Schlesinger Library, Seq. 105; Journal Entry, Schlesinger Library, Seq. 129.

5. Journal Entry, Schlesinger Library, Seq. 99.

6. Dierikx, *Clipping the Clouds*, 2–5.

7. Becker, *Overbooked*, 9.

8. Swinglehurst, *Cook's Tours*.

9. Dierikx, *Clipping the Clouds*, 9–13.

10. Dierikx, *Clipping the Clouds*, 30–31.

11. Dierikx, *Clipping the Clouds*, 23–24.

12. Swinglehurst, *Cook's Tours*, 167; Becker, *Overbooked*, 52.

13. Perkins, "Compagnie Générale," 44; Hazbun, "East as an Exhibit," 23.

14. Dierikx, *Clipping the Clouds*, 33–36; Becker, *Overbooked*, 9–11.

15. Pattullo, *Last Resorts*, 9; Ward, "A Means of Last Resort."

16. Hazbun, "East as an Exhibit," 28; Pattullo, *Last Resorts*, 21.

17. Dierikx, *Clipping the Clouds*, 58.

18. Swinglehurst, *Cook's Tours*, 107–9.

19. Perkins, "Compagnie Générale," 34–37; Hazbun, "East as an Exhibit," 29; Pattullo, *Last Resorts*, 64.

20. Dann, "People of Tourist Brochures," 72; Swinglehurst, *Cook's Tours*, 116.

21. Brohman, "New Direction in Tourism"; Pattullo, *Last Resorts*, 4, 82.

22. Pattullo, *Last Resorts*, 30–32.

23. Western, "Travelers' Philanthropy," 13–18.

24. Hemmati and Koehler, "Financial Leakages in Tourism," 15–18; Wearing, *Volunteer Tourism*, 146; Mowforth and Munt, *Tourism and Sustainability*, 52.

25. Mary Conran, "They Really Love Me," 1454–73; Brohman, "New Direction in Tourism."

26. Pattullo, *Last Resorts*, 38.

27. Hemmati and Koehler, "Financial Leakages."

28. Daniel Dickinson, "Tourism 'Bypasses' Zanzibar's Locals," BBC *News*, February 17, 2004, http://news.bbc.co.uk/go/pr/fr/-/2/hi/africa/3493533.stm.

29. Pattullo, *Last Resorts*, 38.

30. Dickinson, "Tourism 'Bypasses' Zanzibar's Locals."

31. Brendon, *Thomas Cook*, 80.

32. Becker, *Overbooked*, 10.

33. United Nations World Tourism Organization (UNWTO), "UNWTO Tourism Highlights: 2018 Edition."

34. Becker, *Overbooked*, 307.

35. UNWTO, "UNWTO Tourism Highlights: 2018 Edition"; UNWTO, "UNWTO Tourism Highlights: 2016 Edition"; Center for Responsible Travel, "Case for Responsible Travel."

36. Becker, *Overbooked*, 9.

37. Swinglehurst, *Cook's Tours*, 177; Hazbun, "East as an Exhibit," 13.

38. Patricia Mazzei and Frances Robles, "The Costly Toll of Not Shutting Down Spring Break Earlier," *New York Times*, April 11, 2020, https://www.nytimes.com/2020/04/11/us/florida-spring-break-coronavirus.html; UNWTO, "Community Tourism in Asia"; UNWTO, "UNWTO Tourism Highlights: 2015 Edition"; UNWTO, "UNWTO Tourism Highlights: 2016 Edition."

39. UNWTO, "UNWTO Tourism Highlights: 2018 Edition."

40. UNWTO, "UNWTO Tourism Highlights: 2018 Edition."

41. UNWTO, "UNWTO Tourism Highlights: 2015 Edition"; UNWTO, "UNWTO Tourism Highlights: 2016 Edition"; Center for Responsible Travel, "Case for Responsible Travel."

42. UNWTO, "UNWTO Tourism Highlights: 2016 Edition"; Pattullo, *Last Resorts*, 5; Phelan, "Elephants, Orphans and HIV/AIDS," 127–40.

43. Vodopivec and Jaffe, "Save the World in a Week," 111–28.

44. Pattullo, *Last Resorts*, 52, 55.

45. Hazbun, "East as an Exhibit," 22–33; Pattullo, *Last Resorts*, 75, 204.

46. MacCannell, *Ethics of Sightseeing*, 6; Nash, *Study of Tourism*, 223.

47. Hazbun, "East as an Exhibit," 13; Selwyn, "Introduction," 1.

48. Pattullo, *Last Resorts*, 118.

4. ALTERNATIVE TOURISM

1. US Weekly Staff, "Malawi Orphan to Madonna: 'You Are Our God,'" *US Weekly*, October 28, 2009, https://www.usmagazine.com/celebrity-news/news/madonna-and-david-20092810/.

2. O'Conner et al., "Empathy-Based Pathogenic Guilt," 11–15; Anheier and Salamon, "Volunteering in Cross-National Perspective," 43–65; Krueger, "Altruism Gone Mad," 395–405.

3. Madhavan and Oakley, "Too Much of a Good Thing," 237; Sin, "Selling Ethics," 218–34.

4. Anheier and Salamon, "Volunteering in Cross-National Perspective," 45.

5. Fischer, *Making Them Like Us*, 1–21.

6. Fischer, *Making Them Like Us*, 2.

7. Australian Volunteers International, "Our Program," https://www.australianvolunteers.com/about-us/our-program/ (accessed March 14, 2019).

8. Anheier and Salamon, "Volunteering in Cross-National Perspective," 48.

9. International Voluntary Service, "Our History," https://ivsgb.org/history/ (accessed March 14, 2019).

10. Fischer, *Making Them Like Us*, 2–107.

11. Becker, *Overbooked*, 245–47.

12. Gilbert, "Belated Journeys," 255–73.

13. Becker, *Overbooked*, 245–47; Honey, "Origin and Overview," 5; Pattullo, *Last Resorts*, 118–21.

14. Sin, "Selling Ethics"; Center for Responsible Travel, "Case for Responsible Travel"; Conran, "They Really Love Me," 1454–73; Bailey and Russell, "Predictors of Interpersonal Growth," 352–68.

15. Azarya, "Globalization and International Tourism," 949–67; Palacios, "Volunteer Tourism," 861–78; Egmond, *Understanding Western Tourists*; Western, "Travelers' Philanthropy," 13–18; Pattullo, *Last Resorts*, 121.

16. Xie, *Authenticating Ethnic Tourism*.

17. Gilbert, "Belated Journeys," 259.

18. Western, "Travelers' Philanthropy," 15–16.

19. Becker, *Overbooked*, 263–66.

20. Vodopivec and Jaffe, "Save the World in a Week," 111–28.

21. Pattullo, *Last Resorts*, 39.

22. Brohman, "New Direction in Tourism," 48–70.

23. O'Conner et al., "Empathy-Based Pathogenic Guilt," 16; Moyo, *Dead Aid*, xviii–xix.

24. Mostafanezhad, *Volunteer Tourism*, 85.

25. Berofsky, "Is Pathological Altruism Altruism?," 264; Vilardaga and Hayes, "A Contextual Behavioral Approach," 31.

26. Honey, "Origin and Overview," 8.

27. Chen and Chen, "Motivations and Expectations," 435–42; Sin, "Volunteer Tourism"; Coles et al., "Post-Disciplinary Tourism," 80–100.

28. Egmond, *Understanding Western Tourists*, 108; Vodopivec and Jaffe, "Development and Difference"; Sin, "Selling Ethics."

29. Richter, "Inside the Thriving Industry," 6–8.

30. Mowforth and Munt, *Tourism and Sustainability*, 2; Mostafanezhad, *Volunteer Tourism*, 34; Lyons et al., "Gap Year Volunteer Tourism."

5. THE AGE OF VOLUNTOURISM

1. *Invisible Children*, documentary, 2016.

2. Emily Scott, co-creator of *Two Dusty Travelers* blog, in discussion with author, by phone, June 22 and August 14, 2018.

3. Mostafanezhad, *Volunteer Tourism*, 35.

4. Novelli, *Tourism and Development*, 148; Wearing and McGehee, "Volunteer Tourism," 120–30.

5. Mostafanezhad, *Volunteer Tourism*, 35.

6. Wearing and McGehee, "Volunteer Tourism"; McGehee, "Volunteer Tourism," 847–54.

7. Mostafanezhad, *Volunteer Tourism*, 41.

8. Mostafanezhad, *Volunteer Tourism*, 42.

9. McGehee, "Volunteer Tourism," 847; Benson, "Why and How," 100; Chen and Chen, "Motivations and Expectations," 435–42.

10. Wearing and McGehee, "Volunteer Tourism," 121.

11. Wearing and McGehee, "Volunteer Tourism," 121; Lough, "International Volunteering," 1–2; Knott, "Guests on the Aegean," 349–66.

12. Lough, "Volunteering from the United States," 2.

13. Lough, "Volunteering from the United States," 3–4; Mowforth and Munt, *Tourism and Sustainability*, 127; Rehberg, "Altruistic Individualists," 109–22.

14. Wearing, *Volunteer Tourism*, 2.

15. Lough, "Volunteering from the United States," 5; Sin, "Who Are We Responsible To?," 987.

16. Chen and Chen, "Motivations and Expectations," 436; Bailey and Russell, "Volunteer Tourism," 1; Wearing and McGehee, "Volunteer Tourism," 121; McGehee, "Volunteer Tourism," 848.

17. Sin, "Who Are We Responsible To?," 987; Sin et al., "Traveling for a Cause," 119–31.

18. Mowforth and Munt, *Tourism and Sustainability*, 126; Sin et al., "Traveling for a Cause," 120.

19. Sherraden et al., "Effects of International Volunteering," 395–421.

20. Honey, "Origin and Overview," 3–12.

21. Rovner, "Next Generation of American Giving"; Rovner, "Next Generation of Canadian Giving"; Rovner et al., "Next Generation of Australian and New Zealander Giving"; Rovner et al., "Next Generation of UK Giving."

22. McGehee, "Volunteer Tourism," 848; Knott, "Guests on the Aegean."

23. Coghlan and Noakes, "Towards an Understanding," 7.

24. Wearing and McGehee, "Volunteer Tourism," 120.

25. Coghlan and Noakes, "Towards an Understanding," 7.

26. Farley, "Potential Short-Term International Volunteers' Perceptions," 4.

27. Coghlan and Noakes, "Towards an Understanding," 4; Mostafanezhad, *Volunteer Tourism*, 35.

28. Coghlan and Noakes, "Towards an Understanding," 4.

29. McGloin and Georgeou, "'Looks Good on Your CV,'" 403–17; Vodopivec and Jaffe, "Save the World in a Week," 111–28.

30. Chen and Chen, "Motivations and Expectations," 435; Bailey and Russell, "Volunteer Tourism," 1.

31. Lyons et al., "Gap Year Volunteer Tourism," 361–78.

32. Ethan Knight, executive director of Gap Year Association, "Press Question—Market Size," email discussion with author, April 9, 2019.

33. Egmond, *Understanding Western Tourists*, 105; Smith and Font, "Volunteer Tourism, Greenwashing," 942–63; Coghlan and Noakes, "Towards an Understanding," 3; Rattan, "Is Certification the Answer?," 108.

34. ME to WE, "FAQ," https://www.metowe.com/about-us/faq/ (accessed August 30, 2018).

35. ME to WE, "About Us," https://www.metowe.com/about-us/; ME to WE, "FAQ."

36. ME to WE, "FAQ."

37. ME to WE, "Ecuador," https://www.metowe.com/trips/volunteer-travel/university -trips/ecuador/ (accessed April 5, 2019).

38. Jessica Murphy, "WE Charity Scandal—A Simple Guide to the New Crisis for Trudeau," *BBC News*, July 26, 2020, https://www.bbc.com/news/world-us-canada-53494560.

39. Jaren Kerr, "Inside the 'Cult' of Kielburger," Canadaland, June 25, 2019, https://www .canadalandshow.com/inside-the-cult-of-kielburger/.

40. Projects Abroad, "Medicine Internships in Argentina for Teenagers," https://www .projects-abroad.org/projects/medicine-internship-for-teens-spanish-argentina/ (accessed April 5, 2019); Projects Abroad, "Volunteer with Children in Ghana," https://

www.projects-abroad.org/projects/volunteer-childcare-ghana/ (accessed April 5, 2019).

41. Smith and Font, "Volunteer Tourism, Greenwashing," 945.

42. Bailey and Russell, "Predictors of Interpersonal Growth."

43. Laing and Frost, *Explorer Travellers and Adventure Tourism*, 30; Vodopivec and Jaffe, "Development and Difference," 114; Susan Carey, "The Virtuous Vacation?—More Travelers Sweat, Teach as Volunteers on Time Off; The Burden of Do-Gooders," *Wall Street Journal*, July 27, 2001; Chen and Chen, "Motivations and Expectations," 436; Cater, "Meaning of Adventure," 7–18.

44. Freidus, "Unanticipated Outcomes," 1315–18; Boluk et al., "Exploring the Expectations," 272–85; Bornstein, "Impulse of Philanthropy," 622–51.

45. Bjerneld et al., "Motivations, Concerns, and Expectations," 49–58.

46. Rehberg, "Altruistic Individualists," 118; Boluk et al., "Exploring the Expectations," 277; Richter, "Inside the Thriving Industry," 6–8.

47. Bailey and Russell, "Powerful Programs," 7–8; Richter, "Inside the Thriving Industry," 7.

48. Mostafanezhad, *Volunteer Tourism*, 120.

49. Anheier and Salamon, "Volunteering in Cross-National Perspective," 43–65.

50. Vodopivec and Jaffe, "Development and Difference," 117.

51. Palacios, "Volunteer Tourism," 861–78; Vodopivec and Jaffe, "Development and Difference," 122; Anheier and Salamon, "Volunteering in Cross-National Perspective," 65; Rob Oliver, education and advocacy at Stahili, "Re: Questions Re: Stahili and Orphanage Tourism," email discussion with author, July 30, 2018; Simpson, "'Doing Development,'" 681–92.

52. Frank Bruni, "To Get to Harvard, Go to Haiti?," *New York Times*, August 13, 2016, https://www.nytimes.com/2016/08/14/opinion/sunday/to-get-to-harvard-go-to -haiti.html.

53. Boluk et al., "Exploring the Expectations," 277; McGloin and Georgeou, "'Looks Good on Your CV,'" 414.

54. Easterly, *White Man's Burden*, 272.

55. Vodopivec and Jaffe, "Development and Difference," 118.

56. Smith and Font, "Volunteer Tourism, Greenwashing," 943.

57. Mostafanezhad, *Volunteer Tourism*, 41–42; Egmond, *Understanding Western Tourists*, 108; Mowforth and Munt, *Tourism and Sustainability*, 293.

58. Sin, "Selling Ethics," 218–34.

59. Caton and Santos, "Selling Study Abroad," 191–204.

60. Daye, "Re-visioning Caribbean Tourism," 19–43; Dann, "People of Tourist Brochures," 61–81.

61. Butcher, "Against 'Ethical Tourism,'" 244–60; McGloin and Georgeou, "'Looks Good on Your CV,'" 410.

62. United Nations, "Frequently Asked Questions," https://www.un.org/development/desa/youth/what-we-do/faq.html (accessed November 20, 2019).

63. Hartman et al., "Fair Trade Learning," 108–16.

64. Brendon, *Thomas Cook*, 30.

65. WE Charity, "WE Day Events," August 30, 2018, https://www.we.org/we-day/we-day-events/.

66. Chen and Chen, "Motivations and Expectations," 438; Vodopivec and Jaffe, "Development and Difference," 118; Pan, "Motivations of Volunteer Overseas," 1493–1501.

67. Smith and Font, "Volunteer Tourism, Greenwashing," 945–46.

68. Pan, "Motivations," 1497; Phelan, "Elephants, Orphans and HIV/AIDS," 127–40; Sin, "Volunteer Tourism," 480–501.

69. Clary and Snyder, "Motivations to Volunteer," 156–59.

70. Easton and Wise, "Online Portrayals," 141–58; Vodopivec and Jaffe, "Development and Difference," 119–20.

71. Lough, "Volunteering from the United States," 2.

72. Center for Responsible Travel, "Case for Responsible Travel."

73. Wearing and McGehee, "Volunteer Tourism," 123.

74. Lough, "Volunteering from the United States," 2.

75. Volunteering Solutions, "Global Volunteer Abroad Report by Volunteering Solutions," https://www.volunteeringsolutions.com/blog/global-volunteer-abroad-trends/ (accessed November 20, 2019).

76. McGloin and Georgeou, "'Looks Good on Your CV,'" 414.

77. Lough, "Volunteering from the United States," 2.

78. Benjamin Lough, associate professor, University of Illinois, phone interview with author, December 13, 2018.

79. Clary and Snyder, "Motivations to Volunteer," 157.

80. Pan, "Motivations"; Rehberg, "Altruistic Individualists."

6. COLONIAL PATHOLOGIES

1. Gilbert and Johnston, "Introduction," 1–19.

2. Brendon, *Thomas Cook*, 167.

3. Mowforth and Munt, *Tourism and Sustainability*, 76–77; Said, *Orientalism*; Gilbert and Johnston, "Introduction," 7.

4. Mowforth and Munt, *Tourism and Sustainability*, 53.

5. Hazbun, "East as an Exhibit," 3–33.

6. Hazbun, "East as an Exhibit," 30.

7. Pattullo, *Last Resorts*, 63.

8. Teo, "Femininity, Modernity, and Colonial Discourse," 173–90.

9. Mary Adams Abbott Travel Papers (1920–1927), "Journals and Letters of a Trip Around the World—July 1920 to February 1927," Journals of Mary Adams Abbott, Arthur and Elizabeth Schlesinger Library on the History of Women in America, Radcliffe Institute for Advanced Study, Harvard University, https://iiif.lib.harvard.edu/manifests/view/drs:10472616$1i.

10. Sin, "Volunteer Tourism," 480–501.

11. Sin, "Who Are We Responsible To?," 983–92; Pattullo, *Last Resorts*, 82–83.

12. Barbieri et al., "Volunteer Tourism," 509–16.

13. Heddwyn Kyambadde, filmmaker, in discussion with author, October 22, 2018.

14. Sin, "Who Are We Responsible To?," 990.

15. "Greek Coastguard Rescues 242 Migrants as Boat Sinks, Three Drown," *Reuters*, October 28, 2015, https://www.reuters.com/article/us-migrants-greece-shipwreck/greek-coastguard-rescues-242-migrants-as-boat-sinks-three-drown-idUSKCN0SM2MI20151028.

16. Schrode, interviews, March 4, 2016, March 6, 2016, February 19, 2016.

17. Strauss, *Between the Eyes*, 74.

18. Sontag, "In Plato's Cave," 3–24.

19. Palacios, "Volunteer Tourism," 861–78.

20. Campbell and Smith, "What Makes Them Pay?," 84–98; Sin, "Involve Me," 493; Strauss, *Between the Eyes*, 74.

21. Conran, "They Really Love Me," 1454–73.

22. O'Conner et al., "Empathy-Based Pathogenic Guilt," 10–30.

23. Oakley et al., "Pathological Altruism—An Introduction," 3–9.

24. Brin, "Self-Addiction and Self-Righteousness," 77–84; Conran, "They Really Love Me," 1465.

25. Wright, *Very Worst Missionary*, 166–67.

26. O'Conner et al., "Empathy-Based Pathogenic Guilt," 12.

27. Karen Myers, "The Story So Far: Jesus and the Mural," *Chimes*, April 15, 2010, https://chimesnewspaper.com/12800/archives/features/jesus-mural-sofar/.

28. TheJesusMural, "Biola Jesus Mural 'Forum,'" 8:40.

29. Mike Fillon, "The Real Face of Jesus," *Popular Mechanics*, January 13, 2015, https://www.popularmechanics.com/science/health/a234/1282186/.

30. Teju Cole, "The White-Savior Industrial Complex," *The Atlantic*, March 21, 2012, www.theatlantic.com/international/archive/2012/03/the-white-savior-industrial-complex/254843/.

31. Knott, "Guests on the Aegean," 349–66; Caton and Santos, "Selling Study Abroad," 191–204.

32. Pattullo, *Last Resorts*, 62.

33. UNWTO, "UNWTO Tourism Highlights: 2018 Edition," 14.

34. Becker, *Overbooked*, 228.

7. FAITH, PURPOSE, AND MISSION

Epigraph. Matthew 28:19–20 (King James Version).

1. Megan Specia, "American's Death Revives Evangelical Debate over Extreme Missionary Work," *New York Times*, December 2, 2018, https://www.nytimes.com/2018/12/02 / world/asia/john-chau-missionary-evangelical.html.

2. Paxton et al., "Volunteering and the Dimensions of Religiosity," 597–625.

3. Anheier and Salamon, "Volunteering in Cross-National Perspective," 43–65.

4. Jeffrey Gettleman, Kai Schultz, Ayesha Venkataraman, and Hari Kumar, "John Chau Aced Missionary Boot Camp; Reality Proved a Harsher Test," *New York Times*, November 20, 2018, https://www.nytimes.com/2018/11/30/world/asia/john-chau -andaman-missionary.html.

5. Lough, "International Volunteering," 1, 4; Sherraden et al., "Effects of International Volunteering," 395–421.

6. YWAM, "YWAM History," https://www.ywam.org/about-us/history/ (accessed April 1, 2019).

7. YWAM, "How Do I Choose a DTS?," https://www.ywam.org/training/how-do-i -choose-a-dts/ (accessed April 1, 2019).

8. YWAM East London, "Schools," https://www.ywameastlondon.com/products-/ (accessed April 1, 2019, site discontinued).

9. YWAM Yosemite, "Sierra Discipleship Training School," https://www.ywamyosemite .org/sierradts (accessed April 1, 2019).

10. YWAM, "Join Staff," https://www.ywam.org/get-involved-2/join-staff/ (accessed April 1, 2019).

11. "Missionary Group Thrust into Limelight after Colorado Shootings," *FOX News*, December 11, 2007, https://www.foxnews.com/story/missionary-group-thrust-into -limelight-after-colorado-shootings.

12. James Kassaga Arinaitwe and Viviane Rutabingwa, "Why Many Ugandans Are Offended by Music Video Made By U.S. Missionaries," *NPR*, October 21, 2016, https:// www.npr.org/sections/goatsandsoda/2016/10/21/498840456/why-many-ugandans -are-offended-by-music-video-made-by-u-s-missionaries.

13. Gilbert, "Belated Journeys," 255–73.

14. Jackie Kramlich and Emily Worrall, Instagram post, March 7, 2016, https://www .instagram.com/p/BCq-c2csfYR/ (accessed April 12, 2019).

15. Jackie Kramlich and Emily Worrall, Instagram post, March 29, 2016, https://www .instagram.com/p/BDivxtLsfX8/ (accessed April 12, 2019).

16. Jackie Kramlich and Emily Worrall, Instagram post, April 16, 2016, https://www
    .instagram.com/p/BERW7Vvsffu/ (accessed April 12, 2019).

17. Sin and He, "Voluntouring on Facebook and Instagram," 215–37.

18. OBrien, "Business, Management and Poverty Reduction," 33–46; Sin and He, "Vol-
    untouring on Facebook and Instagram," 221; Teju Cole, "When the Camera Was a
    Weapon of Imperialism (And When It Still Is)," *New York Times Magazine*, February
    6, 2019, https://www.nytimes.com/2019/02/06/magazine/when-the-camera-was-a
    -weapon-of-imperialism-and-when-it-still-is.html; Caton and Santos, "Selling Study
    Abroad," 191–204.

19. Edwards, "Postcards," 196–221.

20. MacCannell, *Ethics of Sightseeing*, 10.

21. Mowforth and Munt, *Tourism and Sustainability*, 288; Azarya, "Globalization and
    International Tourism," 949–67; Egmond, *Understanding Western Tourists*, 58.

22. Knott, "Guests on the Aegean," 349–66.

23. Mostafanezhad, *Volunteer Tourism*, 57, 105–6.

24. Emily Worrall, co-creator of Barbie Savior, in discussion with author, August 1, 2018.

25. "Our Story," Ekisa Ministries, https://www.ekisa.org/our-story (accessed April 13,
    2019).

26. Conran, "They Really Love Me," 1454–73; Bjerneld et al., "Motivations, Concerns,
    and Expectations," 49–58.

27. Corey Pigg, creator, Failed Missionary Podcast, in discussion with author, October
    4, 2018.

28. David Joel Hamilton, "Official Letter from David Joel Hamilton to the YWAM
    Community," March 8, 2019, https://static1.squarespace.com/static
    /5854bbb5414fb59a9522c122/t/5c9a9ff58165f53527f4781d/1553637365104/fc
    -General-Letter-on-Sex-and-Marriage-FINAL.pdf.

29. Specia, "American's Death."

30. YWAM, "Join Staff."

31. "Missionary Group Thrust into Limelight."

32. Wright, *Very Worst Missionary*, 135.

33. Specia, "American's Death."

34. Gettleman et al., "John Chau."

35. McGehee, "Volunteer Tourism," 847–54.

36. Wright, *Very Worst Missionary*, 133.

37. Specia, "American's Death."

38. Gettleman et al., "John Chau."

39. Gettleman et al., "John Chau"; Specia, "American's Death."

40. Gettleman et al., "John Chau."

41. Gettleman et al., "John Chau"; Specia, "American's Death."

42. Nick Cocalis, former executive director of Next Step Ministries, in discussion with author, September 7, 2018.

43. Next Step Ministries, "Worship and Programming," https://nextstepministries.com /worship/ (accessed April 28, 2019).

44. Next Step Ministries, "About Us," https://nextstepministries.com/about-us/ (accessed April 25, 2020).

45. MyStep, "MyStep," http://mystep.me/ (accessed April 28, 2019).

46. Next Step Ministries, "Sumpango, Guatemala," https://nextstepministries.com /sumpango-guatemala-2/ (accessed April 28, 2019).

47. Next Step Ministries, "Fairbanks, Alaska," https://nextstepministries.com/fairbanks -alaska/ (accessed April 28, 2019).

48. Next Step Ministries, "About Us."

49. Next Step Ministries, "About Us: Annual Reports," https://nextstepministries.com /about-us/annual-reports/ (accessed April 28, 2019).

50. Next Step Ministries, "Worship and Programming."

8. THE DEVELOPMENT CONUNDRUM

1. Borglund, "Governing the Commons."

2. Sin et al., "Traveling for a Cause," 119–31; UNWTO, "UNWTO Tourism Highlights: 2018 Edition," 5.

3. Sin, "Who Are We Responsible To?," 983–92.

4. Mostafanezhad, *Volunteer Tourism*, 144.

5. "Kielburger to Guelph Students: 'You Can Change the World,'" *Guelph Mercury Tribune*, March 20, 2012, https://www.guelphmercury.com/news-story/2782386 -kielburger-to-guelph-students-you-can-change-the-world-/.

6. Novelli, *Tourism and Development*, 148–51.

7. Smith and Font, "Volunteer Tourism, Greenwashing," 942–63; Fadnis, "Good Travels," 11.

8. Global Crossroad, "Program Fees," https://www.globalcrossroad.com/programfee _go.php (accessed May 7, 2020).

9. Global Crossroad, "Program Fees."

10. Projects Abroad, "Why We Charge a Fee," https://www.projects-abroad.org/how-it -works/why-we-charge-a-fee/ (accessed May 7, 2020).

11. Juliana Ruhfus, "Cambodia's Orphan Business," *Al Jazeera*, June 27, 2012, https:// www.aljazeera.com/programmes/peopleandpower/2012/05/201252243030438171 .html.

12. Barbieri et al., "Volunteer Tourism," 509–16.

13. Carey, "Virtuous Vacation."

14. Lyons et al., "Gap Year Volunteer Tourism," 361–78.

15. Simpson, "'Doing Development,'" 681–92; Bailey and Russell, "Volunteer Tourism," 1–10.

16. Leigh Mathews, founder of ALTO Global Consulting and co-founder of ReThink Orphanages, in discussion with author, December 9, 2018.

17. Mostafanezhad, *Volunteer Tourism*, 119.

18. Ashley and Haysom, "From Philanthropy to a Different Way," 265–80; Coghlan and Noakes, "Towards an Understanding," 123–31.

19. Vodopivec and Jaffe, "Save the World in a Week," 111–28.

20. Sin, "Who Are We Responsible To?," 986–90.

21. Vodopivec and Jaffe, "Development and Difference," 120; Mowforth and Munt, *Tourism and Sustainability*, 79.

22. Rattan, "Is Certification the Answer?," 107; Azarya, "Globalization and International Tourism," 949–67.

23. Alexandra Knott, "Colonialism in Development: Partners' Reflections," *Omprakash Blog*, December 10, 2018, https://www.omprakash.org/blog/colonialism-in-development.

24. Novelli, *Tourism and Development*, 165–66.

25. Novelli, *Tourism and Development*, 165–66; Simpson, "'Doing Development,'" 685, 687–88; Mowforth and Munt, *Tourism and Sustainability*, 79.

26. Greer, *Stop Helping Us*; Sin, "Who Are We Responsible To?," 984, 988; Cole, "White-Savior Industrial Complex."

27. Moyo, *Dead Aid*, 44.

28. Moyo, *Dead Aid*, 44.

29. Freidus, "Unanticipated Outcomes," 1306–21.

30. Vodopivec and Jaffe, "Development and Difference," 117–20.

31. Conran, "They Really Love Me," 1454–73.

32. Mowforth and Munt, *Tourism and Sustainability*, xii.

33. Anonymous business owner, Río Limpio, Dominican Republic, in discussion with Chase Wonderlic on behalf of author, August 1, 2016.

34. Vodopivec and Jaffe, "Development and Difference," 113.

35. Emily Worrall, co-creator of Barbie Savior, in discussion with author, August 1, 2018.

36. Sin, "Who Are We Responsible To?," 991; Madhavan and Oakley, "Too Much of a Good Thing," 237–45; Smith and Font, "Volunteer Tourism, Greenwashing," 947.

37. Wolff, "Survey of Tour Operators," 150–58.

38. Greer, *Stop Helping Us*, 21.

9. PLAYING DOCTOR

1. Larsa Al-Omaishi, in discussion with author, August 12, 2017, August 19, 2017, August 31, 2018.

2. International Volunteer HQ, "Volunteer in Tanzania," https://www.volunteerhq.org/volunteer-in-tanzania/ (accessed May 7, 2019).

3. Save Africa Orphanage, "Homepage," https://saveafricatanzania.weebly.com/ (accessed May 7, 2019).

4. New Hope Initiative, "Homepage," http://newhopeinitiative.org (accessed May 7, 2019).

5. Larsa Al-Omaishi, "Larsa Follow-Up Survey with IVHQ," December 7, 2013 (on file with author).

6. Al-Omaishi, "Larsa Follow-Up Survey with IVHQ."

7. International Volunteer HQ, "Volunteer in Tanzania."

8. Dan Radcliffe, "Why We Support Orphanage Volunteering," *Volunteer Travel Blog*, February 10, 2018, https://www.volunteerhq.org/blog/why-we-support-orphanage-volunteering/.

9. Emily Scott, co-creator of *Two Dusty Travelers* blog, in discussion with author, June 22; August 14, 2018.

10. Carey, "Virtuous Vacation"; Easton and Wise, "Online Portrayals," 141–58.

11. Child Family Health International, "CFHI Impact Report," 2018, https://www.cfhi.org/sites/default/files/pdf/ar2017.pdf; Child Family Health International, "All Programs," https://www.cfhi.org/all-programs (accessed May 7, 2019).

12. Seymour et al., "Voluntourism and Global Health," 1252–57.

13. Jessica Evert, executive director of Child Family Health International, in discussion with author, November 23, 2018.

14. "Nepal Earthquakes: Devastation in Maps and Images," *BBC News*, May 15, 2015, https://www.bbc.com/news/world-asia-32479909.

15. Global Outreach Doctors, "Nepal Earthquake Relief," https://www.globaloutreachdoctors.org/team-work/nepal-earthquake-relief/ (accessed May 7, 2019).

10. TEACHING CHILDREN

1. Sin, "Who Are We Responsible To?," 983–92; Barbieri et al., "Volunteer Tourism," 509–16; Raymond and Hall, "Development of Cross-Cultural (Mis)Understanding," 530–43.

2. Aaron Reddecliffe, co-creator of *Two Dusty Travelers* blog, in discussion with author, November 16, 2018.

3. Sin, "Realities of Doing Responsibilities," 95–193.

4. Raintree Farms, "Raintree Farms," www.raintreefarms.com (accessed May 7, 2019).

5. TMS Ruge, entrepreneur, in discussion with author, June 28, 2018.

6. Mostafanezhad, *Volunteer Tourism*, 104, 107, 111; Knott, "Colonialism in Development"; Palacios, "Volunteer Tourism," 861–78.

7. Sin, "Volunteer Tourism," 480–501; Lyons et al., "Gap Year Volunteer Tourism," 361–78; O'Conner et al., "Empathy-Based Pathogenic Guilt," 10–30.

11. ORPHANAGES

1. A Broader View, "Volunteer Abroad Orphanage Assistance Programs—America, Asia, Africa," https://www.abroaderview.org/programs/orphanage-support (accessed July 10, 2019).

2. Catherine Cottam, volunteer at Stahili, in discussion with author, July 11, 2018.

3. Richter and Norman, "AIDS Orphan Tourism," 217–29.

4. UNICEF, "Orphans," https://www.unicef.org/media/orphans (accessed May 6, 2020).

5. Richter and Norman, "AIDS Orphan Tourism," 219; Havens, "Harms of Orphanage Voluntourism," 1.

6. Phelan, "Elephants, Orphans and HIV/AIDS," 127–40; "Australia Says Orphanage Trafficking Is Modern-Day Slavery," *BBC News*, November 29, 2018, https://www.bbc.com/news/world-australia-46390627; Becker, *Overbooked*, 102; "Bali's Orphanage Scam," *Bali Advertiser* (blog), 2010, https://www.baliadvertiser.biz/orphanage/; Havens, "Harms of Orphanage Voluntourism," 3.

7. Richter and Norman, "AIDS Orphan Tourism," 222–25.

8. Farley, "Potential Short-Term International Volunteers' Perceptions," 4.

9. Ruhfus, "Cambodia's Orphan Business"; Guiney and Mostafanezhad, "Political Economy of Orphanage Tourism," 132–55.

10. "Australia Says"; "Bali's Orphanage Scam."

11. Guiney and Mostafanezhad, "Political Economy of Orphanage Tourism," 143, 147; Sin and He, "Voluntouring on Facebook and Instagram," 215–37.

12. James 1:27 (King James Version).

13. Wright, *Very Worst Missionary*; Havens, "Harms of Orphanage Voluntourism," 19.

14. Brin, "Self-Addiction and Self-Righteousness," 77–84.

15. Boluk et al., "Exploring the Expectations," 272–85.

16. Sin, "Who Are We Responsible To?," 983–92.

17. Peter K. Muthui, founder, Child in Family Focus–Kenya, "Following up from panel," email discussion with author, April 1, 2019.

18. *The Love You Give*, documentary, Better Care Network, UK, 2019.

19. World Challenge, "Orphanage Position Statement," http://www.worldchallenge.com.au/documents/orphanage-position-statement.pdf (accessed April 1, 2019); World Challenge, "Homepage," https://weareworldchallenge.com/northamerica/ (accessed April 1, 2019).

20. Lumos, "Homepage," https://www.wearelumos.org/ (accessed July 10, 2019).

21. Leigh Mathews, founder of Alto Global Consulting and co-founder of ReThink Orphanages, in discussion with author, December 9, 2018.

22. "Australia Says."

23. Sin and He, "Voluntouring on Facebook and Instagram," 235; "Australia Says."

24. Richter, "Inside the Thriving Industry," 6–8; Richter and Norman, "AIDS Orphan Tourism," 221–22.

25. Ainsworth, "Infant–Mother Attachment," 932–37; Bowlby, *Attachment and Loss*.

26. Ruhfus, "Cambodia's Orphan Business"; Mikulincer and Shaver, "Attachment Security," 34–38.

27. "Bali's Orphanage Scam."

28. Christopher Knaus, "The Race to Rescue Cambodian Children from Orphanages Exploiting Them for Profit," *Guardian*, August 18, 2017, https://www.theguardian.com/world/2017/aug/19/the-race-to-rescue-cambodian-children-from-orphanages-exploiting-them-for-profit; Becker, *Overbooked*, 102.

29. Bridie Jabour, "Orphanage Shut down amid Child Abuse Allegations," *Brisbane Times*, March 25, 2013, https://www.brisbanetimes.com.au/national/queensland/orphanage-shut-down-amid-child-abuse-allegations-20130325-2goon.html; Simon Henderson and Phok Dorn, "Police Shut Down Orphanages Accused of Neglect, Sexual Abuse," *Cambodia Daily*, March 26, 2013, https://www.cambodiadaily.com/news/police-shut-down-orphanages-accused-of-neglect-sexual-abuse-15909/.

30. Ruhfus, "Cambodia's Orphan Business."

31. Dallas Franklin, "Judge Sentences Oklahoma Man Convicted of Abusing Orphans to 40 Years in Prison," *KFOR*, March 7, 2016, https://kfor.com/2016/03/07/judge-scheduled-to-hand-down-sentence-for-oklahoma-man-convicted-of-abusing-orphans/.

32. "British Airways Pays Pilot Simon Wood Africa Abuse Victims," *BBC News*, March 4, 2016, https://www.bbc.com/news/uk-england-35724038.

33. "Americans Accused of Defiling Orphans in Bomet."

34. Faith Karimi, "Pennsylvania Missionary Arrested for Allegedly Abusing Children at an Orphanage in Kenya," *CNN*, July 13, 2019, https://www.cnn.com/2019/07/13/us/pennsylvania-man-accused-of-abuse-kenya/index.html.

35. "US Missionary Gregory Dow Pleads Guilty to Sex Crimes in Kenya Orphanage," *BBC News*, June 16, 2020, https://www.bbc.com/news/world-africa-53067259.

36. Havens, "Harms of Orphanage Voluntourism," 17–19.

37. Freidus, "Unanticipated Outcomes," 1306–21.

38. "Bali's Orphanage Scam."

39. Becker, *Overbooked*, 102.

40. Havens, "Harms of Orphanage Voluntourism," 19.

41. Kathryn Joyce, "The Trouble with the Christian Adoption Movement," *New Republic*, January 11, 2016, https://newrepublic.com/article/127311/trouble-christian-adoption-movement; Bethany Christian Services, "About Us," https://bethany.org/about-us (accessed May 15, 2019).

42. Bethany Christian Services, "U.S. International Adoption," https://bethany.org/help -a-child/adoption/us-international-adoption (accessed May 15, 2019).

43. Havens, "Harms of Orphanage Voluntourism," 24.

44. Maura R. O'Connor, "Two Years Later, Haitian Earthquake Death Toll in Dispute," *Columbia Journalism Review*, January 12, 2012, https://archives.cjr.org/behind_the _news/one_year_later_haitian_earthqu.php.

45. Ginger Thompson, "Case Stokes Haiti's Fear for Children, and Itself," *New York Times*, February 1, 2010, https://www.nytimes.com/2010/02/02/world/americas /02orphans.html.

46. Marc Lacey, "Haiti Charges Americans with Child Abduction," *New York Times*, February 4, 2010, https://www.nytimes.com/2010/02/05/world/americas/05orphans.html.

47. Marc Lacey and Ian Urbina, "Adviser to Americans Jailed in Haiti Is Arrested," *New York Times*, March 19, 2010, https://www.nytimes.com/2010/03/20/world/americas /20puello.html.

48. "American Freed from Haitian Jail," *New York Times*, March 8, 2010, https://www .nytimes.com/2010/03/09/world/americas/09haiti.html; CNN Wire Staff, "U.S. Missionary Held in Haiti Is Free, Lawyer Says," *CNN*, May 17, 2010, http://www.cnn .com/2010/CRIME/05/17/haiti.silsby.freed/index.html.

49. Richter, "Inside the Thriving Industry," 7.

50. Ruhfus, "Cambodia's Orphan Business."

51. Stephen Ucembe and Jessica Festa, "What It's Really like to Grow Up in an 'Orphanage' in Kenya," *Epicure & Culture* (blog), May 26, 2016, https://epicureandculture .com/like-grow-orphanage-kenya-around-voluntourists/; Phelan, "Elephants, Orphans and HIV/AIDS," 137–38.

52. Burton, "Pathological Certitude," 131–37.

53. Nick Cocalis, former executive director of Next Step Ministries, in discussion with author, September 7, 2018.

54. Peter K. Muthui, founder, Child in Family Focus–Kenya, "Following Up from Panel," email discussion with author, April 1, 2019.

55. Radcliffe, "Why We Support Orphanage Volunteering."

56. Cottam, interview, July 11, 2018.

57. Krueger, "Altruism Gone Mad," 395–405.

58. Michelle Oliel, executive director of Stahili, in discussion with author, January 7, 2019.

59. Oliel, interview, January 7, 2019.

60. Kirithani Kenya African Orphanage Child Labor, Abuse and Corruption, Facebook page, December 13, 2013, https://www.facebook.com/watotowabaraka/ (accessed November 29, 2018).

61. Palacios, "Volunteer Tourism," 861–78.

12. AN INDICTMENT

1. Dadabhai, "Female Education in India."
2. Mowforth and Munt, *Tourism and Sustainability*, 47; Palacios, "Volunteer Tourism," 861–78; Conran, "They Really Love Me," 1454–73; Sherraden et al., "Effects of International Volunteering," 395–421.
3. TMS Ruge, in discussion with author, June 28, 2018.
4. Easton and Wise, "Online Portrayals," 141–58.
5. Sue et al., "Racial Microaggressions," 271–86.
6. Aaron Reddecliffe, in discussion with author, November 16, 2018.
7. Raymond and Hall, "Development of Cross-Cultural (Mis)Understanding," 530–43.
8. Freidus, "Unanticipated Outcomes," 1306–21; Mostafanezhad, *Volunteer Tourism*; Simpson, "'Doing Development,'" 681.
9. Palacios, "Volunteer Tourism," 861–78; McGloin and Georgeou, "'Looks Good on Your CV,'" 403–17; Vodopivec and Jaffe, "Save the World in a Week," 111–28.
10. Freidus, "Unanticipated Outcomes," 1306–21.
11. Nixon, *Slow Violence*.
12. McGloin and Georgeou, "'Looks Good on Your CV,'" 403–17.
13. Bailey and Russell, "Volunteer Tourism," 1–10.
14. Berofsky, "Is Pathological Altruism Altruism?," 262–71.
15. Oakley et al., "Pathological Altruism—An Introduction," 3–9.
16. Sontag, "In Plato's Cave," 3–24.
17. Manzo, "Imaging Humanitarianism," 632–57.
18. Simpson, "'Doing Development,'" 682.
19. Brin, "Self-Addiction and Self-Righteousness," 77–84.
20. Heddwyn Kyambadde, filmmaker, in discussion with author, October 22, 2018.

13. TURNING TIDE

1. Lydia Ngoma, "Louise Linton's Zambia Is Not the Zambia I Know," *Guardian*, July 6, 2016, https://www.theguardian.com/global-development-professionals-network /2016/jul/06/louise-lintons-zambia-is-not-the-zambia-i-know.
2. Tobias Denskus, "#LintonLies: How Zambians Are Using Social Media to Talk Back," *NPR*, July 6, 2016, https://www.npr.org/sections/goatsandsoda/2016/07/06 /484810475/-lintonlies-how-zambians-are-using-social-media-to-talk-back; Ngoma, "Louise Linton's Zambia."
3. Patrick Smith and Craig Silverman, "The Woman Who Wrote That 'Gap Year in Africa' Memoir Is in a Relationship with Donald Trump's Finance Chief," *BuzzFeed*, July 6, 2016, https://www.buzzfeed.com/patricksmith/the-woman-who-wrote-that -gap-year-in-africa-memoir-is-in-a-r.

4. TMS Ruge, "Dear Africa, Louise Linton Is on Us," *BRIGHT Magazine*, July 8, 2016, https://brightthemag.com/dear-africa-louise-linton-is-on-us-b7177db7ace0.
5. TMS Ruge, entrepreneur, in discussion with author, June 28, 2018.
6. Ruge, in discussion with author, June 28, 2018.
7. Zion Amanda Kente, in discussion with author, October 4, 2018.
8. Burton, "Pathological Certitude," 131–37.
9. Easterly, *White Man's Burden*, 272.
10. No White Saviors, Instagram post, June 5, 2018, https://www.instagram.com/p/BjoeOoyhDRt/, (accessed June 12, 2019).
11. Kelsey Nielsen and Olivia Alaso, co-creators of No White Saviors, "Would love to connect!," email discussion with author, October 1, 2018.
12. No White Saviors, Instagram post, May 5, 2019, https://www.instagram.com/p/BxFmPaUBW00/ (accessed June 12, 2019).

14. THE FUTURE OF VOLUNTOURISM

1. Tara Russell, founder, president, and global impact lead, Fathom (Carnival Cruises), in discussion with author, June 15, 2015.
2. Lucas Peterson, "A 7-Night, $250 Cruise? Yes, and You Might Also Do Some Good," *New York Times*, September 29, 2016, http://nyti.ms/2dcKNrR.
3. Tim Wood, "Fathom Ceasing Operations: Is This a Setback for Voluntourism?," *Travel Pulse*, November 24, 2016, https://www.travelpulse.com/news/cruise/fathom-ceasing-operations-is-this-a-setback-for-voluntourism.html.
4. Jeremy Smith, "Tourism Concern Archive Now Freely Available on Travindy," *Travindy* (blog), June 13, 2019, https://www.travindy.com/2019/06/tourism-concern-archive-now-freely-available-on-travindy/.
5. Tourism Concern, "Ethical Travel Guide FAQs," https://www.tourismconcern.org.uk/ethical-travel/faq/ (accessed July 5, 2019).
6. Smith, "Development and Its Discontents," 272.
7. Coghlan and Noakes, "Towards an Understanding," 123–31; Comhlámh, "Code of Good Practice," https://comhlamh.org/code-of-good-practice/ (accessed July 5, 2019); Year Out Group, "Approved Gap Year Providers," https://yearoutgroup.org/approved-gap-year-providers/ (accessed July 5, 2019); Fair Trade Volunteering, "The Criteria," http://fairtradevolunteering.com/criteria.html (accessed July 5, 2019); Fair Trade Volunteering, "What Is Fair Trade Volunteering?," http://fairtradevolunteering.com/whatis.html (accessed July 5, 2019).
8. Hartman et al., "Fair Trade Learning," 108–16.
9. Rattan, "Is Certification the Answer?," 107.
10. Amizade, *23rd Annual Report and Infographic*; Amizade, *25th Annual Report and Infographic*.

11. Amizade, *25th Annual Report and Infographic.*

12. Willy Oppenheim, "The Problem with 'Placements,'" *Omprakash Blog*, January 22, 2018, https://www.omprakash.org/blog/the-problem-with--placements-.

13. Willy Oppenheim, founder and co-director of Omprakash, phone interview with author, September 5, 2018, and October 10, 2018.

14. Raymond and Hall, "Development of Cross-Cultural (Mis)Understanding," 530–43; Barbieri et al., "Volunteer Tourism," 509–16.

15. Leigh Mathews, founder of Alto Global Consulting and co-founder of ReThink Orphanages, in discussion with author, December 9, 2018.

16. World Challenge, "Costa Rica," https://weareworldchallenge.com/northamerica /destination/costa-rica/ (accessed July 5, 2019); World Challenge, "Botswana," https:// weareworldchallenge.com/northamerica/destination/botswana/ (accessed July 5, 2019); World Challenge, "Borneo," https://weareworldchallenge.com/northamerica /destination/borneo/ (accessed July 5, 2019).

17. Easton and Wise, "Online Portrayals," 141–58.

18. Smith and Font, "Volunteer Tourism, Greenwashing," 942–63.

19. Barbieri et al., "Volunteer Tourism," 514–15.

20. Zhao and Ritchie, "Tourism and Poverty Alleviation," 119–43.

21. Ashley and Haysom, "From Philanthropy to a Different Way," 265–80.

22. Scott Malone, "Want to Go to College in the U.S.? Show Compassion Not Test Scores: Proposal," *Reuters*, January 20, 2016, https://www.reuters.com/article/us-usa -education-idUSKCN0UY2R6.

23. Sin, "Volunteer Tourism," 480–501; Ong et al., "Going Global, Acting Local," 135–46.

24. Barbieri et al., "Volunteer Tourism," 513–14.

25. Wearing, *Volunteer Tourism*, 2; McBride et al., "Perceived Impact of International Service"; Berofsky, "Is Pathological Altruism Altruism?," 269.

26. Cole, "White-Savior Industrial Complex."

27. Egmond, *Understanding Western Tourists*, 135; Illich, "To Hell with Good Intentions."

28. Sontag, "In Plato's Cave," 15; Strauss, *Between the Eyes*, 74.

29. ReThink Orphanages, "ReThink Orphanages 10-Point Volunteering Checklist," https:// rethinkorphanages.org/volunteer-checklist (accessed April 10, 2019).

30. Freidus, "Unanticipated Outcomes," 1306–21.

31. Campbell and Smith, "What Makes Them Pay?," 84–98.

32. Kaitlin Menza, "This Could Be the Youngest Woman Ever Elected to Congress," *Cosmopolitan*, April 4, 2016, https://www.cosmopolitan.com/politics/a56203/erin -schrode-running-for-congress/; Erin Schrode, "#ErinForUs in the News," https:// www.erinschrode.com/erinforus-media (accessed July 5, 2019); "Erin Schrode:

25-Year-Old Running for California Office," ABC News, May 2016, YouTube, 3:04, posted May 10, 2016, https://www.youtube.com/watch?v=u3muDbRDeoQ.

33. World Central Kitchen, "What We Do," https://www.worldcentralkitchen.org/what-we-do (accessed July 5, 2019).

34. World Central Kitchen, "#CHEFSFORPUERTORICO," https://www.worldcentralkitchen.org/category/puerto-rico (accessed July 5, 2019).

35. Erin Schrode, activist, in discussion with author, February 7, 2019.

15. ON TO AN END

1. Mechi Annaís Estévez Cruz, "When Tourism Erases Instead of Elevating," *La Galería*, February 5, 2016, http://www.lagaleriamag.com/when-tourism-erases-instead-of-elevates/.

2. Mowforth and Munt, *Tourism and Sustainability*, 110; Fee, *How to Manage*, 218.

3. UNWTO, "UNWTO Tourism Highlights: 2015 Edition," 2.

4. UNWTO, "UNWTO Tourism Highlights: 2018 Edition," 3–7.

5. Roberts, "Reflections from the Periphery," 156.

6. "Thomas Cook Collapses as Last-Ditch Rescue Talks Fail," *BBC News*, September 23, 2019, https://www.bbc.com/news/business-49791249.

7. Corina Knoll, Azi Paybarah, Jacob Meschke, and Elaine Chen, "11 Numbers That Show How the Coronavirus Has Changed N.Y.C.," *New York Times*, April 20, 2020, https://www.nytimes.com/2020/04/20/nyregion/coronavirus-nyc-numbers-unemployment.html.

8. Conran, "They Really Love Me," 1454–73.

9. Erin Schrode, activist, in discussion with author, February 7, 2019.

10. Nicholas Kristof, "Westerners on White Horses," *New York Times*, July 14, 2010, https://kristof.blogs.nytimes.com/2010/07/14/westerners-on-white-horses/.

BIBLIOGRAPHY

Ainsworth, Mary S. "Infant–Mother Attachment." *American Psychologist, Psychology and Children: Current Research and Practice* 34, no. 10 (1979): 932–37.

"Americans Accused of Defiling Orphans in Bomet: Preying Missionaries." NTV Kenya, March 24, 2019. Online video. YouTube. https://www.youtube.com/watch?v= KOfdDaWy43E.

Amizade. *23rd Annual Report and Infographic*. Pittsburgh: Amizade, 2017. https://amizade .org/wp-content/uploads/2017/12/Amizades-23rd-Annual-Infographic.pdf.

———. *24th Annual Report and Infographic*. Pittsburgh: Amizade, 2018. https://amizade .org/wp-content/uploads/2019/01/Amizade-24th-Annual-Report-FY17-18.pdf.

———. *25th Annual Report and Infographic: FY 2018–2019*. Pittsburgh: Amizade, 2020. https://amizade.org/wp-content/uploads/2020/04/art-25th-infographic_final.pdf.

Anheier, Helmut K., and Lester M. Salamon. "Volunteering in Cross-National Perspective: Initial Comparisons." *Law and Contemporary Problems* 62, no. 4 (1999): 43–65.

Ashley, Caroline, and Gareth Haysom. "From Philanthropy to a Different Way of Doing Business: Strategies and Challenges in Integrating Pro-Poor Approaches into Tourism Business." *Development Southern Africa* 23, no. 2 (June 2006): 265–80.

Auerbach, Jeffery A. *The Great Exhibition of 1851: A Nation on Display*. New Haven CT: Yale University Press, 1999.

Azarya, Victor. "Globalization and International Tourism in Developing Countries: Marginality as a Commercial Commodity." *Current Sociology* 52, no. 6 (2004): 949–67.

Bailey, Andrew W., and Keith C. Russell. "Predictors of Interpersonal Growth in Volunteer Tourism: A Latent Curve Approach." *Leisure Sciences* 32, no. 4 (2010): 352–68.

———. "Volunteer Tourism: Powerful Programs or Predisposed Participants?" *Journal of Hospitality and Tourism Management* 19, no. 1 (2012): 1–10.

Barbieri, Carla, Carla Almeida Santos, and Yasuharu Katsube. "Volunteer Tourism: On-the-Ground Observations from Rwanda." *Tourism Management* 33, no. 3 (2012): 509–16.

Beames, Simon, and Peter Varley. "Eat, Play, Shop: The Disneyization of Adventure." In *Adventure Tourism: Meanings, Experience and Learning*, edited by Steve Taylor, Peter Varley, and Tony Johnston, 77–84. Abingdon: Routledge, 2013.

Becker, Elizabeth. *Overbooked: The Exploding Business of Travel and Tourism.* New York: Simon and Schuster, 2013.

Benson, Angela M. "Why and How Should the International Volunteer Tourism Experience Be Improved?" *Worldwide Hospitality and Tourism Themes* 7, no. 2 (2015): 100.

Berofsky, Bernard. "Is Pathological Altruism Altruism?" In *Pathological Altruism*, edited by Barbara Oakley, Ariel Knafo, Guruprasad Madhavan, and David Sloan Wilson, 262–71. New York: Oxford University Press, 2012.

Bjerneld, Magdalena, Gunilla Lindmark, Lucia Ann McSpadden, and Martha J. Garrett. "Motivations, Concerns, and Expectations of Scandinavian Health Professionals Volunteering for Humanitarian Assignments." *Disaster Management & Response* 4, no. 2 (June 2006): 49–58.

Boluk, Karla, Carol Kline, and Alicia Stroobach. "Exploring the Expectations and Satisfaction Derived from Volunteer Tourism Experiences." *Tourism and Hospitality Research* 17, no. 3 (2017): 272–85.

Borglund, Hanna. "Governing the Commons: A Case-Study of Rio Limpio National Park, Dominican Republic." Undergraduate Thesis, Södertörn University, 2011. https://www.diva-portal.org/smash/get/diva2:440035/FULLTEXT01.pdf.

Bornstein, Erica. "The Impulse of Philanthropy." *Cultural Anthropology* 24, no. 4 (2009): 622–51.

Bowlby, John. *Attachment: Attachment and Loss.* Vol. 1. New York: Basic Books, 1969.

Brendon, Piers. *Thomas Cook: 150 Years of Popular Tourism.* London: Secker and Warburg, 1991.

Brin, David. "Self-Addiction and Self-Righteousness." In *Pathological Altruism*, edited by Barbara Oakley, Ariel Knafo, Guruprasad Madhavan, and David Sloan Wilson, 77–84. New York: Oxford University Press, 2012.

Brohman, John. "New Direction in Tourism for Third World Development." *Annals of Tourism Research* 23, no. 1 (1996): 48–70.

Budge, E. A. Wallis. *Cook's Handbook for Egypt and the Egyptian Sudan with Chapters on Egyptian Archaeology*. 4th ed. London: Cook, 1921.

Burton, Robert A. "Pathological Certitude." In *Pathological Altruism*, edited by Barbara Oakley, Ariel Knafo, Guruprasad Madhavan, and David Sloan Wilson, 131–37. New York: Oxford University Press, 2012.

Butcher, Jim. "Against 'Ethical Tourism.'" In *Philosophical Issues in Tourism*, edited by John Tribe, 244–60. Bristol: Channel View, 2009.

Campbell, Lisa M., and Christy Smith. "What Makes Them Pay? Values of Volunteer Tourists Working for Sea Turtle Conservation." *Environmental Management* 38, no. 1 (2006): 84–98.

Carpenter, J. Estlin. *The Life and Work of Mary Carpenter*. London: Macmillan, 1881.

Carpenter, Mary. *Six Months in India*. 2 vols. London: Longmans, Green, 1868.

Cater, Carl. "The Meaning of Adventure." In *Adventure Tourism: Meanings, Experience and Learning*, edited by Steve Taylor, Peter Varley, and Tony Johnston, 7–18. Abingdon: Routledge, 2013.

Caton, Kellee, and Carla Almeida Santos. "Selling Study Abroad in a Postcolonial World." *Journal of Travel Research* 48, no. 2 (November 2009): 191–204.

Center for Responsible Travel. "The Case for Responsible Travel: Trends and Statistics, 2016." Washington DC: Center for Responsible Travel, 2016. https://www.responsibletravel.org/.

Chen, Li-Ju, and Joseph S. Chen. "The Motivations and Expectations of International Volunteer Tourists: A Case Study of 'Chinese Village Traditions.'" *Tourism Management* 32, no. 2 (2011): 435–42.

Clary, E. Gil, and Mark Snyder. "The Motivations to Volunteer: Theoretical and Practical Considerations." *Current Directions in Psychological Science* 8, no. 5 (1999): 156–59.

Coghlan, Alexandra. "Exploring the Role of Expedition Staff in Volunteer Tourism." *International Journal of Tourism Research* 10, no. 2 (2008): 183–91.

Coghlan, Alexandra, and Steve Noakes. "Towards an Understanding of the Drivers of Commercialisation in the Volunteer Tourism Sector." *Tourism Recreation Research* 37, no. 2 (2012): 123–31.

Coles, Tim C., Michael Hall, and David Timothy Duval. "Post-Disciplinary Tourism." In *Philosophical Issues in Tourism*, edited by John Tribe, 80–100. Bristol: Channel View, 2009.

Conran, Mary. "They Really Love Me! Intimacy in Volunteer Tourism." *Annals of Tourism Research* 38, no. 4 (2011): 1454–73.

Dann, Graham. "The People of Tourist Brochures." In *The Tourist Image: Myths and Myth Making in Tourism*, edited by Tom Selwyn, 61–81. West Sussex: John Wiley & Sons, 1996.

Daye, Marcella. "Re-visioning Caribbean Tourism." In *New Perspectives in Caribbean Tourism*, edited by Marcella Daye, Donna Chambers, and Sherma Roberts, 19–43. New York: Routledge, 2008.

Daye, Marcella, Donna Chambers, and Sherma Roberts, eds. "Foreword." In *New Perspectives in Caribbean Tourism*, edited by Marcella Daye, Donna Chambers, and Sherma Roberts, ix–x. New York: Routledge, 2008.

Dickens, Charles. *Oliver Twist; Or the Parish Boy's Progress*. 3 vols. London: Bentley, 1838.

Dierikx, M. L. J. *Clipping the Clouds: How Air Travel Changed the World*. Westport CT: Praeger, 2008.

Easterly, William. *The White Man's Burden: Why the West's Efforts to Aid the Rest Have Done So Much Ill and So Little Good*. New York: Penguin Books, 2006.

Easton, Siân, and Nicholas Wise. "Online Portrayals of Volunteer Tourism in Nepal: Exploring the Communicated Disparities between Promotional and User-Generated Content." *Worldwide Hospitality and Tourism Themes* 7, no. 2 (2015): 141–58.

Edwards, Elizabeth. "Postcards: Greetings from Another World." In *The Tourist Image: Myths and Myth Making in Tourism*, edited by Tom Selwyn, 196–221. West Sussex: John Wiley & Sons, 1996.

Egmond, T. Van. *Understanding Western Tourists in Developing Countries*. Wallingford, UK: CABI, 2007.

Fadnis, Charuta. "Good Travels: The Philanthropic Profile of the American Traveler." Grand Valley State University: Phocuswright White Paper, 2015.

Farley, James. "Potential Short-Term International Volunteers' Perceptions of Children's Residential Care in Cambodia." Phnom Penh, Cambodia: Friends-International, 2015.

Fee, Derek. *How to Manage an Aid Exit Strategy: The Future of Development Aid*. London: Zed, 2012.

Fernandez, Lauren S., Joseph A. Barbera, and Johan R. van Dorp. "Spontaneous Volunteer Response to Disasters: The Benefits and Consequences of Good Intentions." *Journal of Emergency Management* 4, no. 5 (2006): 57–68.

Fischer, Fritz. *Making Them Like Us: Peace Corps Volunteers in the 1960s*. Washington DC: Smithsonian Institute, 1998.

Freidus, Andrea Lee. "Unanticipated Outcomes of Voluntourism among Malawi's Orphans." *Journal of Sustainable Tourism* 25, no. 9 (2017): 1306–21.

Ghose, Indira. *Women Travellers in Colonial India: The Power of the Female Gaze*. New York: Oxford University Press, 1998.

Gilbert, Helen. "Belated Journeys: Ecotourism as a Style of Travel Performance." In *In Transit: Travel, Text, Empire*, edited by Helen Gilbert and Anna Johnston, 255–73. New York: Peter Lang, 2002.

Gilbert, Helen, and Anna Johnston. "Introduction." In *In Transit: Travel, Text, Empire*, edited by Helen Gilbert and Anna Johnston, 1–19. New York: Peter Lang, 2002.

Greer, Peter. *Stop Helping Us*. Tysons VA: Institute for Faith, Work and Economics, 2014. tifwe.org/wp-content/uploads/2014/06/StopHelpingUs-eBook.pdf.

Guiney, Tess, and Mary Mostafanezhad. "The Political Economy of Orphanage Tourism in Cambodia." *Tourist Studies* 15, no. 2 (2015): 132–55.

Hartman, Eric, Cody Morris Paris, and Brandon Blache-Cohen. "Fair Trade Learning: Ethical Standards for Community-Engaged International Volunteer Tourism." *Tourism and Hospitality Research* 14, no. 1–2 (2014): 108–16.

Havens, Holly. "The Harms of Orphanage Voluntourism: Misperceptions among Volunteers." Master's thesis, Columbia University, 2018. https://doi.org/10.7916/D8C553BS.

Hazbun, Waleed. "The East as an Exhibit: Thomas Cook & Son and the Origins of the International Tourism Industry in Egypt." In *The Business of Tourism*, edited by Philip Scranton and Janet F. Davidson, 3–33. Philadelphia: University of Pennsylvania, 2007.

Hemmati, Minu, and Nina Koehler. "Financial Leakages in Tourism." *Third World Resurgence*, no. 207/208 (2007): 15–18.

Honey, Martha. "Origin and Overview of Travelers' Philanthropy." In *Travelers' Philanthropy Handbook*, edited by Martha Honey, 3–12. Washington DC: Center for Responsible Travel, 2011. http://www.responsibletravel.org/docs/Travelers'_PhilanthropyHandbook_by_CREST.pdf.

Illich, Ivan. "To Hell with Good Intentions." Speech presented at the Conference on InterAmerican Student Projects, Cuernavaca, Mexico, April 20, 1968.

Invisible Children. Directed by Jason Russell, Lauren Poole, and Bobby Bailey. CA: Invisible Children, Inc., 2006. Documentary Film.

TheJesusMural. "Biola Jesus Mural 'Forum,'" Part 1 of 11. October 4, 2009. YouTube. https://www.youtube.com/watch?v=hCxXrPrGytI.

Journals of Mary Adams Abbott. "Journals and Letters of a Trip around the World. July 1920–February 1927." Vol. 2. Arthur and Elizabeth Schlesinger Library, History of Women in America, Radcliffe Institute for Advanced Study at Harvard.

King, Ed. "The Crystal Palace and Great Exhibition of 1851." *British Library Newspapers*. Detroit: Gale, 2007.

Knott, Alexandra. "Guests on the Aegean: Interactions between Migrants and Volunteers at Europe's Southern Border." *Mobilities* 13, no. 3 (2017): 349–66.

Krueger, Joachim I. "Altruism Gone Mad." In *Pathological Altruism*, edited by Barbara Oakley, Ariel Knafo, Guruprasad Madhavan, and David Sloan Wilson, 395–405. New York: Oxford University Press, 2012.

Laing, Jennifer, and Warwick Frost. *Explorer Travellers and Adventure Tourism*. Bristol: Channel View, 2014.

Lough, Benjamin. "International Volunteering from the United States between 2004 and 2012." Research Brief. Saint Louis MO: Center for Social Development, 2013.

The Love You Give. Directed by Will Francome. Kenya: Livity, 2019. Documentary.

Lyons, Kevin, Joanne Hanley, Stephen Wearing, and John Neil. "Gap Year Volunteer Tourism, Myths of Global Citizenship?" *Annals of Tourism Research* 39, no. 1 (2012): 361–78.

MacCannell, Dean. *The Ethics of Sightseeing*. Berkeley: University of California Press, 2011.

Madhavan, Guruprasad, and Barbara Oakley. "Too Much of a Good Thing? Foreign Aid and Pathological Altruism." In *Pathological Altruism*, edited by Barbara Oakley, Ariel Knafo, Guruprasad Madhavan, and David Sloan Wilson, 237–45. New York: Oxford University Press, 2012.

Manzo, Kate. "Imaging Humanitarianism: NGO Identity and the Iconography of Childhood." *Antipode* 40, no. 4 (September 2008): 632–57.

McBride, Amanda Moore, Benjamin J. Lough, and Margaret Sherrard. "Perceived Impact of International Service on Volunteers: Interim Results from a Quasi-Experimental Study." Washington DC: Brookings Institution, 2010. https://www.brookings.edu/wp-content/uploads/2016/06/0621_volunteering_mcbride.pdf.

McGehee, N. G. "Volunteer Tourism: Evolution, Issues and Futures." *Journal of Sustainable Tourism* 22, no. 6 (2014): 847–54.

McGloin, Colleen, and Nichole Georgeou. "'Looks Good on Your CV': The Sociology of Voluntourism Recruitment in Higher Education." *Journal of Sociology* 52, no. 2 (2016): 403–17.

Mikulincer, Mario, and Phillip R. Shaver. "Attachment Security, Compassion, and Altruism." *Current Directions in Psychological Science* 14, no. 1 (2005): 34–38.

"Miss Carpenter's Interview with the Queen." *Friends' Intelligencer*, May 16, 1868. American Periodicals Database.

Mostafanezhad, Mary. *Volunteer Tourism: Popular Humanitarianism in Neoliberal Times*. Surrey and Burlington VT: Ashgate, 2014.

Mowforth, Martin, and Ian Munt. *Tourism and Sustainability: Development and New Tourism in the Third World*. New York: Routledge, 2009.

Moyo, Dambisa. *Dead Aid: Why Aid Is Not Working and How There Is a Better Way for Africa*. New York: Farrar, Strauss and Giroux, 2009.

Mullens, Joseph. *London and Calcutta Compared in Their Heathenism, Their Privileges, and Their Prospects: Showing the Great Claims of Foreign Missions upon the Christian Church*. London: J. Nisbet, 1868.

Nash, Dennison, ed. *The Study of Tourism: Anthropological and Sociological Beginnings*. Bingley, UK: Emerald Group, 2005.

Netto, Alexandre Panosso. "What Is Tourism? Definitions, Theoretical Phases and Principles." In *Philosophical Issues in Tourism*, edited by John Tribe, 43–61. Bristol: Channel View, 2009.

Newmeyer, Trent. "'Under the Wing of Mr. Cook': Transformations in Tourism Governance." *Mobilities* 3, no. 2 (2008): 243–67.

Nixon, Rob. *Slow Violence and the Environmentalism of the Poor*. Cambridge MA: Harvard University Press, 2011.

Novelli, Marina. *Tourism and Development in Sub-Saharan Africa: Current Issues and Local Realities*. London and New York: Routledge, 2016.

Oakley, Barbara, Ariel Knafo, and Michael McGrath. "Pathological Altruism—An Introduction." In *Pathological Altruism*, edited by Barbara Oakley, Ariel Knafo, Guruprasad Madhavan, and David Sloan Wilson, 3–9. New York: Oxford University Press, 2012.

OBrien, Peter W. "Business, Management and Poverty Reduction: A Role for Slum Tourism?" *Journal of Business Diversity* 11, no. 1 (2011): 33–46.

O'Conner, Lynn E., Jack W. Berry, Thomas B. Lewis, and David J. Stiver. "Empathy-Based Pathogenic Guilt, Pathological Altruism, and Psychopathology." In *Pathological Altruism*, edited by Barbara Oakley, Ariel Knafo, Guruprasad Madhavan, and David Sloan Wilson, 10–30. New York: Oxford University Press, 2012.

Ong, Faith, Brian King, Leonie Lockstone-Binney, and Olga Junek. "Going Global, Acting Local: Volunteer Tourists as Prospective Community Builders." *Tourism Recreation Research* 43, no. 2 (2018): 135–46.

Palacios, Carlos M. "Volunteer Tourism, Development and Education in a Postcolonial World: Conceiving Global Connections beyond Aid." *Journal of Sustainable Tourism* 18, no. 7 (2010): 861–78.

Pan, Tze-Jen. "Motivations of Volunteer Overseas and What We Have Learned—The Experience of Taiwanese Students." *Tourism Management* 33, no. 6 (2012): 1493–501.

Pattullo, Polly. *Last Resorts: The Cost of Tourism in the Caribbean*. London: Cassell, 1996.

Paxton, Pamela, Nicholas E. Reith, and Jennifer L. Glanville. "Volunteering and the Dimensions of Religiosity: A Cross-National Analysis." *Review of Religious Research* 56 (2014): 597–625.

Perkins, Kenneth J. "The Compagnie Générale Transatlantique and the Development of Saharan Tourism in North Africa." In *The Business of Tourism*, edited by Philip Scranton and Janet F. Davidson, 34–55. Philadelphia: University of Pennsylvania, 2007.

Phelan, Kelly Virginia. "Elephants, Orphans and HIV/AIDS: Examining the Voluntourist Experience in Botswana." *Worldwide Hospitality and Tourism Themes* 7, no. 2 (2015): 127–40.

Projects Abroad. *Global Impact Report 2018*. New York: Projects Abroad. https://docs.projects-abroad.co.uk/uk/global-impact-report/global-impact-report-2018.pdf. Accessed April 9, 2019.

Rattan, Jasveen K. "Is Certification the Answer to Creating a More Sustainable Volunteer Tourism Sector?" *Worldwide Hospitality and Tourism Themes* 7, no. 2 (2015): 107–26.

Raymond, Eliza Marguerite, and C. Michael Hall. "The Development of Cross-Cultural (Mis)Understanding through Volunteer Tourism." *Journal of Sustainable Tourism* 16, no. 5 (2008): 530–43.

Rehberg, Walter. "Altruistic Individualists: Motivations for International Volunteering among Young Adults in Switzerland." *Voluntas* 16, no. 2 (2005): 109–22.

Richter, Linda M. "Inside the Thriving Industry of AIDS Orphan Tourism." *Human Sciences Research Council Review* 8, no. 2 (2010): 6–8.

Richter, Linda M., and Amy Norman. "AIDS Orphan Tourism: A Threat to Young Children in Residential Care." *Vulnerable Children and Youth Studies* 5, no. 3 (September 2010): 217–29.

Roberts, Sherma. "Reflections from the Periphery: An Analysis of Small Tourism Businesses within the Sustainability Discourse." In *New Perspectives in Caribbean Tourism*, edited by Marcella Daye, Donna Chambers, and Sherma Roberts, 135–61. New York: Routledge, 2008.

Rogers, Eliza M. *Domestic Life in Palestine*. Cincinnati: Poe and Hitchcock, 1865.

Rolfes, Manfred. "Poverty Tourism: Theoretical Reflections and Empirical Findings Regarding an Extraordinary Form of Tourism." *GeoJournal* 75, no. 5 (2010): 421–42.

Rovner, Mark. "The Next Generation of American Giving: The Charitable Habits of Generation Z, Millennials, Generation X, Baby Boomers, and Matures." Charleston SC: Blackbaud Institute, 2018.

———. "The Next Generation of Canadian Giving: The Charitable Habits of Millennials, Generation Xers, Baby Boomers and Civics." Charleston SC: Blackbaud Institute, 2018.

Rovner, Mark, Ashley Thompson, Erin Duff, and Lidia Lal. "The Next Generation of Australian and New Zealander Giving: The Charitable Giving Habits of Generation Zers, Millennials, Generation Xers, Baby Boomers and Matures." Charleston SC: Blackbaud Institute, 2018.

Rovner, Mark, Ashley Thompson, Erin Duff, and Louise Sparks. "The Next Generation of UK Giving: The Charitable Giving Habits of Generation Zers, Millennials, Generation Xers, Baby Boomers and Matures." Charleston SC: Blackbaud Institute, 2018.

Said, Edward. *Orientalism*. New York: Pantheon, 1978.

Scranton, Philip, and Janet F. Davidson, eds. *The Business of Tourism: Place, Faith, and History*. Philadelphia: University of Pennsylvania, 2007.

Selwyn, Tom. "Introduction." In *The Tourist Image: Myths and Myth Making in Tourism*, edited by Tom Selwyn, 1–31. West Sussex: John Wiley & Sons, 1996.

Seymour, Brittany, Habib Benzian, and Elsbeth Kalenderian. "Voluntourism and Global Health: Preparing Dental Students for Responsible Engagement in International Programs." *Journal of Dental Education* 77, no. 10 (2013): 1252–57.

Sherraden, Margaret S., Benjamin Lough, and Amanda Moore McBride. "Effects of International Volunteering and Service: Individual and Institutional Predictors." *Voluntas* 19, no. 4 (2008): 395–421.

Simpson, Kate. "'Doing Development': The Gap Year, Volunteer-Tourists and a Popular Practice of Development." *Journal of International Development* 16, no. 5 (2004): 681–92.

Sin, Harng Luh. "Realities of Doing Responsibilities: Performances and Practices in Tourism." *Geografiska Annaler: Series B, Human Geography* 96, no. 2 (2014): 95–193.

———. "Selling Ethics: Discourses of Responsibility in Tourism." *Annals of the American Association of Geographers* 107, no. 1 (2017): 218–34.

———. "Volunteer Tourism—'Involve Me and I Will Learn'?" *Annals of Tourism Research* 36, no. 3 (2009): 480–501.

———. "Who Are We Responsible To? Locals' Tales of Volunteer Tourism." *Geoforum* 41, no. 6 (2010): 983–92.

Sin, Harng Luh, and Shirleen He. "Voluntouring on Facebook and Instagram: Photography and Social Media in Constructing the 'Third World' Experience." *Tourist Studies* 19, no. 2 (2019): 215–37.

Sin, Harng Luh, Tim Oakes, and Mary Mostafanezhad. "Traveling for a Cause: Critical Examinations of Volunteer Tourism and Social Justice." *Tourist Studies* 15, no. 2 (2015): 119–31.

Smith, George Albert. *Correspondence of Palestine Tourists; Comprising a Series of Letters by George A. Smith, Lorenzo Snow, Paul A. Schettler, and Eliza R. Snow, of Utah—Mostly Written While Traveling in Europe, Asia and Africa—in the Years 1872 and 1873.* Salt Lake City, Utah Territory: Deseret News Steam Printing Establishment, 1875.

Smith, Mick. "Development and Its Discontents: Ego-Tripping Without Ethics or Idea(l)s?" In *Philosophical Issues in Tourism*, edited by John Tribe, 261–77. Bristol: Channel View, 2009.

Smith, Victoria Louise, and Xavier Font. "Volunteer Tourism, Greenwashing and Understanding Responsible Marketing Using Market Signalling Theory." *Journal of Sustainable Tourism* 22, no. 6 (2014): 942–63.

Sontag, Susan. "In Plato's Cave." In *On Photography*, by Susan Sontag, 3–24. London: Farrar, Strauss and Giroux, 1977.

Spicer Brothers. *Official Catalogue of the Great Exhibition of the Works of Industry of All Nations, 1851.* 2nd ed. London: W. Clowes and Sons, 1851.

Strauss, David Levi. *Between the Eyes: Essays on Photography and Politics.* New York: Aperture Foundation, 2004.

Sue, Derald Wing, Christina M. Capodilupo, Gina C. Torino, Jennifer M. Bucceri, Aisha M. B. Holder, Kevin L. Nadal, and Marta Esquilin. "Racial Microaggressions in Everyday Life: Implications for Clinical Practice." *American Psychologist* 62, no. 4 (2007): 271–86.

Swinglehurst, Edmund. *Cook's Tours: The Story of Popular Travel.* Poole, Dorset: Blanford Press, 1982.

Teo, Hsu-Ming. "Femininity, Modernity, and Colonial Discourse." In *In Transit: Travel, Text, Empire*, edited by Helen Gilbert and Anna Johnston, 173–90. New York: Peter Lang, 2002.

United Nations World Tourism Organization. "Community Tourism in Asia: An Introduction." In *Tourism and Community Development: Asian Practices*. 2nd ed. Madrid: United Nations World Tourism Organization, 2009.

——. "UNWTO Tourism Highlights: 2015 Edition." Spain: United Nations World Tourism Organization, 2015.

——. "UNWTO Tourism Highlights: 2016 Edition." Spain: United Nations World Tourism Organization, 2016.

——. "UNWTO Tourism Highlights: 2018 Edition." Spain: United Nations World Tourism Organization, 2018.

Vilardaga, Roger, and Steven C. Hayes. "A Contextual Behavioral Approach to Pathological Altruism." In *Pathological Altruism*, edited by Barbara Oakley, Ariel Knafo, Guruprasad Madhavan, and David Sloan Wilson, 31–48. New York: Oxford University Press, 2012.

Vodopivec, Barbara, and Rivke Jaffe. "Save the World in a Week: Volunteer Tourism, Development and Difference." *European Journal of Development Research* 23, no. 1 (2011): 111–28.

"Volunteering in the United States, 2015." U.S. Bureau of Labor Statistics, 2016. www.bls.gov/news.release/volun.nr0.htm.

Ward, Evan R. "A Means of Last Resort: The European Transformation of the Cuban Hotel Industry and the American Response, 1987–2004." In *The Business of Tourism*, edited by Philip Scranton and Janet F. Davidson, 213–38. Philadelphia: University of Pennsylvania, 2007.

Wearing, Stephen. *Volunteer Tourism: Experiences That Make a Difference*. Wallingford, Oxon: CABI, 2001.

Wearing, Stephen, and Nancy Gard McGehee. "Volunteer Tourism: A Review." *Tourism Management* 38 (2013): 120–30.

Western, David (Jonah). "Travelers' Philanthropy and the Good Samaritan." In *Travelers' Philanthropy Handbook*, edited by Martha Honey, 13–18. Washington DC: Center for Responsible Travel, 2011. http://www.responsibletravel.org/docs/Travelers'_PhilanthropyHandbook_ by_ CREST.pdf.

Wolff, Johanna. "Survey of Tour Operators in Arusha, Tanzania." In *Travelers' Philanthropy Handbook*, edited by Martha Honey, 150–58. Washington DC: Center for Responsible Travel, 2011. http://www.responsibletravel.org/docs/Travelers'_PhilanthropyHandbook _ by_ CREST.pdf.

Wright, Jamie. *The Very Worst Missionary: A Memoir or Whatever*. New York: Convergent Books, 2018.

Xie, Philip Feifan. *Authenticating Ethnic Tourism*. Bristol, UK: Channel View, 2011.

Zhao, Weibing, and J. R. Brent Ritchie. "Tourism and Poverty Alleviation: An Integrative Research Framework." *Current Issues in Tourism* 10, no. 2–3 (2007): 119–43.

INDEX

Abbott, Mary Adams, 25, 64
Abbott, Mary Ogden, 25
abuse, 133–36, 137, 143–44
adoption, 138–39
"The Adventures of Oliver Twist"
   (Dickens), 12
Africans: as part of the problem, 120, 157;
   as tourists, 73
agency, reclaiming, 120–21, 157
Ainsworth, Mary, 132
air travel, 26–27, 28
Alaso, Olivia, 160
all-inclusive trips, 19, 30–31
All Nations, 86
alternative tourism, 40
altruism: locals capitalizing on, 65, 69,
   120; pathological, 67–69, 72
American Express, 25
Amizade, 167–68

Andrés, José, 176
Archarya, Bishwa, 137
arrivals, international tourist, 31–32
artist missionaries, 82–83
Arusha, Tanzania, 103–4
attachment disorders, 132–33
Atwell, Andrew, 86
Australian voluntourism, 37, 131
authenticity, 33–34, 38, 55

baby delivering, 111–12
Barbie Savior, 77–81, 159, 160
Bentley's Miscellany, 12
Bethany Christian Services, 138–39
Bethsaida orphanage, x–xv, 187n1
Better Care Network, 130
Biola University, 67–68, 69–70
Birmingham Conference of 1851, 5
Blache-Cohen, Brandon, 167

Borderless Volunteers, 95
Bowlby, John, 132
British Airways, 135
British Calcutta, 1–3, 62
Broader View Volunteers, 123
Byemba, Robert, 105, 107–8

Calcutta, India, 1–3, 62
Cambodian orphanages, 48, 126, 131, 134, 135, 137, 140
capital and capacity, 95–96
capitalism, 45
Caribbean tourism, 28, 30, 63
Carnival Corporation & PLC, 163, 164
Carpenter, Mary: about, 3–4, 162; colonialism and, 62, 63; criminal justice reform and, 5; in India, 2–3, 5–8, 21–22, 61, 155; Sorabsha Dadabhai and, 7–8, 147–48
carriage riding, 2, 11, 33
certification systems, 40, 166–68
Chau, John Allen, 85–86
Chefs for Puerto Rico, 176
Child Family Health International (CFHI), 112–13, 166
Child in Family Focus–Kenya, 130
"Children Are Not Tourist Attractions" campaign, 140
Children's Umbrella Centre Organization, 135
child sponsorship, 139–40
child trafficking, 131, 135, 138–39, 154
China, 31
Christianity: adoption and, 138–39; Mary Carpenter and, 3, 5, 6; mission-aries and, 83–88; orphanages and, 127; voluntourism and, 70, 74–75, 77, 81–82
Christian privilege, 84–85

"close-but-separate" approach to tourism, 6, 19–20, 29–30
Cocalis, Nick, 86–89, 141
Cole, Teju, 159
colonialism, defined, 62
colonialism and tourism, 24, 27–28, 29
colonialism and voluntourism, 61–73; background and overview of, 61–63; contemporary, 148–51, 153, 157; pathological altruism and, 67–69, 72; playing doctor and, 115; power and image and, 64–67; race and faith and, 69–72; women and, 63–64
Comhlámh, 167
commercial air travel, 26–27, 28
communities: control of, 120–21; development and, 32–33, 40, 91, 93–98, 100–101; medical social contract and, 114; middle class emergence and, 11–12, 13; missionaries and, 88–89; slow violence and, 152; voluntourist reform and, 153–54, 159, 167–68, 172, 175; voluntourists and, 53–54; zooification and, 78
conservation volunteers, 172, 175
contemporary colonialism, 148–51, 153, 157
Cook, John Mason, 10, 18–20, 62–63
Cook, Marianne Mason, 10, 14
Cook, Thomas: about, 9–10, 17–19, 22–23, 162; Far East travel and, 21–22; Great Exhibition and, 15–17; Middle East travel and, 19–20; temperance events and, 13–15. See also Thomas Cook travel company
Cook's Law, 31
Costa Rican tourism, 37–38
Cottam, Catherine, 123–25, 133, 142–43
COVID-19 pandemic, 180
crime, juvenile, 4–5

crisis response teams, 115–16

cruises, 21, 29, 39, 163–65; alternative style of, 39

Cuban tourism, 28, 29

Cunningham, Loren, 75

Current Population Survey data, 46, 59

Dadabhai, Sorabsha, 7–8, 63, 147–48

dame culture, 96–98

Dar es Salaam, Tanzania, x, xiv

"Dear Africa, Louise Linton Is on Us" (Ruge), 157

desire to help, 35–37, 40–41

developing economies and tourism, 32

development of tourism, 29–31, 32, 40

development voluntourism, 90–101; about, 154; *dame* culture and, 96–98; measurable impacts of, 94–96; money and, 91–94; Río Limpio and, 90–91; social development and, 98–99; white elephants and, 99–101

Dickens, Charles, 12

Discipleship Training School (DTS), 75–76

disinhibited social engagement disorder, 132–33

doctor, playing. *See* medical voluntourism

Dominican Republic: Haitian earthquake and, 138–39; voluntourism in, 90–91, 97, 163, 164

donation to placement, 93

Dow, Gregory and Mary Rose, 136

Dow Children's Home, 136

dragomen, 20

Durham, Matthew, 135

East African tourism, 38–39

economic leakage, 30–31, 40, 63

economics of voluntourism, 47–52

ecotourism, 37–40, 41–42

EdGE (Education through Global Engagement), 170

education: in Africa, 158; for females, 3, 5, 6–7, 147; pre-trip voluntourism, 154, 169–70, 172; teaching and, 117–22

Egyptian tourism, 19, 27, 29, 33, 62–63

Ekisa Ministries, 79–81

emotional and physical abuse, 133–34, 143–44

England and tourism, 10–11, 14–15, 27–28, 31

Ethical Student Travel Forum, 170–71

ethical tourism, 166–67

evangelism, 12–13, 15, 75–76. *See also* missionaries

Evert, Jessica, 113–15, 166

experience rooms, 67–68

Failed Missionary podcast, 82, 84–85

Fair Trade Learning Standards, 167–68

Fair Trade Volunteering, 167

faith and adoption, 138–39

faith and voluntourism, 74–85; background and overview of, 74–77, 154; Barbie Savior and, 77–81; Corey Pigg's story and, 81–85; race and, 70. *See also* Christianity; evangelism; missionaries

Fathom cruises, 163–65

financial exploitation of orphans, 137

financial privilege, 46

Fletcher, Pete, 171

flight, 26–27, 28

for-profit voluntourism, 48–52

Free the Children, 50

Frontera Futuro, 90

fulfillment, personal, 53, 54

gap-year industry, 49

Gehrmann, Todd, 86

gender: norms, 6; and voluntourism, 58–59

Ghose, Monomohun, 3, 5

giving, 13, 36, 41, 47, 53

global citizenship, 42, 55

Global Crossroad, xiv, 92

global engagement, 36

Global Outreach Doctors, 115

GoAbroad.com, 48

Golder, Ruth, 134

good, being and doing, 8, 40–41, 68, 152–53, 173–74, 181

"good tourism," 37, 40

government programs for volunteering abroad, 36–37

Great Commission, 74

Great Exhibition, 15–17

greenwashing, 39–40, 166

Haiti earthquake, 138–39

Hamilton, David Joel, 83

Happy Home Orphanage, 137

Hartman, Eric, 167

help, desire to, 35–37, 40–41

history, teaching, 158

Holidays with Pay Act, 27

human trafficking, 131, 135, 138–39, 154

Hurricane Maria, 175–77

Hurricane Sandy, 88–89

identity confirmation, 66–67

illegitimate adoptions, 138–39

imagery: of travel, 55, 56; of voluntourism, 58, 65–67, 78, 172, 174

Industrial Revolution, 11

International Volunteer HQ (IVHQ): Emily Scott story and, 110–12; Larsa Al-Omaishi story and, 102–3, 104–9; Olorien Community Clinic and, 105–9; orphanages and, 103–4, 110, 142; standards of, 105–6, 109–10

Invisible Children (Russell), 43

Iona island, 17

Jaffa, travel to, 19

James 1:27, 127, 138

Jerusalem, 19–20

journal, author's, xiii, xiv–xv

juggernauts, 21–22

Julius Nyerere International Airport, ix

juvenile crime, 4–5

Kalighat Kali Temple, 2–3

Kennedy, John F., 36

Kente, Zion Amanda, 157–59

Kielburger family, 49–50, 91

Knight, Ethan, 49

Kony, Joseph, 43

Kramlich, Jackie, 79–80, 160

Kristof, Nicholas, 181

Kyambadde, Heddwyn, 65, 67–68, 69–71, 155

labor, child, 133

length of voluntourism trips, 45

Linton, Louise, 156–57

local economies and tourism, 30–32

local volunteering, 54

Lord's Resistance Army, 43

Lough, Benjamin, 46, 59

The Love You Give, 130

Luket Ministries, 76–77

Lumos, 131

Manchester Guardian, 7–8, 63, 147–48

marketing of voluntourism, 55–58, 92–93, 172

mass migration, 11–12

Mathews, Leigh, 130–31, 132, 142, 170–71; and ALTO Global Consulting, 130
McWilliams, Nancy, 68
medical schools and voluntourism, 106, 113–14
medical social contract, 114–15, 154
medical voluntourism: about, 154; crisis response teams and, 115–16; Emily Scott story and, 110–12, 115–16, 122; IVHQ and, 103, 105–10; Jessica Evert story and, 113, 114; Larsa Al-Omaishi story and, 102–3, 104–9; social contract and, 114–15; unequal dynamic and, 121–22
metadata, 174
ME to WE, 50–51, 57
microaggressions, 149
micro-exploitation, 149
middle class, 11–12, 13, 14–15
Midland Counties Railway Company, 9, 13–14
missionaries: background and overview of, 70, 74–75, 76–77, 85; Corey Pigg's story and, 81–85; John Allen Chau as, 85–86; Luket Ministries, 76–77; Next Step, 86–89; YWAM, 75–76
Modern Slavery Act, 131
moral economy, 41–42, 45, 54, 71
moral metadata, 174
Mostafanezhad, Mary, 95
Moutafis, Giorgos, 66
Muthui, Peter K., 128–30, 141–42
MyStep, 87

New Hope Initiative, 105
New Life Children's Refuge, 138–39
New York Times, 22–23, 164
Next Step Ministries, 86–89, 141
Ngarenaro Health Centre, 110–12

Nielsen, Kelsey, 160
Nin, Anaïs, 165
Nixon, Rob, 152
nonprofit voluntourism, 48–51
Norman, Amy, 125
North Sentinel Island, 85–86
No White Saviors, 159–62

Oliel, Michelle, 143–46
Olorien Bible Baptist Church, 105
Olorien Community Clinic, 105–9
Omaishi, Larsa Al-: about, 102–3, 175; at Olorien Community Clinic, 104–9; at Save Africa Orphanage, 103–4
Omprakash, 169–70
Oppenheim, Willy, 168, 169–70
orphan, term of, 125
orphanages: Cambodian, 48, 126, 131, 134, 135, 137, 140; crisis of, 125–26; IVHQ and, 103–4, 110. *See also* orphanage voluntourism
orphanage voluntourism, 123–46; abuse and, 133–37, 143–44; anti-orphanage efforts and, 130–32, 140, 143–46; attachment disorders and, 132–33; background and overview of, 125–28, 154; Catherine Cottam story of, 123–25, 143; child sponsorships and, 139–40; financial exploitation and, 137, 139–40; illegitimate adoptions and, 138–39; Peter Muthui and, 128–30; reform and, 174; responsibility and, 140–42; World Challenge and, 130, 142, 170–71
Other, 56, 61–62, 151, 154
outputs and outcomes, 94–95, 99–100

Paris, Cody, 167
pathological altruism, 67–69, 72, 80, 148, 152–53

Peace Corps, 36–37, 41, 53

performances by orphans, 65, 72, 133, 137, 153

Peterson, Lucas, 164

philanthropy of Victorian era, 13

photographs, 65–67, 78, 115, 174

Pigg, Corey, 82–85

placement, volunteer, 93, 110, 154, 168–69

Placement Paradigm, 168–69

playing doctor. *See* medical voluntourism

Porter, Dan, 171

power dynamics, uneven, 72, 117–20, 121–22

presumption of progress, 47

pre-trip education for voluntourism, 154, 169–70, 172

privilege: about, xv–xvi, 64, 122; Christian, 84–85, 86; "collision" and, 89; financial, 46; privileged savior complex and, 71–72; reform and, 161

privileged savior complex, 71–72

profit and voluntourism, 48–52

progress, presumption of, 47

Projects Abroad, 51–52, 93

"The Psychology of the Altruist" (McWilliams), 68

Puello, Jorge Torres, 139

Puerto Rico, 175–77

race: faith and, 70; savior complexes and, 71–72; social development and, 98; teaching and, 120; of voluntourists, 46

racism, 29, 64, 115, 161

Red Cross, 36

Reddecliffe, Aaron, 110–11, 117–20, 122, 149–50, 158

Red Lodge, 5

reforming voluntourism, 165–81; background and overview of, 165–66; certification system and, 166–68; pre-trip education and, 169–70; sustainability and, 179–80; travelers and, 173–75, 177–78, 181; trip providers and, 170–73; volunteer placement and, 168–69

religion at home, 12–13

ReThink Orphanages, 130

Richter, Linda, 125

Río Limpio, Dominican Republic, 90–91, 99–100

river cruises, 21

road trips, 25

Ruge, TMS, 120–21, 149, 157

Ruhfus, Juliana, 93, 135

Ruskin, John, 23

Russell, Jason, 43

Russell, Tara, 163–64

Said, Edward, 61

Save Africa Orphanage, 103–4

Schrode, Erin, 66, 67, 175–77, 180

Scott, Emily, 43–44, 60, 110–12, 115–16, 122, 149–50

service requirements of schools, 57–58

service versus engagement, 174

sex tourism, 135

sexual abuse, 134–36

Silsby, Laura, 138–39

simulations, village, 86

slow violence, 152

Slow Violence and the Environmentalism of the Poor (Nixon), 152

social clout, 53–54

social contract, medical, 114–15, 154

social development, 98–99

social norms, 6, 8

sponsorship of children, 139–40

staging, 66, 72, 153

Stahili Foundation, 145–46

surveys on voluntourism, 41, 46, 47, 48, 59, 126

sustainable development, 67, 91, 94, 97, 100–101, 177, 179–80

sustainable tourism, 40, 172, 179–80

teaching, 95–96, 117–22, 154, 158

temperance, 9, 10, 13–14

Thomas Cook travel company: about, 22–23, 180; Americans and, 18–19; anglicizing by, 20, 61; around the world travel and, 21–22; colonialism and, 61, 62–63; European travel and, 17–18; Far East travel and, 21–22; Great Exhibition and, 15–17; Middle East and Africa travel and, 19–21; temperance events of, 13–15

tourism: Americans and, 18–19, 24–25, 28–29; COVID-19 pandemic and, 180; development of, 29–31, 32, 40; early, 10, 18–19, 22–23, 24; ecotourism, 37–40, 41–42; effects of, 33–34; England and, 10–11, 14–15, 27–28, 31; ethical, 166–67; "good," 37, 40; growth in, 31–33; local economies and, 30–32; sex, 135; sustainable, 40, 172, 179–80; during WWI, 24–26. *See also* voluntourism

Tourism Concern, 166–67

tourism enclaves, 29–31

tourist arrivals, international, 31–32

trafficking, human, 131, 135, 138–39, 154

train travel, 13–14

travel, leisure, 10, 14, 24–25. *See also* tourism

Twitchell, Kent, 69–70

Two Dusty Travelers, 122

uneven power dynamics, 117–20, 121–22

UNICEF, 130–31

universities and voluntourism, 56–57, 113–14, 131

Upendo Children's Home, 135

The Very Worst Missionary (Wright), 85

Victorian-era philanthropy, 13

Volunteer Abroad database, 48

volunteering abroad government programs, 36–37

Volunteering Solutions, 58–59

Volunteers Unleashed, 102, 107–9

Volunteer Vacations guide, 48

voluntourism: age and, 58; background and overview of, xvi, 42, 43–47, 161; definition of, 47; economics of, 47–52; gender and, 58–59; marketing of, 55–58, 92–93, 172; pantomiming progress of, 152–55; power and image and, 64–67; pre-trip education for, 154, 169–70, 172; reasons for buying, 52–54; as slow violence, 151–52. *See also* colonialism and voluntourism; development voluntourism; faith and voluntourism; medical voluntourism; orphanage voluntourism; reforming voluntourism

WE Charity, 50–51, 57

WE Day events, 50, 57

Western benevolence, 54, 55

whiteness. *See* race
white savior complex, 71–72, 156–59
white savior industrial complex, 71, 159
Winks, Joseph Foulkes, 10
Wood, Simon, 135
"The WORD" (Twitchell), 69–70
workhouses, 12, 13
Working and Visiting Society, 4
World Central Kitchen, 176
World Challenge, 130, 142, 170–72

World War I, 24–25, 26
World War II, 26
Worrall, Emily, 78–81, 82, 160
Wright, Jamie, 85

Year Out Group, 167
YWAM (Youth with a Mission), 75–76,
    83–84, 86

zooification, 78